By Being, It Is: The Thesis of Parmenides – **Néstor-Luis Cordero**
ISBN 1-930972-03-2

Errata Insert

Appendix 1
The Poem of Parmenides

The correct words in Greek appear in **bold**.

p. 186:
4.1: λεῦσσε δ′ ὅμως ἀπεόντα **νόῳ** παρεόντα βεβαίως·
5.2: ὁππόθεν ἄρξομαι· τόθι γὰρ πάλιν ἵξομαι **αὖτις**.

p. 187:
6.9: κοὐ **ταὐτόν·** πάντων δὲ παλίντροπός ἐστι κέλευθος.
7.5: καὶ γλῶσσαν· κρῖναι δὲ **λόγῳ** πολύδηριν ἔλεγχον

p. 188:
8.15: ἀλλ′ ἔχει· ἡ δὲ κρίσις περὶ τούτων ἐν **τῷδ′** ἔστιν·
8.22: οὐδὲ διαιρετόν ἐστιν, **ἐπεὶ** πᾶν ἐστιν ὁμοῖον·
8.25: **τῷ** ξυνεχὲς πᾶν ἐστιν· ἐὸν γὰρ ἐόντι πελάζει·
8.29: ταὐτόν τ′ ἐν **ταὐτῷ** τε μένον καθ′ ἑαυτό τε κεῖται
8.35: οὐ γὰρ ἄνευ τοῦ ἐόντος, ἐφ′[705] **ᾧ** πεφατισμένον ἐστίν,
8.38: ὗλον ἀκίνητόν τ′ ἔμμεναι· **τῷ πᾶντ′** ὄνομ′ ἔσται
8.43: πάντοθεν, εὐκύκλου σφαίρης ἐναλίγκιον **ὄγκῳ**,
8.50: ἐν **τῷ** σοι παύω πιστὸν λόγον ἠδὲ νόημα
8.54: τῶν μίαν οὐ χρών ἐστιν -ἐν **ᾧ** πεπλανημένοι εἰσίν-

p. 189:
8.57: ἤπιον ὄν, μέγ′ [ἀραιον] ἐλαφρόν, **ἑωυτῷ** πάντοσε τωὐτόν,
8.58: **τῷ δ′ ἑτέρῳ** μὴ τωὐτόν· ἀτὰρ κἀκεῖνο κατ′ αὐτό
9.4: ἴσων ἀμφοτέρων, ἐπεὶ **οὐδετέρῳ** μέτα μηδέν.
12.1: αἱ γὰρ στεινότεραι **πλῆντο** πυρὸς ἀκρήτοιο,
12.3: ἐν δὲ **μέσῳ** τούτων δαίμων ἣ πάντα κυβερνᾷ·
12.5: πέμπουσ′ ἄρσενι θῆλυ μιγῆν **τό τ′** ἐναντίον αὖτις
12.6: ἄρσεν **θηλυτέρῳ·**

p. 190:
19.3: τοῖς δ′ ὄνομ′ ἄνθρωποι **κατέθεντ′** ἐπίσημον **ἑκάστῳ**.

By Being, It Is

By Being, It Is

THE THESIS OF PARMENIDES

Néstor-Luis Cordero

PARMENIDES
PUBLISHING

PARMENIDES PUBLISHING
Las Vegas 89109

Published 2004
Printed in the United States of America

ISBN: 1-930972-03-2

Publisher's Cataloging-in-Publication Data

Cordero, Nestor-Luis.
By being, it is : the thesis of Parmenides / Néstor-Luis Cordero.

p. ; cm.

Includes bibliographical references and index.
ISBN: 1-930972-03-2

1. Parmenides. 2. Ontology. 3. Eleatics. II. Title.

B187.05 C67 2004
182/.3

English translation by Dinah Livingstone
for Translate-A-Book, Oxford, England

1-888-PARMENIDES
www.parmenides.com

Contents

Prologue

Historians of philosophy usually refer to Plato to confirm the importance that Parmenides' philosophy had acquired, even in his own time. They cite not only the celebrated passage from Plato's *Sophist,* in which the Eleatic philosopher is described as the Athenian's (obviously spiritual) "father" (241d), but also the text of the *Theaetetus,* which calls him "venerable" and "fearsome" (183e), according to the Homeric formula applied to the revered Priam (*Il.* 3.172). Generally speaking, at this point, curiously, quotations from Plato's text peter out. But Plato continues to concern himself with Parmenides, and in the following sentence we find a true confession, proof of the lucidity and sincerity with which the philosopher approaches his ancestor's thought: Parmenides, says Plato, "seemed to me to have a power that denotes a depth absolutely full of nobility. Even so, I am afraid we may not understand his words, and I am even more afraid that what he was thinking of when he said them goes quite beyond us" (184a).

For us these words of Plato's have always been an invitation, indeed, an incitement, to take an interest in Parmenides' philosophy. Less than a century after his death, Plato is already confessing that he is afraid he cannot understand the meaning of the Eleatean's philosophy, but that does not prevent him recognizing its immense value or, especially, from criticizing and even refuting it. This means that *whatever the real meaning of Parmenides' ideas,* they were taken by Plato in a certain way, and that is the Parmenides whom Plato combats, or, if you prefer, revises and even improves. Today, almost twenty-five centuries later, we see that the Parmenideanism that Plato criticizes is a combination of the Eleatean's own ideas with Zenonian and Melissian ingredients, and that this explosive mixture was very probably represented by Antisthenes at the time the *Theaetetus* and *Sophist* were being written[1] (cf. Epilogue). But all this is secondary: it is the image Plato has of Parmenides that leads him to take an interest in him. And this is still going on today. Other philosophers of antiquity (Aristotle, Plutarch, Sextus Empiricus, Simplicius) offer us other aspects of Parmenides, and we might even say they present us with "other" Parmenides. So did the numerous doxographers, who often gave pride of place to a "cosmological" Parmenides.

1 Approximately 369–367 B.C.

This diversity of viewpoints has encouraged us to try to decipher those words that were already enigmatic for Plato. Do we then aspire, from our postmodernist stand, to grasp Parmenides' thought from a more privileged perspective than that from which his successors studied him? Not at all. But we must not fall into the opposite extreme and blindly accept the classical authors' viewpoints, without any critical spirit. Let us not forget that in commenting on their predecessors' thought they were not claiming to be "historians" of philosophy. They were conversing with ideas, not real people. And these real people may have expressed themselves orally, but most of them—including Parmenides—*wrote texts.* Almost miraculously, passages from these texts have come down to us.[2] And in our case, there is the assumption, or if you like, the prejudice that any interpretation of the philosopher must be based on these. When ancient authors comment on these passages, they must be listened to and respected as firsthand witnesses. This is the case with Plato when he cites and comments on the current first two lines of fragment 7 of Parmenides' Poem in the *Sophist* (237a, 258d), or when Sextus Empiricus transcribes nearly the whole of fragment 1 and presents his allegorical interpretation (*Adv. Math.* VII.111). On the other hand, there are cases in which certain passages have not earned the attention in antiquity that they merit for us today; in this case, we can exercise our right to interpret them. This is the case with fragment 2, fragment 6, and the first line of fragment 8, which today appear to expound the nucleus of Parmenides' thought, but which no one in antiquity commented on or cited (unless they did in texts now lost to us) for eleven centuries, until the sixth century of our era.[3]

* * * * *

All these theoretical conditions (or prejudices, if you like) have made us focus for years on the *state* of the Poem's text. Any new interpretation of Parmenides' philosophy, or any criticism of previous interpretations, must be based on a text that is as close as possible to the lost original. The titanic task carried out over centuries by philologists and codicologists offered us a firm starting point, but much still remained to be done. Passages of the Poem remained inexplicably obscure. (For example, why does the Goddess order withdrawal from a true way in line 6.3? How can it be said that thought is expressed in being, as line 8.35 appears to say?) For this reason, since my presence in Europe made it possible, I decided to check the manuscript tradition of citations (wrongly called "fragments") of the Poem, in order to propose a new version of it, purified of certain errors that had

2 In the case of Parmenides, cf. Chapter I (e).

3 In fact, the only citations of these texts occur in Proclus and in Simplicius.

accumulated over the centuries. A first result of my search was presented in 1971[4] as a doctoral thesis. Some years later, my book, *Les deux chemins de Parménide,*[5] completed my work. New research on the manuscript sources of the first editions of the Poem, as well as a change of view in my assessment of "the two ways," allow me to present this new version of Parmenides' "thesis" today. In this work, I also take into account comments and criticism that my previous studies on Parmenides have raised, and when appropriate, (a) I defend myself, or (b) I accept and make certain corrections.

It is impossible to go into Parmenides' philosophy without being "bitten by the bug." I hope that readers of this book will feel the same.

Néstor-Luis Cordero
University of Rennes I
France

4 Paris IV, Sorbonne. Supervisor, Pierre-Maxime Schuhl.

5 **Cordero**, N. L., *Les deux chemins de Parménide* (Paris/Brussels: Vrin/Ousia, 1984; second edition, augmented and corrected, 1997).

Acknowledgments

If Greek philosophy is still alive today it is due to two main factors. The first is the depth of Greek philosophers' thought in questioning the foundation of reality, a depth that continues to be the base of all actual reflection today. That we are aware of this thought, however, and that we are able to appreciate the Greek philosophers in all their magnificence, is due to quite another, usually forgotten, factor, one to which I want to pay tribute in this acknowledgment: the titanic work of those thousands of anonymous intermediates who handed down the ancient texts. It is thanks to these copyists and transcribers, true laborers of the intellect who were at first entirely unknown, that the texts we have today were able to survive. As more experts joined the ranks of dedicated workers intent on perfecting the quality of the texts, little by little the crafts of papyrology, codicology, and philology were born. Our indebtedness and eternal gratitude to these preservers and transmitters of the ideas of the past are fundamental.

In our own time, the task of conserving old texts is close to completion due to the promotion of ancient books and works dedicated to great philosophers of the past. A few publishers continue the tremendous task of the old copyists. In this sense, the work of Parmenides Publishing is exemplary, because it dedicates its efforts to defend Parmenides' place as the true "father" of Philosophy. To be among its selected authors and to partake in this essential promotion of Parmenidean philosophy makes me feel proud. I sincerely thank them.

By Being, It Is

Chapter I: Introduction to Parmenides

(a) The Region

All historians of ancient Greece admit that in the middle of the eighth century B.C., an unprecedented phenomenon occurred within the Hellenic world which, as we know, was made up of a group of autonomous cities, gradually evolving toward what would form the basis of the democratic *pólis* a century later. This was the expansion—wrongly named "colonization"[6]—toward the West.[7] For various reasons, none of which had to do with an idealistic "thirst for adventure"—either the growing shortage of arable land (a phenomenon called *stenokhoría* in Greek), or the need to seek new markets for production surpluses, or simply for individual reasons (invasions, natural disasters),[8] large human groups left what were usually the more prosperous cities in search of new horizons. This happened, above all, in Corinth, Megara, Miletos, and Phocaea. Phocaea is the one that concerns us here.

According to Strabo (XIV, 1, 3 = 633), the Phocians, who came from areas near Parnassus, in Phocis, settled in Ionia at a date that we can set today at around the eleventh to tenth centuries B.C.[9] They not only took part in this later expansion toward the West but, according to Herodotus, "they were the first among the Greeks to accomplish distant voyages. They were the ones who discovered the Adriatic Gulf, Tyrrenia, Iberia, and Tartessos (Cadiz)" (I.163). It is known that in about the year 600 B.C. they founded Massalia (Marseilles) and that in 565 B.C. they also settled in Alalia on the island of Corsica.[10]

While this settlement of the Phocians was taking place, a serious event hastened the departure of a new wave of migrants: in 545 B.C., Harpagon,

---

6 Finley says that during this period of crisis "a safety-valve" was provided by the movement wrongly called "colonization." (**Finley**, M. I., *The Ancient Greeks* [London: Viking Press, 1963], 25).

7 A detailed study of the question can be found in **Boardman**, J., *The Greeks Overseas* (Baltimore: Penguin Books, 1964), especially 175–231.

8 Claude Mossé's chapter titled "L'extension du monde grec a partir du VIIIe siecle" examines the possible causes of this expansion (**Mossé**, C., *La Grèce archaïque d'Homère à Eschyle* [Paris: Seuil, 1997], 79–95).

9 Cf. **Huxley**, G. L., *The Early Ionians* (New York: Faber, 1966), 25.

10 **Béraud**, J., *La colonisation grecque de l'Italie méridionale et de la Sicile dans l'Antiquité* (Paris: P.U.F., 1957), 267.

one of Cyrus the Persian's generals, invaded the mother city, Phocaea, whose inhabitants mostly went into exile.[11] Almost at the same time, an alliance between the Etruscans and the Carthaginians attacked the Corsican Phocians. The Greeks won, but they suffered such heavy losses that they had to abandon the island. That is how the exiled Phocians from the east (Alalia) and the west (Phocaea) joined together and disembarked at present-day Lucania, a few miles south of Naples. There they established the settlement of Elea.[12] A few years later, in the Phocian city in southern Italy, Parmenides was born.

Without coming to any agreement, historians debate about a certain detail, though it is not a very important one for us: in the place chosen to found the new "colony," was there already a local population, or did the Phocians occupy an uninhabited area? The reader who is interested in this question can refer to the documented works of E. Ciaceri,[13] J. Béraud,[14] G. Vallet and F. Villard,[15] M. Napoli,[16] E. Lepore,[17] and especially, J. P. Morel.[18] Herodotus (I.167) says that, in fact, the Phocians took over the city in southern Italy that the Enotrians called "Hyele." There must be some truth in this viewpoint, because Strabo (VI, 1, 1 = 252) confirms that the later Greeks gave the name of "Elea" to the place that the founders knew as Hyele, and that this name was of pre-Greek origin.[19] However that may be, we can state that Parmenides was born and lived among a Phocian community, that is, Ionian. Consequently, we can say at once that the arbitrary system usually to be found in certain history of philosophy manuals (whose origin goes back to Diogenes Laertius: I.13), which separates an "Ionian" school from an "Italic" school, does not make sense. Not only was the founder of the so-called Italic school, Pythagoras, born in Samos (an island from which Ionia can be seen), but Elea's most important philosopher, Parmenides, was of pure Ionian stock.

---

11 Cf. **Huxley**, *Early Ionians*, 117.

12 Cf. **Pugliese Carratelli**, G., "Nascita di Velia," *La parola del passato* 25 (1970) 60.

13 **Ciaceri**, E., *Storia della Magna Grecia* (Milan: Albrighi, Segati & Co., 1927).

14 **Béraud**, *La colonisation grecque*.

15 **Vallet**, V. and Villard, F., "Les Phocéens en Méditerranée Occidentale à l'époque archaïque et la fondation de Hyélè," *La parola del passato* 21 (1966) 166–90.

16 **Napoli**, M., *Civilità della Magna Grecia* (Rome: Eurodes, 1978) and "La ricerca archeologica di Velia," *La parola del passato* 21 (1966) 191–226.

17 **Lepore**, E., "Strutture della colonizzazione focea in Occident," *La parola del passato* 25 (1970) 19–54.

18 **Morel**, J. P., "Les Phocéens en Occident: certitudes et hypothèses," *La parola del passato* 21 (1966) 379–420, and "Sondages sur l'acropole de Vélia (Contribution aux premiers temps de la cité)," *La parola del passato* 25 (1970) 131–45.

19 Cf. **Capizzi**, A., *Introduzzione a Parmenide* (Bari: Laterza, 1975), 16. According to **Untersteiner** (1958), 41, the root of the name is Tyrrenian.

To complete this geographical sketch, we may add that Elea was a harbor city known as Velia by the Romans and in the Middle Ages called Castellamare di Veglia or Della Bruca. Nowadays it has lost its access to the sea because the coast has withdrawn by half a mile, and it is known as Ascea.

(b) Chronology

All the ancient witnesses assert that Parmenides was born in Elea.[20] However, nothing certain is known about his possible date of birth. As there can be no doubt that Parmenides is an Eleatean, a *post quem* date applies: Parmenides could not have been born before the foundation of Elea, an event that, as we have seen, took place shortly after 545 B.C. From then on, researchers have a free field in which to propose all sorts of hypotheses. Nevertheless, this freedom is not total: we may say that there are two possibilities to take into account, and as usually happens, there is a happy medium between the two. Hence we find that three probable chronologies have been proposed.

As a last resort, everything depends on the source chosen. In our case, as we said, there are two different dates proposed by two different sources, although in both cases, as we shall see, we have to resort to sophisticated deductions. One of the sources is a historian; the other, a philosopher. Which witness should we choose? The question is important because nearly thirty years separate the dates proposed by these two sources. However, we might say that the question could be resolved *a priori:* as it is a question of establishing a date, that is, a historical fact, it would appear that the last word should lie with the historian. In the present case, things are not that simple, because the historian uses data that enable us to *deduce* a date, but do not establish it for certain. The philosopher in question is Plato, whose authority specialists usually reverently accept regarding everything he said, including statements about historical events.

Let us begin with the historian. He is Diogenes Laertius, whose work, *Lives of Eminent Philosophers,* is an inexhaustible source of facts. Nevertheless, we know that this work should be referenced with caution because its reliability depends on the sources used by Diogenes himself, and when no source is cited, then doubts arise. However, with his chronologies there is a certain consensus among commentators to consider them fairly reliable, because they depend on Apollodorus' heavily documented *Chronicles* (sec-

20 Cf., among others, **Diogenes Laertius**, IX.21; **Proclus**, *In Parm.*, I, 619, 4; **Strabo**, VI, I, 252.

ond century B.C.),[21] which use the dates of the Olympiads as benchmarks.[22] With respect to Parmenides, we read in Diogenes Laertius (who, in this case, probably also takes the information from Apollodorus, although he does not say so) that the philosopher reached his *akmē* (that is, the height of his activity, which usually coincides with his forties) during the sixty-ninth Olympiad[23] (IX.23). If this is true, Parmenides must have been born between 544 and 541 B.C., that is, just about when the Phocians arrived in Elea. His parents may have belonged to the party that founded the city.

Let us now look at what Plato has to say. As we know, the dialogue *Parmenides* describes a visit to Athens by Zeno of Elea for the purpose of making known orally (through conferences, as we would say today) the contents of his book. Still according to Plato, Zeno arrived accompanied by his master, Parmenides, and one of those present at the conference was Socrates. Unexpectedly, the introduction of these characters gives us material of priceless value for the Parmenidean chronology, because for reasons unknown to us, Plato is unstinting with details referring to the precise ages of the protagonists: Zeno is approaching his forties; Parmenides, despite his noble presence, has white hair and is fairly old, about sixty-five. For his part, Socrates is a mere stripling (*Parm.* 127b–c).

In order to be able to deduce the date of Parmenides' birth, we need to know what year this philosophical encounter in Athens took place. Plato only says that the meeting took place during the Pan-Athenian Festival, and that at that time Socrates was very young. Historians have established that this festival, celebrated every four years, took place in 454 B.C., 450 B.C., and 446 B.C. during Socrates' youth. Hence, as Socrates was not only present at the conference but appeared as a young philosopher already propounding the real existences of Forms or Ideas, the first date must be discounted. A fifteen-year-old adolescent (Socrates was born, as we know, in 469 B.C.) would have found it difficult to assume that role. We must also discount the year 446 B.C., because a twenty-three-year-old is no longer "a stripling" (*sphódra néos*, 127c). That leaves only 450 B.C., the year in which Socrates would have been nineteen. And if Parmenides, as Plato states, was then sixty-five, he must have been born in the year 515 B.C., that is, almost thirty

---

21 This lost work has partly been reconstructed by **Jacoby**, F., *Apollodoros Chronik, Eine Sammlung der Fragmente* (Berlin: Weidmann, 1902).

22 On the importance of this work, cf. **Untersteiner**, M., in *Problemi di filologia filosofica*, ed. Sichirollo, L., and Venturi Ferriolo, M. (Milan: Cislapino-Goliardica, 1980), 244. Cf. also **Diels**, H., "Chronologische Untersuchungen über Apollodors Chronik," *Rheinisches Museum* 31 (1876) 1–54.

23 Years 504–501 B.C., because the first Olympiad is thought to have taken place in 740–737 B.C.

years later than the date proposed by Diogenes Laertius and Apollodorus. The difference is very important, especially when we want to position a philosopher's thought in relation to someone else's ideas, in this case, Heraclitus (as we shall see).

As usually happens, attempts to reconcile both dates were not slow in coming, but most of them were based on modifications of the original texts, a mortal sin that any serious philologist must avoid. I mention, as a curiosity, that a desperate but ingenious solution was proposed in 1924 by Heinrich Gomperz.[24] He retained Plato's authority, but saw a contradiction between the description of Parmenides as someone very old (*mála presbúten,* 127b) and the fact that he was "barely" sixty-five years old. His interpretation was that Plato meant that the philosopher "appeared" to be that age, whereas he was really much older ("he might have been eighty," Gomperz supposed). Thence he proposed the year 530 B.C. as Parmenides' date of birth.[25]

Which testimony is the most reliable? Given the characteristics of the Platonic text, I am inclined to opt for the Diogenes Laertius/Apollodorus chronology. Let me say why. Plato is a philosopher, not a historian.[26] His interest in the first part of *Parmenides* is to criticize certain aspects of his theory of Forms. So imagine the scene: only a philosopher with great prestige, especially if he is a "venerable" person (as Parmenides had already been described in the *Theaetetus,* 183e), would have the necessary authority to admonish a stripling claiming to have "already" found a definitive truth, as is the case with the character interpreted by Socrates. I say "interpreted" because, although there may be doubts in other dialogues about the philosophical opinions expressed by Socrates (which might belong, according to some scholars, to the historical Socrates), in the case of the *Parmenides,* Plato puts into Socrates' mouth a rigorous and orthodox presentation of his own theory of Forms. This turns the great philosopher into an almost fictional character, a sort of ventriloquist through whom Plato's own voice speaks. And just as he had to rejuvenate Socrates in order to attribute the difficulties he found in defending his ideas to his inexperience, Plato had to resort to the great Parmenides to make a criticism, which is in fact a self-criticism.

Everything indicates that Plato does not set real characters on his stage but symbolic ones: the young philosopher, enthusiastic but dogmatic; the

---

24 **Gomperz,** H., "Psychologische Beobachtungen an griechischen Philosophen," *Imago* 10 (1924).

25 Other possibilities are found in **Bicknell,** P. J., "Dating the Eleatics," in *For Service of Classical Studies, Essays in Honor of F. Letters,* ed. Kelly, M. (Melbourne: Cheshire, 1966), 1–14.

26 On Plato as a "historian," cf. **Chiereghin,** F., *Implicazioni etiche della storiografia filosofica di Platone* (Padua: Liviana, 1976), Chapter III.

old master, experienced and didactic. R. E. Allen admits no doubt in maintaining that the encounter is just a fiction,[27] which only confirms that lack of confidence already shown in antiquity about the reality of this fact. Athenaeus had stated that its historicity was highly unlikely, and to back this judgment he cited an epigram by Timon, who alluded to Plato's "fictions" (or "simulations": *peplasména: Deip.*, XI, 505f). For his part, Macrobius quoted the case of the *Protagoras,* in which Plato presented two characters who had already died of the plague some time before and, ironically, stated that he did not claim to "count" his characters' ages on his fingers" (*Saturn.* I, 1.5).

From the beginning of the dialogue, Plato does everything he can to make the reader "de-realize" the story: the encounter is narrated by Cephalus, who heard it from Antiphon, who in his turn heard it from Pythodorus (126a–127b). After this series of "Russian dolls" (or "Chinese boxes," as Allen calls them),[28] any similarity to real events, as certain movies declare, is pure coincidence.[29] Lastly, we should not forget that Plato is accustomed, doubtless on purpose, to dropping into anachronisms. As M. Untersteiner[30] remarks, in *Timaeus* 20d, Solon becomes younger by twenty and even by thirty years. For all these reasons, I am inclined to accept the date proposed by Diogenes Laertius/Apollodorus, which, incidentally, has an unexpected secondary consequence. It puts an end to the sterile question of Parmenides' supposed criticism of Heraclitus, because if Parmenides was born between 544 and 541 B.C., he was practically contemporary with the Chiaroscuro of Ephesus. Both philosophers reached their intellectual zenith during the sixty-ninth Olympiad and, apparently, they were totally unknown to one another.

(c) Life

Little or nothing is known about Parmenides' life, except for the name of his father, Pyres. A few years ago, the discovery in Elea of a statue pedestal inscribed "Parmenides, son of Pyres, doctor philosopher" encouraged the idea of the existence of a school of medicine in the region, to which our philosopher may have belonged or of which he may have even been the

27 In **Plato**, *Parmenides*, trans. Allen, R. E. (Oxford: Blackwell, 1983), 63.

28 **Plato**, *Parmenides*, 61.

29 Although **Gómez-Lobo** (1985), 19, believes, as I do, that the encounter is imaginary, he thinks that Plato wanted to convince the reader of its reality, hence his precision in giving the ages.

30 **Untersteiner** (1958), 19.

head. Much has been written about this.[31] The only certainty we can draw for our knowledge of Parmenides is the confirmation of his social importance, which was already substantiated in antiquity by authors like Plutarch (*Adv. Col.* 32, p. 1126A) and Strabo (VI, 1), who related that the philosopher compiled the laws of Elea and that even many years later the citizens of that city still swore obedience to those laws. Other details about Parmenides' life are the fruit of interpreters' imagination. One interpreter, Karl Popper, goes beyond what should be expected from a sensible researcher; referring to Parmenidean terminology on light, he does not hesitate to state that our philosopher was "brought up by and with a beloved blind sister, three years older than himself."[32] The classical authors do not fall into these excesses of imagination. Diogenes Laertius, for example, bases himself on Sotion and says that Parmenides belonged to an illustrious and wealthy family (IX.21), which enabled him to put up a mausoleum in memory of his friend Ameinias, a Pythagorean philosopher. This detail brings us to a secondary question, much debated not only in antiquity but also in our own days: the problem of "Parmenides' masters."

Diogenes Laertius is very explicit in this respect: "It was by Ameinias and not by Xenophanes that he [Parmenides] was led to dedicate himself to the contemplative life" (IX.21). Despite Diogenes Laertius' opinion, the belief that Parmenides was a faithful disciple of Xenophanes (the origin of which, as we shall see, goes back to Plato) is usually held.

Let us begin, like Diogenes Laertius, with Ameinias. Nothing is known of this person except that he was a Pythagorean.[33] In fact, Pythagorism had spread over the south of Italy since the year 530 B.C., when Pythagoras had settled in Croton (Calabria), fleeing from Policrates, the tyrant of Samos, his country.[34] It cannot be denied that Parmenides knew about Pythagorean philosophy,[35] and it was his friendship with Ameinias that awoke a sort of

---

31 Cf. the works of **Nutton**, V., "The Medical School of Velia," *La parola del passato* 25 (1970) 211–25; **Gigante**, M., "Velina gens," *La parola del passato* 19 (1964) 135–37; and the three articles by **Pugliese Carratelli**, G., "*Pholarkhós*," *La parola del passato* 18 (1963) 385–86, "Parmenídes *phusikós*," *La parola del passato* 20 (1965) 306, and "Ancora su *pholarkhós*," *La parola del passato* 25 (1970) 134–38.

32 **Popper**, K., *The World of Parmenides* (London/New York: Routledge, 1998), 78.

33 The only mention of the name Ameinias (or Aminias) is to be found in **Diogenes Laertius** IX.21. Cf. *Dictionnaire des philosophes antiques*, ed. Goulet, R. (Paris: CNRS, 1989), 159.

34 On Pythagorean influences on southern Italy, cf. the classic work of **Raven**, J. E., *Pythagoreans and Eleatics* (Cambridge, England: Cambridge University Press, 1948).

35 The principles that Aristotle attributed to the Pythagoreans included *phôs* and *skótos* (*Met.* A,5,986a22), which are picked up by Parmenides in 8.56–59 (*pûr . . . nuktós*) and in 14.3 (*phaòs kaì nuktós*). And in 8.41, Parmenides speaks of *khrôs*, which, according to Aetios, was the term used by Pythagoreans to refer to the surface of a body (I,15.2).

philosophical vocation in him. But we cannot be sure, despite certain rather hasty judgments (for example, Proclus, *In Parm.* I, p. 619, 4; Strabo, VI, 1, p. 252) that he himself was a Pythagorean.

The case of Xenophanes is very different. No ancient source was able to establish the slightest personal connection between Parmenides and Xenophanes. Apparently, the latter, a peripatetic poet-philosopher, wrote an ode in homage to the founders of Elea,[36] but this does not imply his physical presence in the city, especially as the Phocians were almost neighbors of Colophon, Xenophanes' city, where he may well have written the ode in question. Moreover, no evidence exists for the presence of Xenophanes in Elea.[37] Diogenes Laertius relates that the philosopher passed through Sicily (IX, 18), but the weight of prejudices insisting that Xenophanes was Parmenides' master was so heavy that a researcher of the H. Diels stamp did not hesitate to state that there was a gap in the Diogenes text and that the missing text should read: "he was also in Elea, where he taught." In other words, although no ancient source had said so, the presence of Xenophanes in Elea was indubitable, and the modification of a classic text now made it possible. Luckily, the editors of Diogenes Laertius' text did not adopt this hypothesis, which is only to be found in *Die Fragmente der Vorsokratiker* (1903) by H. Diels and in bad translations that rely blindly on this text. A brisk summing-up of the *status quaestionis* can be found in G. Cerri: "In reality, Xenophanes of Colophon never had anything to do with Elea."[38]

As I have already mentioned, it was Plato who first established a relationship between Xenophanes and Parmenides[39]—in an allusive, indirect way. The relationship is a doctrinal one. In a passage in the *Sophist,* Plato wants to refute the philosophers who approach "being" in a quantitative way, whether they are monists or pluralists. When he comes to the monists, Plato, who finds this conception explicitly in Melissus of Samos (cf. *Theaetetus,* 180e, 183e), confronts Parmenides in the *Sophist* as the presumed master of this philosopher to whom he attributes the same idea, an idea belonging to the "Eleatics." And when Plato gives the genealogy of this "group"

36 Cf. **Diogenes Laertius**, IX.20.

37 Cf. **Corbato**, C., "Studi Senofanei," *Annali Triestini* XXII (1952), 200 and **Woodbury**, L., "Apollodorus, Xenophanes and the foundation of Massilia," *The Phoenix* 15 (1961) 134–55.

38 **Cerri**, G., "Elea, Senofane e Leucothea," in *Forme di religiosità e tradizioni sapienziali in Magna Grecia,* ed. Casio, A. C., and Poccetti, P. (Pisa/Rome: Istituti Editoriali e Poligrafici Internazionali, 1993), 138.

39 On this Platonic fiction, cf. **Cordero**, N. L., "Simplicius et l''école' éléate," in *Simplicius, sa vie, son oeuvre, sa survie,* ed. Hadot, I. (Berlin/New York: Walter de Gruyter, 1987) 166–82; and "L'invention de l'école éléatique (Platon, *Sophiste* 242d)," in *Études sur le "Sophiste" de Platon,* ed. Aubenque, P. (Naples: Bibliopolis, 1991), 91–124.

(*éthnos,* 242d), he says that it began with Xenophanes or even before.[40] That is all.[41]

Firstly, I should say that even Xenophanes' "monism" is problematic, because his writings only speak about one single "god" (fr. 23), whereas his "physics" is eminently pluralist (cf. frs. 29, 32, and especially 33, where he says we come from earth and water). As for Parmenides' "monism," as I shall try to show, this was merely a didactic generalization proposed by Plato,[42] considered as a sort of revealed truth by later tradition, which associated his name with Xenophanes'. In short, we can state that Parmenides followed his own way and his philosophy is eminently personal and original.

(d) Works

Tradition unanimously recognizes that Parmenides wrote one single work: a poem (cf. D.L. I.16). There is nothing exceptional about his writing just one text; Diogenes Laertius says that the same was true of Melissus and Anaxagoras. It is difficult in our postmodernity to imagine such unprolific philosophers. But we should not forget that these "sages" had multiple occupations (the "contemplative life" was an ideal, for some, only after Aristotle). Very probably they wrote to leave a statement of their work, which, perhaps, they expounded in oral lectures and which they would certainly have used as a rule of life.[43] So there is nothing surprising about a single work, as in the case of Parmenides, or just a few small treatises, as was the case with most of the Presocratics, being enough to establish the fame of a thinker and become an important stage in the establishment of this new type of knowledge directed toward action, which was later called "philosophy."

---

40 It is curious that the defenders of Eleatic "monism" have not paid any heed to the ironic character of Plato's expression "even before." Plato had already used it in the *Theaetetus* 179e when, in speaking about Heraclitism, he says that these ideas come from Homer "and even from an earlier time." Strictly speaking, it is difficult to imagine witnesses earlier than Homer. With respect to the doctrine attributed to the Eleatics, an ironical spirit might recall that the only philosopher who wrote that "everything [is] one" was Heraclitus (fr. 50).

41 Cf. **Cordero**, "Simplicius et l''école'."

42 This is not the case with Aristotle, who cautiously states: "it is said (*légetai*) that Parmenides came to be his disciple" (*Met.* I, V, 986b22). On the other hand, the lexicon *Suidas* states it clearly.

43 On ancient philosophy as a way of life, cf. **Hadot**, P., *Qu'est-ce que la philosophie antique?* (Paris: Gallimard, 1995).

(e) The Poem

(1) The Reconstruction

Parmenides expressed his ideas in a poem, but his work has been irreparably lost for at least fifteen centuries. *Nothing* remains of Parmenides' original Poem. The work was probably written at the end of the sixth or beginning of the fifth century B.C.[44] Without any doubt, it was copied and recopied (always by hand) over the course of many years, but all traces of it were lost in the sixth century of our era, that is, practically a millennium after it was written by Parmenides. The last concrete reference to the book appears in the neo-Platonic philosopher Simplicius (who is known to have left Athens in 526 A.D. because the Platonic Academy was closed down).[45] After quoting some lines from the Poem, Simplicius explains that he is taking that liberty "because of the rarity (*dià tḗn spánin*) of Parmenides' book" (*Commentary on Aristotle's Physics,* p. 144). From then on, nothing is known about Parmenides' work.[46]

So how do we explain the fact that today we can read, quote, and comment on Parmenides' Poem? It is thanks to the work of a large number of scholars who managed to *reconstruct* the lost text, though unfortunately only in part. Thus Parmenides' fate is like that of most philosophers known as "Presocratic."[47] Their writings were lost, but before that happened, their texts were abundantly quoted by authors from all sorts of disciplines (not only philosophers but also historians, doctors, mathematicians, tragic playwrights, etc.) whose works lasted for very different reasons. Thanks to these *passages* of Parmenides' Poem, sometimes cited to support authors' ideas or sometimes out of simple erudition by a long series of witnesses, it became possible to reconstruct a good part of the original work.[48] As may be deduced from this brief overview, the word "fragment" applied to these

---

44 **Cornford** (1939), 1, suggests that "the poem was written in about the year 485 B.C." Bowra says that the poem was contemporary with Pindar's *Pythica* X, written in 498 B.C., and Aeschylus' *Suplicantes,* written before 490 B.C. (**Bowra**, C. M., "The Poem of Parmenides," *Classical Quarterly* 32 [1937]).

45 Cf. the works of **Hadot**, I., "La vie et l'oeuvre de Simplicius d'après des sources grecques et arabes," 3–39; and **Tardieu**, M., "Les calendriers à usage à Harrân d'après les sources arabes et le Commentaire de Simplicius à la Physique d'Aristote," 40–57, both in Hadot, *Simplicius, sa vie.*

46 With hindsight we find, at most, indirect references to Parmenides' system. Cf. **Baldwin**, B., "Parmenides in Byzantium," *Liverpool Classical Monthly* (1990) 115–16.

47 I say "most" because there are some very rare exceptions: we have received in direct form (that is, not through quotations collected by sources) a fragmentary text by Antiphon, a few discourses by Gorgias, and, recently, a previously unknown fragment of Empedocles.

48 Cf. **Cordero**, N. L., "L'histoire du texte de Parménide" in *Études sur Parménide, Volume II: Problèmes d'interprétation,* ed. Aubenque, P. (Paris: Vrin, 1987) 3–24.

passages does not make sense; they are *quotations*—literal, we may presume (the philologists do not have the last word on that, but they do have the tools to enable them to estimate the reliability of the text)—from *lost* texts.

Quotations from Parmenides' Poem begin at an early date: the first source is Plato, less than a century after the philosopher's death. Plato transcribes a few lines in the *Sophist,* the *Theaetetus,* and the *Symposium.*[49] Then it is the turn of Aristotle, Plutarch, Sextus Empiricus, and so on, until we reach Simplicius. The quotations are sometimes very short (two or three words) but sometimes, especially in the cases of Sextus and Simplicius, they may be more than thirty lines long. On more than one occasion the same passage is quoted a number of times (this is the ideal situation, because when there are divergences, we can choose the version that appears to coincide most closely with the original). In other cases, there exists a single source and our whole interpretation depends on it.

In order to try to *reconstruct* the lost text, it was necessary to assemble all the *quotations* from it that could be found. The success of the task depends to a large extent on the state of the *sources,* that is, the book that assembles every quotation from the Poem. Some of these texts have come down to us in complete form and it has been possible to reconstruct them because various manuscript copies of them have withstood the passage of time.[50] Other works have been ill-treated by history, and their reconstruction requires Homeric efforts. Attempts to reconstruct Parmenides' Poem began shortly after the Renaissance, but although they were very praiseworthy, there were classical texts still unknown at that time, and the quotations from Parmenides contained in them were not discovered until several centuries later. These attempts at reconstruction go from Henri Estienne (*Poesis philosophica,* 1573) to Hermann Diels (*Die Fragmente der Vorsokratiker,* 1903).[51] Thanks to their work, which went on over many centuries, today we can *read* a good part of Parmenides' Poem. Nineteen different quotations were found (one of them translated into Latin!). These were unfortunately labeled "fragments," which is why, for the sake of convenience, works on Parmenides speak about "fragment 3" or "fragment 5." As each fragment includes a number of lines, it is customary to write "fr. 8.34," for example, when quoting line 34 of "fragment" 8.

From what I have said, it can be seen that the version of Parmenides' Poem we possess *is not complete.* Passages *that weren't quoted by anybody* will

---

49 On the decisive importance of Parmenides' philosophy to Plato, cf. **Palmer**, J. H., *Plato's Reception of Parmenides* (Oxford: Oxford University Press, 1999), passim.

50 This is the case with Simplicius' indispensable *Commentary* on Aristotle's *Physics.* A new edition of it, edited by Leonardo Tarán, is eagerly awaited by all Hellenists.

51 One of the first attempts, undertaken in about 1600 by Joseph J. Scaliger, remained unpublished until 1982, when I discovered this version in the archives of Leyden University

remain unknown forever. Of course, the authors we use today as sources (perhaps abusively, because these authors were writing to express their own ideas, rather than to leave testimonies of other thinkers, except in the case of "historians" of thought such as Theophrastus) quoted only those passages that interested them. There is nothing more subjective than a scholar's interest. A paradigmatic case is the vital Parmenides text, our present fragment 2, which postulates the existence of being, quoted for the first time by Proclus (*In Tim.* I.345) a thousand years after it was written. Probably the discovery of the fact of being by Parmenides seemed so "obvious" that nobody thought to quote it. Perhaps the same thing happened with other passages of the Poem; we will never know. Even so, today we possess nearly 152 lines of Parmenides, and these are an inexhaustible source of reflection. So let us take advantage of them.

(2) The Form

At a time when sages, who would later be called philosophers, expressed themselves in prose, albeit in brief treatises or epigrams, Parmenides decided to compose a Poem. Xenophanes had done it before him (although this writer was a poet sporadically introducing philosophical reflections into his compositions, rather than a philosopher expressing himself through poetry). But most of Xenophanes' works are semi-satirical poems called *Silloi* (literally, "jokes"), along with two elegies dedicated to the foundation of Colophon and Elea. In contrast, Parmenides' poetry takes its cue from Homer and from Hesiod's epic hexameter.[52] Although Parmenides is of Ionian stock and most of the inhabitants of the Elea region are Dorians, the poem is written in the pan-Hellenic dialect of the Homeric poems.[53] All these details combine to fulfill a common aim: Parmenides wants to interest (and be understood by) the widest possible public.[54]

The epic hexameter is easy to remember; the educated and even semi-educated public of his time knew long passages, or even the whole works, of Homer and Hesiod by heart. W. Jaeger rightly shows no doubt in stating

---

Library and made this known in "La version de Joseph Scaliger du Poème de Parménide," *Hermes* 110 (1982).

52 An exhaustive study of Parmenides' metrics can be found in **Mourelatos** (1970), 2 and 264–68, and on Parmenides' poetry in general (especially the formulas inherited from tradition) in **Böhme**, R., *Die verkannte Muse. Dichtersprache und geistige Tradition des Parmenides* (Berne: Francke, 1986), especially 33–85.

53 Cf. **Jaeger** (1947), 92.

54 Floyd finds a deeper relationship between Parmenides and Homer, as the philosopher is inspired by the poet when he too presents his teaching by means of the opposing notions of Truth and Opinion (**Floyd**, E. D., "Why Parmenides wrote in verse" *Ancient Philosophy* 12 [1992] 251, 263).

that Parmenides uses a "didactic epic."[55] Indeed, Parmenides, convinced he has discovered an essential, basic, and fundamental *truth,*[56] wants to communicate his discovery, and in order to do so he presents his Poem as a real course in philosophy, in which a professor (in the text, an anonymous goddess) explains to a pupil (in the text, an enthusiastic but inexperienced youth) how to go about seeking truth.[57] Parmenides deploys all the didactic resources at his disposal: allegorical images, persuasion, demonstration through the absurd. It is highly suggestive that, despite the Master's (that is, the Goddess's) intellectual superiority, the criterion of authority, as well as any claim to a "revelation," are absent from the Poem. The Goddess orders that anything she says is to be judged by reasoning (*lógos,* fr. 7.5).

We said that Parmenides is claiming to be the bearer of a "truth." This is another way in which his Poem stands in the Homeric and Hesiodic tradition. Both Homeric poems, like Hesiod's *Theogony* and *Works and Days,* begin with an invocation to the Muses or to a goddess to relate a truth. Parmenides allegorically replaces the invocation with a journey toward the Goddess's home.[58] And as in the case of epic poetry, a truth will be proclaimed. On this occasion, it is not about the consequences of Achilles' rage, the vicissitudes suffered by Odysseus on his journey home, the genealogy of the gods, the invention of women, the ages of humanity, or the propitious days for carrying out particular activities, all these realities expounded by the muses who "when they wish, know how to proclaim true things" (*Theogony* 28). Parmenides' truth will be different. The discourses of the muses, daughters of Memory, would be incapable of presenting it, because from Parmenides onward, truth will not come from the past; it will arise from well-directed, methodological reflection that is respectful of certain principles and aware of the abyss that opens with the possibility of error.

(3) The Content

I have said that, up until now, nineteen quotations from Parmenides' lost Poem have been found, and that with these, part of the text has been recon-

---

55 Cf. **Jaeger** (1947), 92.

56 According to Arrighetti, Parmenides decided to write in verse to differentiate himself from the "physicists," because his Poem follows "another way" (**Arrighetti**, G., "L'heredità dell'epica in Parmenide," in *Festschrift für Robert Muth zum 65. Geburtstag,* ed. Haendel, P., and Meid, W. [Innsbruck: Institut für Sprachwissenschaft der Universität Innsbruck, 1983], 11).

57 Cf. **Cordero**, N. L., "La Déesse de Parménide, maîtresse de philosophie," in *La naissance de la raison en Grèce,* ed. Mattéi, J. F. (Paris: P.U.F., 1990) 207–14.

58 As Montaner points out, Empedocles, a disciple of Parmenides, reverts to attributing the teaching he presents to the Muse (cf. frs. 131.1, 3.3, and 4.2) (**Montaner**, A., "La struttura

structed. It is impossible to know (except in one case) what place in the Poem each of these quotations should occupy. Since the first attempts at reconstruction, they have been arranged in accordance with the conceptual content of each "fragment." However, it must be recognized that Parmenides represents a special case among the philosophers called Presocratic. Quotations from the other Presocratics have mostly been arranged in accordance with the arranger's criterion. This is the case, for example, with Heraclitus: every scholar arranges the "fragments" in the order that he or she thinks is right, and an "index of concordances" is usually added as an appendix to the works to help the reader find the text in the classic version of Diels and Kranz's *Die Fragmente der Vorsokratiker.* Parmenides is an exception because, given the systematic character of his philosophy, there are passages of his text that have to precede or come after others. Brief texts of a general nature are difficult to place, and it can be said that in the present state of the reconstruction,[59] Fragment 4 is the most disputed of all "fragments." Placed logically between fragment 3 and fragment 5 by most interpreters, it is considered as a sort of enclave within fragment 8 by certain scholars—Zeller[60] among them—or is thought to belong directly between fragments 6 and 7.[61]

The exception I referred to in the placing of the fragments is the text considered today to be "fragment 1." The sole source of the first twenty-eight lines of this quotation is Sextus Empiricus, and in the passage preceding his transcription of Parmenides' lines, the skeptic philosopher explains that "at the beginning of his [text] on nature [Parmenides] writes . . ." (*Adv. Math.* VII.111). So nobody can object to considering the extensive quotation presented by Sextus to be "fragment 1."

This quotation ends with a sort of project: the Goddess invites the youth who wants "to know" to consider two ways: that of truth and that of opinions. A text that begins precisely with the presentation of these two possibilities seems to be the logical continuation of "fragment 1," and for that reason it is considered to be "fragment 2." A single line that speaks of the identity between being and thinking was placed next as fragment 3, because toward the end of fragment 2, Parmenides alludes to the impossi-

---

del Proemio di Parmenide," *Annali dell'Istituto Italiano per gli Studi Filosofici* V [1976–78] 138).

59 Which, nevertheless, is always capable of being improved: cf. **Bicknell**, P. J., "A New Arrangement of Some Parmenidean Verses," *Symbolae Osloensis* 42 (1968) 44–50; and **Kent Sprague**, R., "Parmenides: A Suggested Rearrangement of Fragments in the Way of Truth," *Classical Philology* 50 (1955) 124–26.

60 **Zeller**, E., *Die Philosophie der Griechen in ihrer geschichtlichen Entwicklung* (Leipzig: G. R. Reisland, 1892), 693.

61 **Reinhardt** (1916) 48–49.

bility of saying and thinking what is not, which would establish a relationship between what is and what is thought. Next comes the enigmatic fragment 4, which can be placed where the interpreter sees fit, as well as the quotation called "fragment 5," which is eminently methodological or programmatic. In contrast, the text considered to be fragment 6 seems to pick up on the final lines of fragment 2, and the quotation called "fragment 7" naturally continues the content of fragment 6. Fragment 7 is prolonged directly without any break into the extensive fragment 8. This fragment 8 ends with a negative allusion regarding any possible "cosmology," which, according to Parmenides, would form part of "the opinions of mortals." As the eleven remaining quotations (frs. 9–19) also refer to cosmological questions, they have always been placed, fairly coherently, after fragment 8. The current fragment 19 is a sort of conclusion to the Poem.

According to this reconstruction of the Poem, we can state the following: (a) Parmenides begins with an *allegorical* presentation of his philosophy in which, by means of a series of images easily interpretable by the public of his time, he describes two ways of seeking offered to thought (fr. 1); (b) he presents both possibilities *philosophically* and shows that one is viable and the other is a blind alley (fr. 2); (c) he shows why anyone who tries to pursue both ways will reach the conclusion that only one possibility can be admitted (frs. 6 and 7); (d) a long list of "properties" are deduced from the single possibility that accompanies truth (fr. 8.1–52); and (e) despite everything—even though they are deceptive—it is necessary to be aware of the opinions of mortals, illustrated, for example, by illusory "cosmologies" (fr. 8.53–fr. 19).

Let us now see how this project takes shape in terms of Parmenides' *theoría,* that is, his way of confronting the reality of things.

Chapter II: Prolegomena to Parmenides' Thesis

(a) Parmenides' theoría

All philosophical systems have aspired to understand reality. With the Greek philosophers, at least in the early stages, the object of this interest was "everything that is" as a whole, because when a Greek thinks of the notion of what—from a Latin root—we call "reality," he thinks of everything that "possesses" the fact of being, that is, the totality of beings. With this outlook they tried to establish a certain familiarity between human beings and things, which would make possible a way of life in accordance with this *vision* of reality. The Greek word for "vision," "contemplation," or "viewpoint" is *theoría.* This noun, related to the verbs *theoréo̱* and *theáomai,* originally meant observing with precise interest, a kind of scrutiny that goes beyond mere "looking" (*blépo̱*). In the title of this section I have put the word in italics because this is a direct transliteration of the Greek. The moment has not yet come to present Parmenides' "theory" (not in quotation marks, this time), which would be synonymous with his philosophy. That will be the consequence of a certain way of "contemplating" the reality of things, and for the moment I present this rather special way of looking at the Greek word *theoría,* alluding, I repeat, to a preliminary but fundamental stage: anyone who simply "looks at" things will never reach amazement, that state of mind (*páthos*) which both Plato (*Theaet.* 155d) and Aristotle (*Met.* A, 2, 982b 12) make the starting point for doing philosophy. In contrast, anyone who *observes* reality as if it were a theatrical representation ("theater" derives from *theáomai*) will surely be interested in the play's plot and will ask questions about how the action happens; instead of just "looking," they will "ad-mire" (that is, they will be amazed), and thus will become a lover of knowledge, a "philosopher."

Parmenides' *theoría* is different from that of his predecessors. For more than a century, this new activity (which gradually became a kind of "knowledge") had been acquiring a certain specificity. Although we may not blindly trust the didactic outlines drawn up later by Aristotle (which reached posterity through Theophrastus), there is an air of kinship between the thinkers of Miletos, the first Pythagoreans, and another isolated thinker who did philosophy before Parmenides. And this atmosphere will reappear later among the last "Presocratics," the atomists. To a greater or lesser extent, these philosophers observed reality (that is, put into practice a *theoría*) with the intention of explaining it through principles or elements, from which, as the case might be, either internal or external forces could be derived that justified the developmental stages leading from the first germ to reality as it was now constituted.

The task of these lovers of wisdom was titanic. If we had preserved their original writings, we would have to invent an even more grandiose adjective to describe their discoveries. But—and there is nothing pejorative about this "but"; I am simply trying to point out the difference between these *theorías* (which are fairly similar to each other) and that of Parmenides—this way of confronting reality assumed a basic fact, without which it would have been impossible to reflect on the principles or elements of things: the existence of things. As "there are" things (we will look at this notion of "thing" later), it was reasonable to investigate them and question their origins, their components, their connections, and their disconnections. We can say that everything was questioned, except this apparently obvious fact: the existence of these things.

Parmenides' *theoría* is set on a different plane. He is interested in this basic fact *assumed* by his predecessors: "there are" things. What does it mean to assume that "there are" things? It would appear that Thales stated that the first principle of reality was water (or rather moisture), that Anaximander proposed an indefinite first principle (*tò ápeiron*), and that Anaximenes inclined toward air and the Pythagoreans toward mathematical entities. But no one asked what it means that this first principle should exist, and even less, why it exists. The first principle exists; things exist. Isn't that amazing? Why is it amazing? Because there could have been nothing, yet there is something. Why? This is not asking about a possible "creation," because, as we know, that notion has no place in Greek thought. The establishment of the fact that there is a reality (which later becomes Parmenides' "thesis") opens up unexpected horizons for the philosopher, contains undreamt-of riches, and displays an inexhaustible fruitfulness, to the point that it would appear that for Parmenides the inescapable, basic task of the philosopher must consist in grasping the ultimate consequence and total scope of the formula "there are things." And Parmenides gives the example, because his Poem undertakes to do this.

There can be no doubt that Parmenides was aware of the vital importance of the message he proposed to transmit to his contemporaries. That is why he used poetry as his medium of expression and why, in his own way, he methodically "demonstrated" his intuitions. As we saw in the previous chapter, his use of the epic hexameter shows a clear desire to address listeners didactically, or possibly also readers (since few people could read), who were not necessarily already attracted to the new philosophical adventure. Doubtless, this is the reason that the Poem begins with a sort of introduction abounding in easily recognizable Hesiodic images (day and night roads, ethereal gates, winged chariots, gracious daughters of the Sun, and so forth). Through this ploy, once the listener/reader finds himself on familiar ground, the dryness of the philosophical discourse that begins at the end of this introduction seems almost familiar.

Parmenides presents his ideas as stages on a way or road to be traveled, along which a future philosopher will have the privilege of being guided by an anonymous Goddess, who acts as a real professor expounding a kind of master's course. This forces him to follow a "method" (remember that this term comes from the Greek "*hodós,*" "way"), with axioms, stages, conclusions, demonstrations through the absurd, principles, and so on. Parmenides wants to suggest the unsuspected universe hiding under the apparently banal assertion "there are things." And this assertion does appear banal, because in Greek to assert that *there are things* is (or would be) a tautology. Indeed, the word "things" does not exist in Greek (there are terms to refer to certain *types* of things, for example, utensils, *khrḗmata;* productions or matters, *prágmata;* but not for "things" in general). So, with the same meaning that the word "things" has in English (or "cosas," or "Dinge," or "choses," or "cose"), a Greek uses the present participle of the verb "to be" *tà ónta* (as a plural noun), that is, literally, "beings," "that which is" or "that which is being" (in the plural), "the [things] that are." As E. Benveniste wrote, "the linguistic structure of Greek created the predisposition for the notion 'to be' to have a philosophical vocation."[62] Or, as I said, to assert solemnly, as Parmenides does, that *there are things* means admitting that "there is what is being" or, more generally, "by being, it is."

(b) The Allegorical Presentation of the Content of the Poem

Sextus Empiricus, the single source of the first twenty-eight lines of Parmenides' fragment 1, tells us that this passage corresponded to the beginning of the Poem.[63] This fact is of priceless value, since the beginning of a work is usually where the keys to understanding the rest of it are to be found. A century after Parmenides, Plato uses the same procedure in his dialogues. Let us look at just two examples (because this is not our main subject). The *Timaeus,* a dialogue that uses numbers and mathematical cal-

---

62 **Benveniste**, E., *Problèmes de linguistique générale* (Paris: Gallimard, reprinted 1966), 73.

63 **Sextus Empiricus**, *Adv. Math.* VII.111: "In fact, [Parmenides] wrote in this way at the beginning (*enarkhómenos*) of his *Perì Phúseo̱s . . .*"

culations to propound a structure of the universe, begins thus: "One, two, three, who is the fourth?" (17a). And in the *Sophist,* where Plato presents his philosophy's *dernier cri,* which will consist in assimilating non-being with "the different," the dialogue begins by saying that the Stranger of Elea is "different" (*héteron,* and not *hetaîro*)[64] from the Parmenideans.

Given the eminently didactic character of Parmenides' Poem, it is not surprising that the text should begin with poetic images and direct allusions to traditional epic, as if trying to grab the attention of the reader/ listener (as I already said, few people, even the educated, could read at that period: ideas were transmitted, as M. Detienne graphically expressed it, "by mouth and by ear").[65] As we shall see, the origin of certain clichés are easily detectable by the reader/listener of the period, and once the author has established communication, he can transmit the nucleus of his thought. Once the introduction had grabbed the reader's/listener's attention, the philosophy course could begin.

The Poem begins with the story of a journey. In every journey there is a way to travel (a way that assumes a starting point and a goal), there is a traveler, there is a means of transport, and when the traveler is inexperienced, there are guides or leaders to help him in his task. All these elements are present in the first fragment of the Poem, and all have a symbolic value. First of all, we may note that Parmenides does not use suspense: the first lines confirm the successful outcome of the journey, because the traveler refers to his experience as something that has "already" happened, and speaks of himself as someone who "already" possesses the knowledge he sought.[66] This is the reason why he decides to convey his experience, which amounts to relating the events of his journey along a way by which he arrived at the goal: complete success—perfection, if we use this term in its etymological sense, the achievement or finishing ("per-") of an undertaking.

It is precisely the image of the journey and the way (that is, route), which is both physical and intellectual, that will be central in Parmenides' philosophy. *Indeed, this will become the presentation of the single way for thought to travel, and the demonstration of the foundations establishing that only*

64 Cf. my translations of **Plato**, *Sofista, Diálogos,* Vol. V (Madrid: 1988), 332, and **Plato**, *Le Sophiste* (Paris: GF-Flammarion, 1993), 73.

65 Cf. **Detienne**, M., "Par la bouche et par l'oreille," in *L'invention de la mythologie* (Paris: Gallimard, 1981).

66 According to **Ruggiu** (1975), 21, the first lines describe a return journey. Other authors, like **Tarán** (1965), 30, prefer to speak of a repetitive experience, which also presupposes that he has already arrived at the end of the journey and is starting out again. Finally, **Gómez-Lobo** (1985), 30, sees "two stages of the journey: one in which Parmenides is led towards the way, and another in which he travels along the way."

this way exists. The notion of "way," represented by various different terms,[67] but mainly by *hodós,* appears fifteen times in the Poem (*hodós,* nine; *kéleuthos,* three; *pátos,* one; *amaxitós,* one; *atarpós* one). This fact, which is not accidental, shows that for Parmenides, knowledge is gained by a "route," a "journey," a conceptual course, that is, through a *method.* Indeed, as we have already seen, "method" comes from *metà hodón,* "making for," "being on the way." Of course, the ways Parmenides proposes are conceptual ones, that is, methods to follow, but their presentation constantly swings between a rigorous description and allegorical images, especially in this first fragment. Finally, we may say that with Parmenides' Poem, the image of the way, or more broadly, that of a "journey" as a method of access to the truth, makes its entry in definitive form into the domain of philosophy.[68]

As I have said, fragment 1 tells a story. It is not simply a "literary artifice," as L. Tarán[69] asserted, but a summary of the Poem in general. A. Marsoner, who stresses the first fragment's "architectonic" character, does not hesitate to state that this prologue is a sort of pediment to the temple that harbors "the secret of truth."[70] To gain access to this "secret," the traveler has to progress in a particular direction (method?). But the undertaking will be difficult, because obstacles will appear that will have to be overcome; however, finally, the quest will be crowned with success. Looking back, the traveler will see that he has passed from a dark road to a light one, but he could never have reached the light road without going along the dark one first. The rest of the Poem develops these elements.

Various unknowns have to be resolved in order to understand the scope of this fragment 1. The first concerns the character we have hitherto called "the traveler." He is a character speaking in the first person who says he has decided to go on a journey "as far as his *thumós* will take him" (fr. 1.1). This notion (which Plato will resume again in his division of the

---

67 These terms are synonymous, and Parmenides chooses one or another for metric reasons. For example, in fragment 2, after saying that there are only two *hodoí* (ways) of investigation, Parmenides points out that one of them is the *kéleuthos* (way) of persuasion. There are scholars who have found differences between the terms. For example, Wyatt says that Parmenides wants to exploit the wealth of the Greek roots of each term, and that "the different words he uses for way have different meanings" (**Wyatt**, W. F., "The Root of Parmenides," *Harvard Studies in Classical Philology* 94 [1992] 114).

68 We need only remember the "journey" of Plato's prisoner, who escapes the cave and goes in search of the Sun (*Rep.* VII, 514a–517a). On the image of the "way" in general, there are two classic works: **Misch**, G., *Der Weg in die Philosophie* (Berlin/Leipzig: 1926); and **Becker**, O., "Das Bild des Weges und verwandte Vorstellungen im frühgriechischen Denken," *Hermes* Einzelschriften 4 (1937) 1–223. With respect to this image in Parmenides, the most complete study continues to be Chapter 1 of **Mourelatos** (1970), especially 16–24.

69 **Tarán** (1965), 31.

70 **Marsoner**, A., "La struttura del Proemio di Parmenide," *Annali dell'Istituto Italiano per gli Studi Storici* 5 (1976–78) 181.

soul into three parts in the *Republic*)[71] refers in Homer not just to courage and impulse[72] (which for us would be equivalent to "will"),[73] but also includes a certain capacity to discern. When Circe presents Odysseus with the two routes (*hodoí:* ways, routes) available for him to navigate (Scylla and Carybdis) she tells him he will have to decide in his *thumós* which one to take (*Od.* 12.58). So here *thumós* is also connected with deliberation. It has to do with a reflexive will that meditates, a kind of sensible impulse that decides upon an action with a clear and precise aim that has to be reached, even at great risk. Or rather, Parmenides, as a master of philosophy, demands a voluntary and conscious impulse on the part of anyone who wants to learn.[74] This way of confronting the approach to knowledge contrasts with the more passive attitude of the listener to the Muses and other traditional "masters of truth," who can deceive as well as teach.[75] In these cases, the listener has to trust the master who announces a truth when he likes (or "if he likes"; cf. Hesiod, *Theog.* 28). Parmenides' traveler sets out in search of truth impelled by his *thumós.* Once he has taken in the Goddess's message, he will judge "by reasoning" the arguments he has just heard (fr. 7.5).

Nothing is known about this traveler. The Goddess describes him as "*koûros*" ("young") when she receives him, once the introduction to the journey is over (fr. 1.24), but this adjective can be interpreted in very different ways.[76] Despite the fact that nothing could be more natural than that it should be a young person wanting to be educated, this epithet heightened the imagination of various scholars, so that the account in fragment 1 was even interpreted as autobiographical. According to this point of view, Parmenides did not reach his *akmḗ* during his forties (the usual arbitrary reck-

71 Cf. **Plato**, *Republic,* 439e–441c.

72 It is *thumós* that impels Demodocos to sing before the gods (*Od.* VIII, 45).

73 "Ardor," **Riaux** (1840), 207, and **Cassin** (1998), 71; "will," **Untersteiner** (1958), 121; "heart," **Tarán** (1965), 8; "boldness," **Gómez-Lobo** (1985), 27, and "vital impulse, will," 30; "desire," **Conche** (1996), 42, and **Collobert** (1993), 10; "spirit," **Coxon** (1986), 44. For **Casertano** (1978), 13, it is an "intellectual passion," and he therefore translates it "impulse of my mind."

74 As Arrighetti says, "the man who knows [. . .] has already reached total awareness of the strength of his intellect and its capacities" (**Arrighetti**, G., "L'eredità dell'epica in Parmenide," in *Festschrift für Robert Muth zum 65. Geburtstag,* ed. Haendel, P., and Meid, W. [Innsbruck: Institut für Sprachwissenschaft der Universität Innsbruck, 1983], 13).

75 Cf. **Detienne**, M., *Les maîtres de vérité dans la Grèce archaïque* (Paris: Maspéro, 1967), 77: "Un maître de Vérité est aussi un maître de tromperie."

76 Cosgrove analyses the term *koûros,* "young," in a context of initiation and deduces that it means "without experience," which does not necessarily imply that this is a "young person" (**Cosgrove**, M. R., "The *koûros* Motif in Parmenides," *Phronesis* 19 [1974] 94). As here it is a goddess addressing a disciple, Marsoner proposes the translation "oh, son" (**Marsoner**, "La struttura del Proemio," 155).

oning) but much earlier.[77] There is nothing to authorize this interpretation. As occurred in Plato's dialogues, Parmenides speaks through his mouthpiece: the Goddess, in his case; Socrates (and sporadically, the Stranger of Elea, Timaeus, the Athenian, and so forth) in Plato's. If the Goddess addresses a "young" listener, this listener can only be a possible "pupil" of Parmenides.

The traveler is carried in a chariot drawn by mares. It is normal that it should be a chariot:[78] gods and heroes (including the Sun) travel in chariots when their route is a journey by land . . . or in the sky.[79] In contrast, sea voyages are made using all kinds of ships. For its part, the reference to mares has been the subject of very different interpretations. For Gómez-Lobo, the fact is almost banal, because it is "the custom of Homeric heroes."[80] But this is not always the case. Sometimes (for example, *Il.* 24.326, 11.615) heroes are drawn by stallions. As the Orphics usually use mares, the suggestion has been made of an Orphic influence on Parmenides.[81] A. H. Coxon believes that Parmenides preferred "female" horses because everything concerning the feminine is "warmer" than the masculine, and therefore nearer to fire and light.[82] Lastly, there has also been the suggestion of Parmenides' "feminism" *avant la lettre,* because most or nearly all of the mythical figures in the Poem are feminine.[83]

Much more interesting than the problem of the horses' sex is the description of the "maiden guides" on his journey, because both the traveler and the mares are practically dragged by the Daughters of the Sun, the Heliades. The choice of these divinities by Parmenides is not accidental but decisive. I said earlier that an educated reader/listener of the period would be capable of recognizing the poetic images of fragment 1. So we should remember that the Heliades, whether they are just two (Homer, *Od.* 12.127),

77 On the autobiographical nature of the reference, cf. **Reinhardt** (1916), 111, and **Kranz**, W. "Vorsokratisches," *Hermes* 69 (1934) 118.

78 Even so, it is interesting to point out that Pindar, a contemporary of Parmenides (**Bowra**, "The Poem of Parmenides," 38), states that the Poem's composition coincides with that of the *Pythic Ode* X; he associates the image of the chariot with the Muses, that is, with poetry: cf. *Ol.* 9, 80; *Isth.* 2, 1 and 8, 62. On the relationship between Parmenides and Pindar, see **Martinelli**, F., "Fra Omero e Pindaro: Parmenide poeta," in *Forme del sapere nei Presocratici,* ed. Capizzi, A., and Casertano, G. (Athens/Rome: Edizione dell'Ateneo, 1987) 169–86.

79 Both Zeus (*Il.* VIII, 41, 438; XIII, 23) and Hera (*Il.* V, 748, 380) usually cross the sky by chariot, which they themselves drive.

80 **Gómez-Lobo** (1985), 30.

81 Cf. **Tarán** (1965), 9.

82 **Coxon** (1986), 157.

83 Cf. **Merlan**, P., "Neues Licht auf Parmenides," *Archiv für Geschichte der Philosophie* 48 (1966) 267–76.

five, or seven,[84] have a brother, Phaeton, whose story is well known. When he wanted to take his father's place and drive the Sun's chariot, his inexperience produced such great catastrophes that Zeus struck him with his thunderbolt.[85] What caused Phaeton's disaster? The cause was double: (1) the rebel son did not have the *right* to do what he did, and (2) he undertook a journey *without knowing* the way to go; he drove forward at random, without any guide, without obeying any kind of parameter. Thus, Phaeton becomes a negative image of the Parmenidean traveler, whose journey does have those elements that were absent from the unfortunate child of the Sun's feckless dash: (1) the guarantee of right and justice (as we shall see) and (2) maiden guides who know the right direction. So the Goddess will be on his side. The choice of the Heliades as guiding divinities spells a message which Parmenides' contemporary reader/listener would certainly pick up.

Having presented the characters, now let us look at the journey. The structure of this fragment 1 is very complex, because Parmenides swings continually between the present (when the traveler has already arrived at the Goddess's realm) and the past, when he followed the ways that led to his goal. A very detailed analysis of Parmenides' method *in annello* can be found in A. Marsoner's excellent work, to which I refer the reader,[86] and also in C. M. Bowra's classic article, "The Proem of Parmenides."[87] The three first lines confirm that the traveler was taken toward the way of the Goddess, a way that is abundant with signs (*polúphe̱mon*). When we analyze the content of this way which is found in the extensive fragment 8, we will study the meaning of these "signs." For the moment, we may say that, faithful to his method, Parmenides will present arguments in support of his theory and that each argument will be a sort of proof (in the legal sense) of it. Each proof will be a sort of *phé̱me̱*, meaning a sign or oracular word, an announcement.[88]

Along this way, the Goddess leads "the man who knows."[89] Anyone familiar with Parmenides' text will be surprised not to find in my summary the formula according to which the Goddess (or the way, for those who believe "way" is the subject of "lead"[90]) leads the man who knows through

84 Cf. **Falcón Martínez**, C., **Fernández-Galiano**, E., and **López Melero**, R., *Diccionario de mitología clásica,* Vol. I (Madrid: Alianza, 1980), 292.

85 Cf. **Euripides**, fragments of the tragedy *Phaeton,* 771–86.

86 **Marsoner**, "La struttura del Proemio."

87 **Bowra**, "The Poem of Parmenides," 97–112.

88 Cf. **Sophocles**, *Oedipus Rex,* 86: "What message (*phé̱me̱n*) from the god do you bring us?"

89 An analysis of these three lines can be found in **Cordero** (1997) 176–78.

90 In line 1.3 there is a feminine relative pronoun, and its antecedent can be either "the Goddess" or "the way" (feminine, in Greek). In the first case, it is the Goddess who leads, and we adopt this possibility, given that it is she who acts pedagogically toward the trav-

all *cities* (*áste̱*). In fact, classical texts evolve, and the word "cities," which was introduced into a gap in line 1.3 of the Poem in 1909 due to an editor's mistaken reading of a manuscript by Sextus,[91] disappeared in 1969 when another scholar[92] demonstrated that the codex in question presented the same state of incompleteness as the whole of the manuscript tradition. So for more than thirty years, it has been known again that fragment 1.3 has a gap that must be filled if we want to complete the text with conjectures.[93] Even so, regrettable though it is that recent translations ignore the inexistence of "cities," a really pathetic case is that of G. Reale, who asserts that this nonexistent word is "la meglio attestata."[94]

So the journey has an arrival point, which is the realm of the Goddess (and which is, according to our interpretation, the enigmatic "there"), but what was the starting point? There can be no doubt: the answer is darkness. Parmenides does not say so clearly, but the traveler and his guides and companions make "toward the light" (1.10),[95] and the Heliades, who accom-

---

eler and, as is well-known, in the root of the term "pedagogy" we find the idea of "leading" (*ágein*). Our choice is also supported by the role Parmenides attributes to the Goddess, who "rules *all*" (fr. 12.3). In contrast, most interpreters opt for "the way," and in that case, the man who knows would be led "by" (and not "along") a way.

91 This was Mutschmann, who thought, erroneously, he had seen this term in the manuscript *Laurentianus* 85.19 (cf. **Mutschmann**, H., "Die Überlieferung der Schriften des Sextus Empiricus," *Rheinisches Museum* 69 [1909]).

92 **Coxon**, A. H., "The Text of Parmenides Fr. 1.3," *Classical Quarterly* 18 (1968) 69. Direct consultation of the *Laurentianus* manuscript 85.19 in the Laurenziana library in Florence proved to us that the text of folio 124 confirms that Coxon's thesis is correct.

93 I proposed the word "there," and interpreted the preceding phrase as "in every respect," which does not contaminate the text in question too much (the fact that the Goddess leads "in every respect" will be confirmed by fr. 1.28, and the enigmatic "there" appears various times in fragment 1: cf. **Cordero**, N. L., "Le vers 1.3 de Parménide," *La revue philosophique* 107(2) (1982) 159–79, where I also examine all the conjectures proposed to date). For other interpretations, cf. **Cerri**, G., "Il v. 1.3 di Parmenide: la ricognizione dell'esperienza," in *Mousa, Scritti in onore di Giuseppe Morelli* (Bologna: Patron, 1997), 57–63. Fairly recent works, which commit the mortal sin of disinformation and continue translating a nonexistent text, include *Les Présocratiques,* trans. Dumont, J. P., and others (Paris: Gallimard, 1988), 255 (translation re-used in the compendium *Les écoles Présocratiques* [Paris: Gallimard, 1991], 345); **Parmenides,** *I frammenti,* trans. Trabattoni, F. (Milan: Marcos y Marcos, 1985), 15; *De Tales a Demócrito. Fragmentos Presocráticos,* trans. Bernabé, A. (Madrid: Alianza, 1988), 159; **Tzavaras**, G. *Tò Poíe̱ma toû Parmeníde̱* (Athens: Domos, 1980), 20; etc.

94 **Parmenides**, *Poema sulla natura,* trans. Reale, G. (Milan: Rusconi, 1991), 85. On this publication, cf. **Cordero** (1997), 13–14. More coherent is the position of Lesher, who admits the term's nonexistence, but proposes it as an "acceptable" conjecture (**Lesher**, J. H., "The Significance of *katà pánt'á<s>te̱* in Parmenides Fr. 1.3," *Ancient Philosophy* 14 [1994] 15), and of Günther, who speaks of a "Minimalkonjektur" (**Günther**, H. C., *Aletheia und Doxa, Das Proömium des Gedichtes des Parmenides* [Berlin: Dunker & Humblot,1998] 15).

95 Most interpreters are of this opinion (among them, **Kahn** [1968/69], 704; and **Vlastos**, G., "Parmenides' Theory of Knowledge," *Transactions and Proceedings of the Amer. Philol. Assoc.* 77 [1946] 73, note 43). A contrary viewpoint can be found in **Burkert**, W., "Das Proömion des Parmenides und die Katabasis des Pythagoras," *Phronesis* 14 (1961) 1–30.

pany the traveler (1.9, 1.24) and show him the way (1.5), "abandon the realm of night" (1.9).[96]

Consequently, we may suppose that the young traveler also leaves the domain of darkness, otherwise it cannot be explained how the maidens can guide him or drive him (1.8) until he reaches some gates (1.11), which appear to close off one region and open the way to a different sphere. So there can be no doubt that the beginning of the journey takes place along a road belonging to the realm of night, and he must continue until he comes to the home of the Goddess, represented by an opposite way. It is interesting to point out the assimilation Parmenides makes between "way" and "domain," an analogy that becomes plain when the Goddess congratulates the traveler for having taken "this way" (*tḗnd'hodón,* fr. 1.27), which is none other, she says, than "my home," (*hḗméteron dô̱,* fr. 1.25), whereas "night's home" (*dṓmata nuktós,* fr. 1.9) corresponds to the "way of night" (fr. 1.11).

The gates the traveler finds in line 1.11 are "the gates of the ways of night and day." Parmenides makes use of an image already used by Homer and Hesiod to refer allegorically to two incompatible, contradictory, exclusive spheres. Both ways are close (*eggús*) to each other—as we read in *Od.* X.86—but one comes after the other; they are successive.[97] The same shepherd cannot look after his flocks by day and by night; to do so he would have to do without sleep, and in that case, the author of the *Odyssey* says ironically, he would earn a double wage. When Hesiod takes up the image of night and day he confirms that the same home (*dô̱*) does not shelter both at once: when one enters, the other goes out (*Theog.* 748–51).

The journey along the way of night ends, as I said, when the traveler and his companions come to two heavy, closed gates, which prevent them from going any further (1.11).[98] They have encountered an obstacle that prevents them from entering the way of day (symbolized by light), that is, access to truth. The possible opening of these gates depends on Dike, a sort of porter who, together with her sisters, the Hours, keeps the keys of the sky, which enable them to regulate the seasons. In Parmenides she holds the keys "that alternate" (1.14) and that will open the gates of the realm of truth. Here, too, the philosopher resorts to classical images, because Dike

96 **Kern**, O., "Zu Parmenides," *Archiv für Geschichte der Philosophie* 3 (1890) 173–76, analyzed the Orphic origin of the image of the realm of night, as well as the decisive role of Eros (in Parmenides, cf. fr. 19), father of the night.

97 According to Becker, *eggús* has a temporal value in this passage (**Becker** [1937], 12, note 7).

98 On the position and number of these gates, cf. **Cordero**, N. L., "Acerca de tres pasajes del Poema de Parmenides," *Revista latinoamericana de filosofía* 1 (1975) 237–43, and **Cordero** (1997), 179–81; for a polemical viewpoint, cf. **Gómez-Lobo**, A., "Parménides. Las puertas de la noche y del día," *Revista latinoamericana de filosofía* 3 (1977) 185–88.

is traditionally associated with truth: "between Justice and Truth there is no distance at all."[99] Dike, together with Themis, who will appear in line 1.28, represents justice and right.[100] Already in Parmenides' time her sentences, like lawyers' submissions, are supported by "arguments" (*lógoi*). In the case we are concerned with, these *lógoi* are presented by the Heliades: they are persuasive or enveloping (1.15)[101] arguments that show, we presume, that the traveler, unlike the unfortunate Phaeton, has the "right" to continue on his way. Indeed, Dike, who "abundantly chastises" (she is *polúpoinos,* 1. 14), allows the traveler to enter the realm of truth. These arguments "persuade," "convince"[102] (*peîsan,* 1.16) the severe Dike. The heavy gates are opened and a new "great way" (*amaxitós,* 1.21), belonging (*hēméteron,* 1.25) to the anonymous Goddess, awaits the travelers. The philosophy course can begin.

Up to this point in his Poem's prologue, how do we assess our understanding of Parmenides' philosophy? Two spheres monopolize the scene of the journey: darkness, night on the one hand; light, day on the other. Both are represented by ways or roads, each having their own gates, which open and shut at a certain point ("There stand the gates of the ways of night *and* day" [1.11]) through which the traveler can pass. According to A. Pieri's expression, the gates "divide two regions, two ways, one towards darkness and the other towards light."[103] The analogy between darkness and ignorance is perfectly plain.[104] Someone wanting to know *is ignorant* of the truth, and his mind is dark, fogged. Even so, this total absence of knowledge *potentially* possesses all knowing. Much has been written about the Hesiod passage that inspired Parmenides' image.[105] This comes in lines 744 onward in the *Theogony,* which describe this dark, underground realm in which

99 **Detienne**, *Les maîtres de vérité,* 34, note 14. In support of his statement, Detienne cites texts by Mimnermos, Solon, and Plutarch, as well as Hesychius' *Lexicon.*

100 Cf. **Deichgräber**, K., *Parmenides' Auffahrt zur Göttin des Rechts* (Wiesbaden: Akademie der Wissenschaften und der Literatur in Mainz, 1959). According to Burkert, Dike controls the "legal" exchange between Day and Night (**Burkert**, *Das Proömion des Parmenides,* 10, note 34).

101 Parmenides takes the expression "enveloping arguments" from Homer and Hesiod: Patroclus tries to calm Eurypilos' sufferings with these types of arguments (*Il.* XV. 390), Calypso wants to detain Odysseus (*Od.* I.56), Zeus deceives Metis so that he can swallow her (*Theog.* 890), and Apollo sets them in Pandora's breast (*Works* 78).

102 When we look at line 2.4, we will analyze the notion of "persuasion" (*peithṓ*) in Parmenides.

103 **Pieri**, A., "Parmenide e la lingua della tradizione epica greca," *Studi Italiani di filologia classica* 49 (1977) 80.

104 Plato's cave allegory is the most widely-known example, but even in everyday language "obscurantism" is synonymous with ignorance.

105 Cf., for example, **Pellikaan-Engel**, M. E., *Hesiod and Parmenides: A New View on Their Cosmologies and on Parmenides' Poem* (Amsterdam: Adolf M. Hakkert, 1974), and **Schwabl**, H., "Hesiod und Parmenides," *Rheinisches Museum* 106 (1963) 134–42.

"the sources (*pe̱gaí*) of everything are found" (809). As in Anaximander's "indefinite" (*ápeiron*), everything is programmed in that kind of already-fertilized nothing that is ignorance. When they go through the gates, darkness vanishes and truth begins to show. At that moment the Heliades, who hid their brightness (inherited from their father the Sun), drop the veils that covered their heads (1.10).[106] Anachronistically, we might say that from now on, *fiat lux*.

(c) "You Must Inquire About Everything*" (1.28)*

The traveler's efforts have not been in vain: the Goddess receives him readily and tells him what his task will be if he wants to become "a man who knows." "So it is necessary for you to inquire about everything; on the one hand, the unshakable heart of well-rounded truth, and, on the other, the opinions of mortals, in which there is no true conviction" (1.28b–30). As the Goddess will guide him, she begins by proclaiming what the content of her philosophy course will be, and the reference to the totality of things being the object of her teaching encourages me to propose the conjecture "about everything" (*katà pân*) to make sense of the corrupt passage in 1.3.[107] *A priori,* the project looks excessive, because the Goddess invites him to "inquire" about *everything* (*pánta*), but the scope of this "everything" is defined in the following lines: it consists of two contents that are complementary but, apparently, necessary: (1) the heart of truth, and (2) the opinions of mortals.

Firstly, let us say that after the division of knowledge illustrated by the first twenty-eight lines of fragment 1 into two possibilities (ignorance, truth), this new pair (which will also turn out to be necessary [*khreò̱*, 1.28],

---

106 In this unveiling Somville finds a reference to the wedding ceremony of "*anakalupté̱ria,*" literally, "the removal of the veil" (**Somville**, P., *Parménide d'Élée: Son temps et le nôtre* [Paris: Vrin, 1976], 37). When I read this Parmenides text, I cannot help thinking of the characteristic of "un-veiling," "dis-covery," the notion that truth has for **Heiddeger**, M. (cf. especially *Sein und Zeit*, 9th ed. [Tübingen: Max Niemeyer, 1960], § 44). So it is strange that Heidegger did not use this passage to support his thesis (indeed, Heidegger's *Parmenides* [*Gesamtausgabe II: Abteilung, Vorlesungen 1923–1944,* Vol. 54 (Frankfurt am Main: Klostermann, 1982)] contains no reference to fragment 1.10). This absence accords with Heidegger's habit of not seeing things where they are and seeking them where they are not. The most significant examples of this tendency are his analysis of truth in a work entitled *Alétheia,* which studies this idea in a text of Heraclitus (fr. 16), from which this notion is absent, and his writing on truth in Plato, based on the cave allegory, where the idea only appears in allusive form, whereas it appears abusively in the *Euthydemus,* the *Cratylus,* the *Theaetetus,* and especially in the *Sophist,* where it is stated that the *tópos* of truth is the *lógos,* a phrase which Heidegger repeats *ad nauseam* in *Sein und Zeit.*

107 Cf. **Cordero**, "Le vers 1.3."

since just as there was no knowledge without previous ignorance, there will be no truth without opinion) seems to resume the preceding lines' dichotomous presentation, in which, *a priori,* only two possibilities could be taken into account.

So the task is to "inquire" about two possibilities. The Goddess does not say "know" or "learn," because, according to Parmenides' assessment of certain concepts, one of the possibilities will prove to be completely unknowable (*panapeuthéa,* fr. 2.6). Later on he will say that there are two possibilities offered to thought, but not that both are "thinkable" (fr. 2.2). It is only a matter of being abreast of "everything," even though the scope of this "everything" has now been delimited. On the one hand there is *the heart of truth.* The image was exhaustively analyzed by E. Martineau,[108] and its content is plain: the heart is not only the vital core but also the central nucleus of the individual. Truth also has its "heart," and for truth to be truth, that nucleus cannot change from moment to moment; it must be unalterable, firm, constant, or literally "intrepid" (*atremès,* 1.29). The rest of the Poem will show that this nucleus will be proof of the fact of being, and that the way that proclaims this "accompanies the truth" (fr. 2.4). But as the manner of approaching truth will be "circular" (cf. fr. 5: "It is common for me that where I begin, there I shall return again"), truth itself is considered here as "well-rounded" (*eukukléos,* 1.29).[109] And on the other hand, there are the *opinions*[110] *of mortals.* It is worth pointing out the fact that in Parmenides, opinions are always a prerogative belonging to mortals. The genitive "opinions *of* mortals" is subjective: the mortals have the opinions; it does not mean opinions about mortals. This point is important because, in Parmenides, *dóxa* is always a point of view, an "opinion," and never an "image" or an "appearance." Parmenides is not Plato, who distinguishes between "being" and "appearing." Unfortunately, a retroactive application of Platonic schemes to Parmenides is one of the hindrances unnecessarily obscuring our understanding of the philosopher of Elea.[111]

So the content of the apprenticeship of the future philosopher includes truth (especially its central nucleus) and opinions. The formula used in Greek by Parmenides leaves no doubt: he says clearly *ēmèn* (on the one

---

108 **Martineau**, M., "Le 'coeur' de l'Alétheia," *Revue de philosophie ancienne* 4 (1986) 33–86.

109 There is an interminable dispute between those who accept Simplicius' version at this point, *eukukléos,* and the partisans of the version given by Plutarch, Diogenes, and Clement, *eupeithéos* ("well persuasive"). Among the latter recently to be found are **Coxon** (1986), 51; **Conche** (1996), 61; and **Cassin** (1998), 73. My choice is based on the greater reliability of Simplicius' testimony.

110 On the notion of *dóxa,* cf. the excellent work by **Lafrance**, Y., *La théorie platonicienne de la Doxa* (Paris/Montreal: Bellarmin—Les Belles Lettres, 1981).

111 Cf. **Cordero**, N. L., "Parménide platonisé," *Revue de philosophie ancienne* 18(1) (2000) 15–24.

hand) and *e̱dè* (on the other): it is necessary to inquire about both. So it is hard to understand why most scholars of Parmenides' thought are surprised when the Goddess completes her project and *also* expounds a possible model for "opinions." Truth is absent from opinions, but knowing that opinions are not true, *is true.* As mistress of philosophy, the Goddess must didactically show the disciple what the error consists in. In M. Detienne's text, which I cited in note 14, the author stated that a genuine "master of truth" is also a "master of deception."

Parmenides is not the only one to present an erroneous doctrine in order to show its essential flaw. Mathematicians of Euclid's school presented students with false reasonings called *pseudaria* to accustom them to recognizing formal flaws and thus be on their guard against error. Proclus says that Euclid presented a method for detecting paralogisms and wrote a treatise on this called *Fallacies,* a work that is both "cathartic and gymnastic" (*In primun Euclidis elementorum librum commentarii,* 69). Opinions fulfill this same function in Parmenides. Indeed, opinions must *also* be the object of study, but even from line 30 of fragment 1, Parmenides indicates unambiguously that opinions are not reliable, and one cannot have any real confidence (*pístis ale̱thé̱s*) in them. It is not exaggerated to deduce from this expression that opinions "are not true," given the dichotomous way in which Parmenides' thought is presented. In another passage of the Poem, the Goddess says: "Henceforward learn the opinions of mortals, listening to the deceitful order of my words" (8.51–52), which directly suggests that opinions are wrong.

Why learn something that is not true, which may also be a source of errors, deception, as is the case with opinions? Parmenides is aware of the unusualness of his proposal, so he explains. After having stated that opinions are not true, he uses a strongly concessive formula: *all'émpe̱s* (1.31), "*yet, nevertheless,* you will also learn these things."[112] This formula had already been used in Homer to allude to a "restriction in relation to what has just been written."[113] Opinions are not true, but nevertheless, it is necessary to learn them. Why? Lines 1.31b–32 explicitly answer this question, and, given the precision of Parmenides' text, I can't help being surprised by the sterile debate which, as we shall see, this passage has aroused.

---

112 An excellent and subtle analysis of this passage can be found in **Dehon**, P. J., "Les recommendations de la déesse. Parménide, fr. 1.28–32," *Revue de philosophie ancienne* 6(2) (1988) 271–89. However, I do not agree with the conclusion that the author derives from his analysis.

113 **Dehon**, "Les recommendations de la déesse," 273. In *Il.* 2.297, Odysseus recognizes that the Achaens are uneasy because even if they do not fight, *nevertheless,* they would be ashamed to return empty-handed. In *Il.* 8.33, Athena knows that her father has decided on the destruction of the Danaos, *but nevertheless,* her heart is sad.

The term *"taûta"* ("these things," "this") in 1.31 resumes the notion of opinion,[114] which will appear in the following line, once again in the plural in the expression *"tà dokoûnta"* ("what appears in opinions"). As W. Wiersma says, this expression does not refer to *"tà phainómena"* ("appearances") but to *"hà dokeî"* ("the things that seem," "the things that are thought")[115] among mortals. Heraclitus uses the term in the same sense in the ironical fragment 28, which may refer both to Homer and Hesiod, both victims[116] of his sharp comments: "The most renowned only knows and stores up *dokéonta* (opinions)."[117] Mortals "see" the world in a certain way and *tà dokoûnta* is "the world as they see it."[118] But Parmenides' Poem is didactic: that way of responding to the question about the reality of things (the "being" of beings, if you prefer) makes no sense if the truth is known. Nevertheless, the future philosopher must be alert: *if* truth were inaccessible, *then only opinions would exist.* Happily this is not so, and therefore that possibility is presented in a hypothetical manner, but the temptation to be carried along by daily inertia (cf. the reference to "long habit" in fr. 7.3) is great, and Parmenides also has to expound a "probable cosmic order so that no viewpoint of mortals will prevail over you" (fr. 8.60–61).

This shows that line 1.31 resumes the content of the preceding line and that, consequently, it does not introduce a new element, beyond truth and opinions, as some interpreters have believed.[119]

The text of 1.31b–32 expounds this impossible possibility: opinions are not true; "yet, nevertheless, you will also learn this: how it might have been

---

114 **García Calvo**, A., translates, "And, all the same, you will have to learn even those" (*Lecturas Presocráticas* [Madrid: Lucina, 1981], 188).

115 **Wiersma**, W., "Notes on Greek Philosophy (Parm. 1.17, 2.4, 8.61)," *Mnemosyne* 20 (1967) 405. My point of view is that an opionion is a way to think that takes one reality (even Being) in a subjective way. "Appearances" has no ontological status in Parmenides' philosophy: Parmenides is not Plato . . . The appearance is in thought, not in reality. "Appearances" are "things" as they appear in opinions.

116 Homer is criticized in fragment 56; Hesiod, in fragments 40 and 57.

117 Guthrie, W. K. C., translates this as "opinion" (**Guthrie** [1965], 413); **Marcovich**, M., translates it as "fantasie" (or: "false opinion") (*Eraclito. Frammenti* [Florence: La Nuova Italia, 1978], 53); **Kahn**, C. H., translates it as "imagining things" (*The Art and Thought of Heraclitus* [Cambridge, England: Cambridge University Press, 1978], 69); **Eggers Lan**, C., translates it as "las cosas que le parece" (*Los filósofos Presocráticos,* I [Madrid: Gredos, 1978], 384); **Bernabé**, A., translates it as "meras creencias" (*De Tales a Demócrito: Fragmentos presocráticos* [Madrid: Alianza, 1988], 135); **Lami**, A., translates it as "credibile sono le conoscenze . . ." (*I Presocratici* [Milan: Rizzoli, 1991], 209).

118 **Schwabl**, H., "Sein und Doxa bei Parmenides," *Wiener Studien* 66 (1953) 401.

119 For example, **Mourelatos** (1970), 209. We think, like Tarán, that the meaning of the phrase is " . . . the opinions of mortals, despite (*áll'émpe̱s*) the fact that they are false" (**Tarán** [1965], 211). Cf. also **De Rijk**, L. M., "Did Parmenides Reject the Sensible World?" in *Graceful Reason,* ed. Gerson, L. P. (Toronto: Pontifical Institute of Mediaeval Studies, 1983), 31.

necessary that the things that appear in opinions really existed, ranging over everything incessantly." The decisive terms in the passage are the verb *khrê̱n*[120] (would have been necessary) and the adverb *dokímo̱s*[121] ("really," "truly"). Most scholars believe that *dokímo̱s* in this context means "acceptable,"[122] "plausible," but this is only possible if we go back to the word's etymology, which derives from the verb *dokéo̱* ("seem," "believe"). In the few examples of this term that have been preserved despite the passage of time (collected in the Liddell, Scott, and Jones *Lexicon*) it has the meaning "really," "truly." It is true that, as P. J. Dehon says,[123] "few translators have adopted the meaning proposed by the dictionary," but this is due to a misunderstanding of the passage. These writers have used the following logic: (1) the passage refers to "appearances"; (2) Parmenides cannot assert that appearances "really exist"; therefore, (3) they do exist, but only apparently, and only acceptably, and that is the meaning of *dokímo̱s*. These three stages are wrong: (1) Parmenides is not referring to appearances but to opinions; (2) Parmenides does not say that these are "real"; but holds that (3) they *might have really existed* (that is, they might have occupied the place of true, real knowledge) if truth did not exist. We should not forget that the imperfect *khrê̱n* is a *casus irrealis,* as W. Kranz[124] and R. Falus[125] said, because it alludes to something that might have happened if you do not take the true thesis into account.[126]

The hypothetical phrase (starting with *hôs,* "namely," "that," "as," qualifying the notion of "learn") containing the imperfect *khrê̱n,* is completed in the following phrase, in which *tà dokoûnta* ("things as they appear in opinions") is the subject, *eînai* ("existed") is the verb, and *dokímo̱s* ("really") is

---

120 The correction *khrê̱,* proposed by **Peyron**, A., *Empedoclis et Parmenidis fragmenta ex codice Taurinensis Bibliothecae restituta et illustrata* (Leipzig: I. A. G. Weigel, 1810), 55, and accepted by **Stahl**, J. M. (*Kritisch-historischer Syntax des griechischen Verbums der klassischen Zeit* [Heidelberg: C. Winter, 1907], 536), had scant echo.

121 The possibility *dokimó̱s(ai),* proposed by **Diels** (1897), 57 ss., and accepted, among others, by **Untersteiner** (1958), clxvii, note 7, is based on an elision (of "*ai*") that is difficult to accept in a hexameter, as **Wilamowitz**, U. v., pointed out ("Lesefrüchte," *Hermes* 34 [1899] 204).

122 For example, **Dehon**, "Les recommendations de la déesse," 286; **Tarán** (1965), 213, note 27; **Bormann** (1971), 33; **Verdenius** (1942), 49; "doivent être en leur apparaître," **Cassin** (1998), 73.

123 **Dehon**, "Les recommendations de la déesse," 283.

124 **Kranz** (1916), 1170: "*tà dokoûnta* . . . Bestand haben müssten."

125 **Falus** (1960), 286.

126 Examples of this imperfect *khrê̱n* are found in **Herodotus** VII, 9, 25; in **Euripides**, *Hyppolitus,* 297; and again in **Herodotus**, II, 20, 8, in a passage in which the historian eliminates the *unreal hypothesis,* according to which the Ethesian winds might be the cause of the rising of the Nile; if this was the case, then this cause *might have been* (*khrê̱n*) valid for other rivers too. Cf. *contra* Brague, for whom the verb is in the past, that is, in a tense that "expresses that the illusion has been dispelled" (**Brague**, R., "La vraisemblance du faux," in *Études sur Parménide,* Vol. II, ed. Aubenque, P. [Paris: Vrin, 1987] 59).

the predicate. That is, with the previous apprenticeship of the first thesis, which is the only true one, this second possibility (according to which opinions really exist) makes no sense. However, the previous history of philosophy has in fact fallen into this error. The unreal imperfect *khrē̱n* shows that this hypothesis is impossible *if* we accept Parmenides' thesis, which takes it for granted that there is no truth in opinions (fr. 1.30). If we do not know this truth, opinions would range over everything incessantly (as in fact, they do: cf. fr. 19: "thus these things arose according to opinion [*katà dóxan*], and thus they are present now . . ."). The participle *perō̱̂nta*[127] ("ranging over") refers to opinions, and the formula *dià pantós* should, I believe, be interpreted in the temporal sense of "always"—as is the case in Plato[128]—incessantly, "throughout the length of all [times]."[129] All these elements have led me to translate lines 31–32 as I have: "but nevertheless, you will also learn this: how it might have been necessary that things that appear in opinions really existed, ranging over everything incessantly."

Some interpreters have seen in these lines the appearance of a third type of teaching content, apart from truth and opinions. This would be "appearances," which they believe Parmenides also wanted to include. But we have already seen that *tà dokoûnta* does not mean "appearance," but harks back to the notion of "opinions." Moreover, a new content of learning could not have been presented in a phrase of the adversative-concessive type, beginning with "yet, nevertheless." It is true that the phrase contains the word "also" (*kaí*), but this refers to the preceding phrase and not to the following passage: despite the non-truth of opinions they *also* have to be learned. P. J. Dehon showed that the meaning of "*kaí*" here is adverbial,[130] "even," and the reason for learning a thought-content that is wrong is explained by Parmenides himself toward the end of fragment 8, where, after having expounded on "the opinions of mortals" with reference to a sort of cosmology, he says that he states (*phatízo̱*) this totally plausible (*pánta eoikóta*) cosmic order (*diákosmon*) "*so that no viewpoint (gnṓme̱) of mortals will prevail over you (parelásse̱i).*" The plausibility of the discourse can convince anyone who does not know the truth. Only after traveling along the way of truth will you have the necessary elements to grasp the falseness of opinions. That is why anyone claiming "to know" must be abreast of them.

---

127 Some Simplicius manuscripts offer the reading *per ónta*. Gómez-Lobo adopts this possibility and translates "[siendo la totalidad] de las cosas" (**Gómez-Lobo** [1985], 29). A passionate defense of *per ónta* can be found in **Brague**, "La vraisemblance du faux," 44–68.

128 Cf. *Statesman* 294c8: "*tò dià pantòs gignómenon,*" "that which remains always."

129 This is the meaning of *dià pantós* in **Sophocles**, *Ajax*, 105; **Xenophon**, *Anábasis*, VII, 8, 11; **Herodotus**, I, 12, and **Thucydides**, V.105: "we know that the gods reign always (*dià pantós*) through the necessity of their nature." The temporal meaning arises particularly from the combining of *pánta* with *dià pantós*, as in **Hippocrates**, *De victu* 1,1.

130 **Dehon**, "Les recommendations de la déesse," 273.

Chapter III: Parmenides' Thesis and Its Negation

(a) The Alternative in Fragment 2

After allegorically presenting the content of his philosophy and, in particular, after didactically showing that truth can only be reached if thought is *directed* correctly (that is, if it pursues a way, a *hodós,* which means adopting a *met-hodós,* that is, a "method"), Parmenides, through the intermediary of the Goddess, offers the future philosopher a rigorous presentation of his thesis. Curiously, this fundamental text was only quoted for the first time more than a millennium after it was written by Parmenides, as its oldest sources are Proclus and Simplicius, two authors from the sixth century A.D.[131] Proclus quotes seven lines of it in his commentary on Plato's *Timaeus* (I.345, 18–27) and repeats lines 5b and 6 in his commentary on the *Parmenides* (1078, 4–5). Simplicius only transcribes lines 3–8. Conventionally, this text has been considered to be "fragment 2," because its content seems to follow immediately on from the ideas expressed in the last lines of what is called "fragment 1."[132] This text begins in the following manner: "Well then, I will tell."[133] Let us now see what the Goddess will say.

Just as in fragment 1 Parmenides had shown that anyone who wants to know cannot advance blindly, chaotically, with no fixed direction, the

131 On this curious fact, cf. my work "L'histoire du texte de Parménide," in *Études sur Parménide,* Vol. II, ed. Aubenque, P. (Paris: Vrin, 1987), 3–24.

132 However, in the first editions of the Poem, this text was considered to be "fragment 4." Cf. the work quoted in the preceding note.

133 The first words of the text, which I have translated somewhat freely as "Well, I . . ." (*ei d'ág'egò̲n*), are habitually used by Homer to indicate the continuity of an account (cf. *Il.* 1.302, 19.108; *Od.* 1.169, 1.271). With respect to this text, I should point out that the manuscript tradition unanimously offers the version *ei d'áge tô̲n,* which does not appear to make any sense (and which may be based on the existing confusion between "*t*" and "*g*" with lower-case transliterating of classical texts, which were written, as we know, in capitals). The conjecture accepted today almost unanimously (with the exception of **Vitali** [1977], 33, who proposes "*ág'etô̲n eréo̲*" and translates "Orsù, io amo le cose vere") belongs to **Karsten** (1835), 70, who proposes the resumption of the Homeric formula. If Parmenides really did use the pronoun "*egó̲n,*" that would confirm his wish to give his text the easily memorizable style of the classical epic, since *egò̲n eréo̲* is a habitual formula in Homer (cf. *Il.* 1.76, 1.103, 13.735). If he is not using an archaic cliché, then Parmenides is using the current form *egó̲:* cf. 8.60. However, although Parmenides uses the pan-Hellenic Ionian of Homer, he sometimes departs from it. Cf. examples in **Pieri**, A., "Parmenide e la lingua della tradizione epica greca," *Studi Italiani di filologia classica* 49 (1977) 69, 73.

rigorous presentation of the thesis we shall find in this fragment 2 will take the form of a *way,* along which anyone wanting to reach the "heart of truth" must direct his or her thought. As I have said, Parmenides is the first philosopher who *argues,* who *gives reasons* in support of his thesis. Later philosophy will coin the formula "*lógon didónai*" to express this idea of giving the reason for something, and Parmenides himself will use the term *lógos* in fragment 7.5 to mean "reasoning." A reasoning is not a thought; it is a series of thoughts related in a certain way. But this series of thoughts requires an ordered, methodical succession. That is why Parmenides proposes to "lead" thoughts, that is, create a reasoning from them. The term *lógos* alludes precisely to this ordered and coherent series of thoughts, expressed in a discourse.

Let us return to the speech the Goddess presents at the beginning of fragment 2. It will be presenting a thesis, but the Goddess's presentation of this thesis will be double. This procedure is habitual in Parmenides: the truth of a notion is reinforced when the falsehood (or impossibility) of the contrary notion is shown. In fragment 2 we find the repetition of the general scheme presented in lines 28–30 of fragment 1, which stated the necessity of inquiring both about the heart of truth and the opinions of mortals, which were not true (because "there is no true conviction in them"). This alternative between truth and non-truth reappears when, after allegorically presenting his teaching, Parmenides puts into the mouth of the Goddess the rigorous exposition of a true course of philosophy. The Goddess will present a method (or, as we saw, a "way"), that is persuasive and convincing (because it goes with the truth). At the same time she will expound a completely unknowable way, which will be described as "not true" in line 18 of fragment 8. The future philosopher must inquire about the content of both ways, and once he is in possession of the elements that will make possible his *decision* (fr. 8.15), he will choose the single way that will enable him to reason, that is, direct his thought. This way is Parmenides' thesis.

Just as in line 28 of fragment 1 the Goddess began her speech with an exhortation about the necessity of inquiring into everything ("it is necessary"), in the first line of fragment 2 she addresses her listener with an imperative accent: "you, who listens (*akoúsas*), receive (*kómisai*) my word (*mûthon*)."[134] The Goddess invites the listener to make the *mûthos* that she

134 The accusative *mûthon* can relate both to *kómisai* and *akoúsas.* The expression "*mûthon akoúsas*" is common in Homer (*Il.* 17.694, *Od.* 3.94, 4.597), but in the passage we are concerned with *mûthon* appears to be the object of *kómisai.* Collobert shares this viewpoint: "et toi écoutant, acueille ma parole" (**Collobert** [1993], 13); as does Couloubaritsis: "et toi, m'ayant écouté, prend soin de ma parole" (**Couloubaritsis** [1990], 370); Vitali links "listen" with "*mûthos*" ("ascoltando il discorso," **Vitali** [1977], 32), and the great majority of interpreters, without taking into account the difference between the conjugated verb "*kóm-*

proclaims his own. The verb I have translated as "receive" (*kómisai*) has the meaning of "look after," "make your own," "preserve something by taking it with you."[135] That is to say, the teaching that will be offered must form part of the disciple's intellectual baggage. Henceforth he will not be able to judge without using the Goddess's *mûthos* as a reference point.

What does *mûthos* mean in line 1 of fragment 2?[136] Whatever the verb on which this term depends ("listen" or "receive"; my preference inclines toward the latter), *mûthos* simply means "account," "word," or even "discourse."[137] It is interesting to point out that all the wealth implicit in this single "word" ("is") will be expounded in what follows in an extensive . . . *lógos*. That is to say, there is no fundamental distinction between *mûthos* and *lógos* in Parmenides either.

(b) The Only Two Ways of "Leading" Thought

The Goddess's account expounds "the only two ways of investigation there are to think" (fr. 2.2). This phrase deserves an explanation. The term "only" (*moûnai*) cannot be relativized. Nevertheless, most scholars of Parmenides' thought have not taken it literally. The Prologue itself of the Poem presented two ways in allegorical form (ways of day and night), and toward the end, the Goddess spoke of truth as a way far from that of mortals (fr. 1.27). Be that as it may, only two possibilities emerged from this presentation. When Parmenides resumes the subject in fragment 2, before describing the content of each way, he says that these are the "only" (*moûnai*) ways that exist for thought. Parmenides could not have written "only" by chance; the numeral adjective indicates with precision that it would be illusory to try to seek other ways apart from the two that will be presented in what follows in lines 2.3 and 2.5.

Even so, there are scholars who underrate the force of this term and interpret it in a relative sense. A symptomatic case is that of M. Conche, who rejects my literal reading of the text:[138] "certainly, these two ways are the only *legitimate* ones, *a priori*, the only ones that *rightly* exist; but that

isai" and the participle "*akoúsas*," make *mûthos* the object of both terms ("tú preserva el relato, después de escucharlo," **Gómez-Lobo** [1985], 57; "pay attention to the account when you have heard it," **Tarán** [1965], 32; "mais toi, charge-toi du récit que tu auras entendu," **Cassin** [1998], 77).

135 Cf. *Il.* 1.594, 8.284, 6.278.

136 An exhaustive analysis of this question can be found in **Couloubaritsis** (1990), passim.

137 As is well known, the distinction between *mûthos* and *lógos* in early Greek thought is an invention of historians of philosophy: both terms means exactly the same. Cf. **Vernant**, "Raisons du mythe," in *Mythe et société en Grèce ancienne* (Paris: Maspéro, 1974).

138 **Conche** (1996), 76.

does not prevent the fact that others can exist, and do exist."[139] If that is so, these will be ways invented by interpreters: Parmenides is innocent.

Various authors before Conche had maintained that really Parmenides was speaking here of (1) the only two ways "of investigation," or (2) the only two ways that are "thinkable" (or that "it is possible to think," *eisi* is given potential value). Let us look at both possibilities. (1) If it is a matter of the only ways "of investigation," say the partisans of this position, there is nothing to stop another way appearing later that is not suitable for investigation. This would refer to the way formulated in fragments 6 and 7. It is true that in fragment 6 it only says that this way was "created by men, who know nothing" (fr. 6.4), but the description of this way continues in fragment 7, and there Parmenides says that "this way *of investigation*" (fr. 7.2) is to be avoided. So this way of investigation has to be one of the "only" two presented in fragment 2.

Case (2) is even more debatable. In Parmenides' philosophy, a way of investigation that, at least *a priori,* is not "thinkable" (if we base ourselves on those who give the verb "*noḗsai*" a passive sense), would not even have been presented. Even the way that is condemned in line 8.17 as "unthinkable" was one of the ways offered to thought in fragment 2, as the term reappears at the beginning of fragment 8, once reasoning has suppressed one of the ways of investigation, and on that occasion the Goddess declared that "so there remains one single *mûthos* of the way: is." Moreover, those who see a new way appearing in fragment 6 (a way that is not "thinkable") admit that the two "thinkable" ways were already presented in fragment 2, but as it happens, one of these two ways is already described in fragment 2 as "completely unknowable,"[140] as it tries to assert that it is necessary not to be.

Regarding the relation between the two ways and the notion of "think," we generally witness a wrong interpretation of the term *noḗsai* in fragment 2.2. The verb "think" (*noḗsai*) is evidently a final or consecutive infinitive,[141] but it has always been read as if it had passive value, either directly or as if "*eisí*" was interpreted as having potential value. Consequently, it has

139 **Conche** (1996), 76.

140 On the equivalence in Parmenides between "think" (*noeîn*) and "know" (*gignóskein*), cf. **Mansfeld** (1964), 57, note 1.

141 Cf. **Kahn** (1968/69), 703: "for knowing." Aalto maintains that this nuance of the infinitive, assimilated by him to the dative, has its origin in certain forms of Indo-European: "*ji-se,*" for example, is equivalent to "*zu siegen*" (**Aalto**, *Studien zur Geschichte des Infinitivs im Griechischen* [Helsinki: P. Katara, 1953], 11). Constantineau rejects the final value of *noḗsai* because the aorist has a temporal and not an absolute meaning, and, according to him, one of the ways only has an ephemeral existence (**Constantineau**, "La vérité chez Parménide," *Phoenix* 41 [1987] 220). The same argument is valid for the "ephemeral" character of a way that can only direct thought *a priori.*

generally been translated as a passive participle. This is what happened with translations of this type: "welche Wege der Forschung allein *denkbar sind*,"[142] "the only ways of inquiry that can be conceived,"[143] "quali sole vie di ricerca siano logicamente pensabili,"[144] "pensables,"[145] "conceivable,"[146] "à penser,"[147] "da pensare, pensabili,"[148] "zu bedenken."[149] Nevertheless, H. Gomperz already related the infinitive—with active value—to an indefinite subject: "(Strassen) die man erkennend betritt,"[150] whereas Mourelatos proposed a long list of potential subjects: "logically speaking, the subject of the infinitive is something like 'you' or 'men' or 'mortals' [. . .] and an object such as *ti* or *khē̂ma* or even *eón* is implicit,"[151] which was interpreted by J. Jantzen: "welche Wege es für dich allein sind, etwas zu denken."[152] I prefer to leave both the subject and the object of the infinitive indefinite, because this is not a verb inserted into a sentence but an isolated infinitive, and I reject any "passive" nuance, which, as we saw, would be incompatible with one of the ways.

Therefore, the ways proposed in line 2.2 are ways "to think," that is, ways along which, *a priori*, you can direct thought,[153] just as you use a knife "to cut" (without it being "cuttable" itself) or you use a chair "to sit on" (without it being "sittable" itself). An almost literal equivalent of the expression "existing ways *to think* (*eisi noē̂sai*)" can be found in Empedocles, "*póros esti noē̂sai*" (fr. 3). The text asserts the role of the senses as organs of knowledge, since in each of them there is a "pore" that enables us to know. Clearly it is not the pore itself that is "knowable." The pore is the way through which we know something.

Moreover, the final character of the infinitive *noē̂sai* is the only way of explaining the four declarative conjunctions (*hópōs* once and *hōs* three times), which introduce lines 3 and 5 of fragment 2. In fact, in these lines,

---

142 **Diels** (1897), 33.

143 **Tarán** (1965), 32.

144 **Untersteiner** (1958), 129.

145 **Gómez-Lobo** (1985), 57.

146 **Coxon** (1986), 52.

147 **Conche** (1996), 75; **Cassin** (1998), 77.

148 **Cerri**, G., *Parmenide di Elea: Poema sulla natura* (Milan: Rizzoli, 1999), 188.

149 **Wiesner** (1996), 251.

150 **Gomperz**, H., "Psychologische Beobachtungen an griechischen Philosophen," *Imago* 10 (1924) 7, note 19.

151 **Mourelatos** (1970), 55, note 26. In fact, only "you" deserves to be kept, because the Goddess is not speaking for "men" or "mortals," but only for the youth who has made a journey in order to listen to her.

152 **Jantzen**, J., *Parmenides zum Verhältnis von Sprache und Wirklichkeit* (Zetemata H. 63) (Munich: C. H. Bech'sche Verlagsbuchhandlung, 1976), 117.

153 So "thinking" is an activity to carry out in the future. Cf. Chantraine: "the aorist infinitive often refers to the future" (**Chantraine**, *Grammaire homérique, II: Syntaxe* [Paris: Klienck-sieck, 1953], 189).

the content of the two ways of thinking is expounded (one being valid and the other wrong). As both contents depend on the term "way," interpreters who give *noê̱sai* a passive value ("thinkable") have to include an understood verb on which to make the declarative conjunction depend. Thus we find translations such as: "the one <says> . . .";[154] "l'un (dit) . . .";[155] "Weg, welcher besagt . . .".[156] The way does not speak. The way is a way of thinking,[157] and when you think you think *that* . . . The declarative conjunctions correspond to the activity of thinking proposed by each way: on one hand there is a (way to think) *that* . . .; and on the other hand, there is another (way to think) *that* . . .[158] This is normal, since there are only two single ways *to* think, and each corresponds to the two contents of thought expounded toward the end of the first fragment: the heart of truth, and the opinions of mortals. One of the two ways of thinking is valid and fruitful, whereas the other will be revealed as inadequate, sterile, closed, and, finally, unthinkable (fr. 8.17), because it is based on . . . nothing. Nevertheless, *a priori,* an investigation can be based on either way. Both are "ways of investigation" (*dizé̱sios*) (fr. 2.2). "Of investigation" is subjective genitive: investigation has two ways available to it. Once it has been demonstrated that one of the ways is not viable, since the conclusion has been reached, *a posteriori,* that it was not the true way, then the Goddess orders: "Withdraw thought from this way *of investigation*" (fr. 7.2).

(c) Lines 3 and 5 of Fragment 2

The *only* two ways of investigation are stated in lines 3 and 5 of fragment 2 (line 4 is a commentary on the first way and lines 6–8 show why the second way is impracticable). Each formulation is preceded by the particles "*he̱ mèn*" ("on the one hand," "in the first place") for the first and "*he̱ de*" ("on the other hand," "and then") for the second. Both formulas, customary in the case of an enumeration, resume fragment 1's double program of study: "on the one hand" (*e̱mén*), truth; "on the other hand" (*e̱dè*), opinions (fr. 1.29–30). Therefore the reader/listener presumes that the two formulas in fragment 2 coincide with those in fragment 1, but doubtless expects that

154 **Tarán** (1965), 32.

155 **Couloubaritsis** (1990), 370.

156 **Wiesner** (1996), 251.

157 The English term "way," which means both way as "road" and way as "manner," is a literal translation of *hodós.*

158 Günther translates thus: "der eine Weg ist (besteht darin), zu denken, dass . . ." (**Günther,** H. C., "Der Satz des Parmenides von der Identität von Denken und Sein," *Studi Italiani di filologia classica* 15(2) (1997) 166).

now that the philosophy course has begun, the Goddess will go more deeply into both possibilities; indeed she will say "what is truth" and "what are opinions," or if you prefer, what is the "heart" (the nucleus, the perhaps hidden core) of both. The Goddess will amply fulfill these expectations.

Despite the parallelism that I have tried to demonstrate between lines 1.29–30 and 2.3 and 2.5, there is a difference. In the first fragment the expressions "*e̱mèn*" and "*e̱dè*" are conjunctions, that is, neutral terms with respect to the content that follows; anything at all can be stated "on the one hand" and "on the other," and it is the context that gives the passage its meaning. In contrast, in fragment 2, the formulas "*he̱ mèn*" and "*he̱ de*" are made up of a relative ("*he̱*," feminine singular) followed by the particles "*mèn*" and "*dè*." This means that in fragment 2, lines 3 and 5 presuppose a feminine subject, a subject about which something is said on the one hand and something else on the other. The only feminine subject provided by the passage is "way" (*hodós* is feminine in Greek), but this term cannot be a candidate to be taken up by the relatives (cf. *infra*, note 31). Both lines 2.3 and 2.5 present "ways." But as I have said, both lines begin with declarative conjunctions: "*hópo̱s*"[159] (2.3) and "*ho̱s*" (2.5). This means that each way is a way *to think that . . .*

The content of each thought is expressed through a double phrase, made up of two coordinated formulas which, from now on, we shall call "hemistiches." The first way, expounded in line 2.3, is a way "to think that A and that B"; the second way, expounded in line 2.5 is, as we said, the negation of this first way: it is a way "to think that not-A and that not-B." In Greek, A is represented by *éstin*[160] and not-A by *ouk éstin;* B is represented by *ouk esti me̱ eînai* and not-B (as I shall show, because it is not clear) by "*khreó̱n esti me̱ eînai.*" The first way, which thinks that "*éstin te kaí ouk esti mé̱ einai*" is a way that is accompanied by truth, it is (we could say) "true." It is the only way possible, which, once it has been explained in the following fragments, will be **Parmenides' thesis.** The second way that thinks exactly the opposite, viz. "*ouk éstin te kaì khreó̱n esti me̱ eînai,*" will be considered by the Goddess as the negative aspect of the thesis, and for this reason it cannot even be approached as a viable way, because thought cannot direct itself along it.

In the didactic scheme I set out above, the first way of investigation thinks, first, that "*éstin*" ("A" in our scheme) and then also that "*ouk esti me̱*

159 A different interpretation, according to which this "*hópo̱s*" has a modal meaning, has been maintained by **Untersteiner** (1958), lxxxv.

160 The original texts have "*esti.*" These were changed to "*éstin*" by Mullach in order to respect the meter (**Mullach**, F. G. A., *Fragmenta Philosophorum Graecorum* [Paris: Didot, 1860], 113). Although this modification is not important, Diels wrongly attributes it to H. Stein (**Diels's** edition of Simplicius, *In Phys.*, 116).

eînai" (= B). As we know, "*éstin*" is the third person singular of the present of the verb "to be," "*eînai*." This third person appears either on its own or negated, in the two first hemistiches of each way. Let us begin by analyzing these first hemistiches.

(1) *Éstin* on Its Own and Its Negation

First of all, we should say that "A" can be translated literally as "is," and "not-A" as "is not." When we analyze the value of the verb "to be" in Parmenides' philosophy, which will be the central point of our quest, we shall see what Parmenides meant by saying "is" or "is not." However, at once we come to a difficulty: a simple reading of the text upon which we wish to comment shows us that Parmenides says "is" in one line and "is not" in the other (and we shall see with what intention), but he does not tell us *who* or *what* is or is not.

This means the verb "is" (in the affirmative or negative) has no subject. It is true that Greek, like various modern languages, does not require an explicit subject in the third person (and other languages require "it" as a purely formal subject, but to say "it is" is not saying anything; indeed, to understand the meaning of the sentence, we have to know "what" or "who" is the "it" that is), but, in parallel passages, the preceding context usually indicates what is the subject in question. Parmenides' truncated phrase ("*ho̱s/hópo̱s éstin*") is also found in other authors, but in all the parallel passages the subject is made explicit by the context. This is the case with Protagoras' famous statement "man is the measure of all things," which continues in the following way: "of the things that are (*tô̱n ónto̱n*), that are (*ho̱s éstin*) . . ." The phrase "that are," identical to the one in Parmenides (since it is in the singular in Greek) has no subject, but the subject has already been mentioned and we know that it is "the things that are." The same occurs in the famous passage in the *Sophist* (263b) in which Plato says that true speech tells "the things (*tà ónta*) that are [or 'as they are'] (*ho̱s éstin*) about you." The subject of "*ho̱s éstin*" (once again, the phrase is identical to that of Parmenides) is undoubtedly "the things."

In the case of Parmenides, nothing indicates or suggests what the possible subject is.[161] Various explanations can be proposed to give a reason for this unusual fact. But it occurs to us that there is a previous question to answer that is generally overlooked, and which is essential: *if* a subject is proposed (or found) for the *ésti* that occurs in both 2.3a and 2.5a, *this subject*

161 Untersteiner asserts that the subject is "the way" (**Untersteiner** [1958], lxxxvi), but this position is incompatible with the "properties" (*sé̱mata*) that fragment 8 will deduce from the so-called subject.

must be the same for both occurrences of the verb. This is obvious even if the two ways that are stated in lines 2.3 and 2.5 are *opposite* ways. The only way to respect the value of the *opposites* that the Goddess propounds (one way is accompanied by truth, whereas the other is completely unknowable) is to suggest or keep the same subject for both of them. This is the position adopted by, among others, A. Finkelberg, for whom line 2.3 states "that to be is . . . ," whereas line 2.5 says "that to be is not . . . "[162] Thus, when something appropriate is said about this subject, the way is true; when something incorrect is said *about the same subject,* the way is wrong. In contrast, if opposing subjects are proposed, the value judgments about each way would have to be identical. On this point, J. Mansfeld says that *tò eón* could be the subject of *ésti,* but it is mistaken to assert that "*tò mḛ eón* could be the subject of line 2.5.". If that were so, 2.5a would say "*[tò mḛ eón] ouk esti,*" that is, "that which is not, is not," a thesis that cannot be described as wrong, as we read in the following line (2.6), where it repeats almost word for word the second hemistich of line 2.3: "it is not possible not to be," "there is no non-being." In contrast, if the subject of 2.5a were the same as that of 2.3a, 2.5a would state: "*[tò eón] ouk esti,*" that is, "that which is, is not," an absurd and aberrant thesis that Parmenides criticizes. Montero Moliner fell into the same error as Mansfeld when he wrote that the first way states that "the being [beings] are" and the second that "the non-being [non-beings] are not" (or not-being is not).[163] The same happens with Coxon, who states that the only possible subject of "is not and must needs not be" is "Nothing."[164] J. Wiesner also commits a similar error when he says that the "second way" states that "Nichts gibt es nicht."[165] In that case Parmenides would be saying that nothing or non-being is not, and that they necessarily are not. If he were saying that, how could it be said that that thesis is not true?

For his part, L. Tarán criticizes those who assume, as I do, that both ways must have the same subject (if there is one), because, according to him, in that case, Parmenides would have had to demonstrate why one way is valid and the other not, whereas the absence of a subject makes that demonstration unnecessary.[166] To this it can be answered that within the limits of his "logic" Parmenides at least demonstrates the impossibility of the wrong way, and that this impossibility assumes the possibility (and even the necessity) of the true way.

---

162 **Finkelberg**, A., "Parmenides' Foundation of the Way of Truth," *Oxford Studies in Ancient Philosophy* 6 (1988) 47.

163 **Montero Moliner**, F., *Parménides* (Madrid: Gredos, 1960), 68.

164 **Coxon** (1986), 182.

165 **Wiesner** (1996), 177.

166 **Tarán** (1965), 38. Cf. *contra* **Mansfeld**, J., review of Tarán, *Mnemosyne* 20 (1967) 317.

Let us return to the explanations proposed to resolve the problem of the subject of *éstin.*[167] I think there are four possibilities: it could be suggested (1) that there is an error in the transmission of the text (if this is so, it must be corrected to introduce the absent subject); (2) that there is an implicit conceptual subject that has to be sought in the rest of the Poem; (3) that there is no possible subject; and (4) that the subject must be extracted from the isolated verb: "*éstin*" "produces" its own subject. All four of these possibilities have had their champions.[168]

(1) F. M. Cornford held that now at this stage of the text the subject is *tò eón,* and stated that "the absence of a subject for *éstin* suggests that Parmenides wrote '*he̱ mèn hópo̱s eón éstin.*'"[169] His thesis is based on the similarity there is between 2.3 and line 6.1, which, effectively, reads "*eón émmenai.*"[170] However, this analogy does not authorize the modification of a passage situated in a different context and, especially, at a *previous* stage of the argument. J. Loenen also proposed modifying the Parmenides text and adding the subject "*ti*" ("something").[171] According to his correction, hemistich 2.3a would say "*éstin ti.*" According to this scholar, the proposed correction is confirmed by an analogous expression that appears in the reading some manuscripts proposed for 8.1: "*dé ti,*" instead of the generally accepted text, "*d'éti.*" Moreover, Melissus (fr. 1) and Gorgias (fr. 3) also spoke about "*ti,*" but J. Mansfeld correctly observed that in the case of those scholars, the presence of "*ti*" is also conjectural.[172] To sum up, I consider it very risky to introduce modifications into a text (2.3a) that has come down to us in identical form, both in Proclus' and Simplicius' versions.

(2) Most scholars adopted this second possibility and asked the following question: about what could Parmenides say "*éstin*" in line 2.3a and "*ouk éstin*" in 2.5a? The favorite candidates were "*eón*" and "*eînai,*" generally and literally translated as "that which is being," or "that which is," or "being," considered as synonymous.[173] Thus, for example, Diels translates: "dass (das Seiende) ist";[174] O. Becker, "dass es ein Sein gibt";[175] F. M. Riaux, "que

---

167 In tackling the thorny subject of the "subject" of Parmenides' thesis, we have to differentiate between the problem of the grammatical subject, absent from lines 2.3 and 2.5 (about whose absence various hypotheses can be proposed) and the subject around which the whole Poem revolves, which is obsessively present: "[*tò*] *eón,*" meaning "that which is being," "the fact of being." Cf. *infra.*

168 More lavishly, Meijer proposes twelve possibilities (**Meijer** [1997], 114).

169 **Cornford** (1939), 30, note 2.

170 "*Émmenai*" is the epic form of the infinitive "*eînai,*" and the formula means "*that which is,* is," or "*that which is being,* exists," or "by being, it is."

171 **Loenen** (1959), 12.

172 **Mansfeld** (1964), 52, note 2.

173 Cf. **Tarán** (1965), 37.

174 **Diels** (1897), 33.

175 **Becker** (1937), 141.

l'être est."[176] Some scholars postulate the pronoun "it" (which may be "il," "él," or "es") as the subject, but once more, its antecedent is "being" or "the being."

This possibility attracted most researchers because it seems evident that the first way of investigation states, as its central thesis, that "being is" or "there is being," that "being exists," as K. Reinhardt stressed strongly.[177] R. Mondolfo finds an indirect proof of the existence of this subject in lines 2.7–8, where it is stated that "*mḕ eón*" ("that which is not") is unknowable and inexpressible. The knowable and expressible would then be the contrary of that negation, that is to say, "*eón,*" which is then confirmed in 6.1: "It is necessary to say and to think that that which is, is."[178] Continuing with this viewpoint, we could also cite the case of line 8.3, "since that which is (*eón*) is unbegotten and indestructible," where it is difficult to deny that the subject is *eón;* and even more clearly in 8.19, "how then could *tò eón* perish?"; and in 8.25, "*eón* touches *eón.*" In this latter case, if we consider that "*eón,*" without article, is not the subject but a participle referring to another subject, then this tacit subject would "touch *eón*" but what could "touch" that which is, except "that which is"? Let us not forget that *eón* is unique; only *eón* can be the subject of "touches," since "it is impossible to force that which is (*eón*) not to be connected with that which is (*eón*)" (fr. 4.2).

One thing is clear: all these examples show something obvious, that is, that Parmenides' Poem, and especially the "characteristics" of fragment 8, concern "that which is being" (*eón*). But the partisans of this possibility do not explain why, in certain passages (especially at the beginning of his exposition, in fragment 2, and when he returns to the single remaining way again, in line 8.2), that subject does not appear. Given this certainty, we can only share the opinions of R. Falus: "the subject *eón* **may** complete the thesis '*esti*'";[179] and of G. E. L. Owen: "no one will deny that, as the argument goes, *tò eón* is a correct description of the subject."[180] Thus we arrive at a position that admits the existence of *eón* as subject, *but only* at later stages than fragment 2. For example, J. Mansfeld maintains that in 2.3a and 2.5a there is no subject because here we have the premises of a disjunctive syllogism "that is valid for statements (*Aussagen*) but not for concepts (*Begriffen*),"[181] and that any possible subject would have foreseen the conclusion

---

176 **Riaux** (1840), 209; cf. also **Robin**, L., *La pensée grecque et les origines de l'esprit scientifique,* 3rd ed. (Paris: La Renaissance du Livre, 1963), 103.

177 **Reinhardt** (1916), 36.

178 **Mondolfo**, R. "Discusioni su un testo parmenideo (fr. 8.5–6)," *Rivista critica di storia della filosofia* 19 (1964) 311.

179 **Falus** (1960), 274, note 30.

180 **Owen** (1960), 90.

181 **Mansfeld** (1964), 58.

of the syllogism in advance. Nevertheless, still according to Mansfeld, fragments 3 and 8.4 ff. authorize the introduction of the subject, so that "es ist" means "das absolut Seiende ist."[182] On the same tack, we may include here an apparently independent—and clearly original—thesis to which I have already alluded. This is the point of view of M. Untersteiner, for whom the subject is the way, but this, in its turn, "is an *eón*," since "the reality of this way will become the reality of *eón*," so that we reach "a total confusion between the *hodòs alethés* (= the true way) and *eón* itself."[183] However that may be, there can be no doubt that it is difficult to do without the concept of *eón*, even if we agree to leave the *esti* of fragment 2 standing on its own.

Other scholars prefer to propose a general subject, either abstract or concrete. The former is the case with S. Tugwell, for example, for whom the alternative in fragment 2 takes this form: "that which can be known, must exist, or not."[184] This position is shared by Owen and a large number of Anglo-Saxon researchers, for whom the subject is "that whereof one may speak or think."[185] For his part, C. H. Kahn states that the first way does not have a grammatical subject, but does have a logical one: "the object of knowing, what is or can be known."[186] Among those authors who have proposed a general, but concrete, subject, we find L. Woodbury, who maintained that the subject is "the real world," which embraces everything about which we can say "*éstin*," since "Being is the *name* of the world."[187] Relying on a reading by J. Burnet, for whom the subject is "what we call Body,"[188] and on the interest shown by Parmenides in cosmological questions,[189] Y. Lafrance says that the subject is the material universe.[190] T. M.

---

182 Ibid., 45.

183 **Untersteiner** (1958), lxxxix. Casertano shares this hypothesis. For him, "Parmenides only says that there exists one way" (**Casertano** [1978], 63).

184 **Tugwell**, S., "The Way of Truth," *Classical Quarterly* 14 (1964), 36.

185 **Owen** (1960), 95. Nevertheless, the way followed by Owen is curious, since he arrives at his interpretation through an analysis of 2.7, where it says that "*tò mè eón*" is unthinkable and inexpressible. If that is so, Owen notwithstanding, that which is thinkable and expressible (which would be the subject) is . . . *eón*.

186 **Kahn** (1968/69), 710.

187 **Woodbury** (1958), 152. Also **Casertano** (1978), 94, "ciò che è, è il mondo." **Wiesner** (1996), 232, shares this position: the Poem is about the "Welt."

188 **Burnet**, *Early Greek Philosophy*, 4a ed. (London: A. & C. Black, 1930), 178.

189 A "cosmological" Parmenides monopolizes the work of **Popper**, K., *The World of Parmenides* (London/New York: Routledge, 1998), 114: "So, Parmenides was, in my opinion, essentially a cosmologist." Cf. also **Bollack**, J., "La cosmologie parménidienne de Parménide," in *Herméneutique et ontologie, Hommage à Pierre Aubenque,* ed. Bragué, R., and Courtine, J. F. (Paris : P. U. F., 1990), 17–53.

190 **Lafrance**, Y. "Le sujet du Poème de Parménide: L'être ou l'univers?" *Elenchos* 20(2) (1999) 302. According to this scholar, the inscription discovered in 1962 in Elea stating that Parmenides was a doctor ("*ouliádes*") demonstrates, according to one possible etymology of the term, that the philosopher was concerned with the whole, the "*oûlon*" (268).

Robinson adopts the expression "all that is collectively real,"[191] a position perhaps inspired by W. J. Verdenius, for whom the subject of *éstin* "is so obvious [that it] is not stated,"[192] and is none other than Reality, that is, the totality of things. This position has the merit of bringing out the breadth of Parmenides' thesis, but it is more a commentary on the Poem than a decision on the absent subject. Literally, Verdenius's position would be unsustainable, since it would assume that reality is different from being, "since being refers to reality, instead of being identical with it."[193] A few years later, Verdenius abandoned this opinion and wrote: "if Truth is the subject of the Goddess's discourse, it is by implication the subject of *éstin*"[194] insofar as truth is the real nature of things. With this new viewpoint, Verdenius was perhaps pointing to a more primordial concept than reality; if that is so, he could continue his research further, since there is an even more primary notion, the "*heart* of truth," that the Goddess exhorts the seeker to know first and foremost (fr. 1.29). Moreover, in 2.4 Parmenides says that truth is accompanied (or escorted: *ope̱deî*) by the way announced in 2.3, but that it is not identical with this way or with any part of it.[195] Finally, we may add the most general hypothesis concerning the subject of *éstin,* which, while acknowledging a certain debt to Owen and Kahn, is much more generous, since it holds that the verb refers to "any object." This is the interpretation of A. Gómez-Lobo, for whom Parmenides is saying that "there are two and only two ways for the investigation of any object"; one assumes that it is, and the other assumes that it is not.[196] J. E. Raven[197] and W. K. C. Guthrie[198] had said something similar.

(3) There are scholars who have said that there is no subject in 2.3a and 2.5a. All the proposed interpretations of this kind follow G. Calogero's view, who, from an analysis of line 8.34, wrote "*ésti* does not have a defined subject, as the specific expression of a given reality," but keeps the indeterminacy of "a purely logical and verbal element of affirmation."[199] Moreover,

---

191 **Robinson**, T. M., "Parmenides on the Ascertainment of Real," *Canadian Journal of Philosophy* 4 (1975) 56.

192 **Verdenius** (1942), 32.

193 **Fränkel** (1930), 162.

194 **Verdenius**, W. J., "Parmenides B 2.3," *Mnemosyne* 15 (1962) 237.

195 Even Wiersma, one of the very few scholars who do not adopt Bywater's conjecture "*ale̱theíe̱i*" in line 2.4 (he conserves "*ale̱theíe̱*") states that "truth accompanies this way" (**Wiersma**, W., "Notes on Greek Philosophy," *Mnemosyne* 20 [1967] 407).

196 **Gómez-Lobo** (1985), 68.

197 For Raven there is no defined subject, since one can say "it is or it is not" about *everything* (**Kirk**, G. S., and **Raven**, J. E., *The Presocratic Philosophers,* 1st ed. [Cambridge, England: Cambridge University Press, 1957], 270).

198 According to this scholar, *éstin* is the belief in the existence of something, to which the word *éstin* fully refers (**Guthrie** [1965], 22).

199 **Calogero** (1932), 18.

it would be inconsistent to state that *eón* is the tacit subject, since *eón* is actually Parmenides' invention, and so, it would have been difficult for a reader of his own time to assume it.[200] This is the reason why "anyone who does not want to make Parmenides an idiot (*sciocco*), and Plato another idiot for considering Parmenides to be 'venerable and fearsome,' must give up stating that the subject of *éstin* and of *ouk éstin* is the implicit *eón*."[201] The way of truth says "is"; the way of error says "is not"; and the two formulas translate "the two ways belonging to the logical-verbal process." This means that *for Parmenides, being is being as in the verbal copula,* and that only a confusion between the predicative value and the existential value of the verb could have led Parmenides to state, for example, that "being exists."

A. P. D. Mourelatos's position is, if anything, even more extreme: *éstin* is just a certain way of linking *any subject* to *any* predicate, and therefore the structure of Parmenides' thesis is the following: ". . . is . . ." Mourelatos calls the scheme "speculative predication."[202]

Calogero's thesis was revolutionary in his time,[203] but an interpretation that, from my point of view, intolerably weakens Parmenides' *éstin* aroused very violent criticisms. If we take into account the rigorous analysis of being that is developed in fragment 8, we may well ask whether, contrary to Calogero's thesis, the predicative value that he maintains could not be a usage derived from a deeper reality: the absolute and necessary value of being. We shall return to this point, but we can say now that being's *sḗmata,* expounded in fragment 8, cannot belong to a mere formal and empty *éstin.*

H. Fränkel also held that *éstin* has no subject, but his arguments differ from Calogero's. For Fränkel it is an *impersonal* verb, like "rain" or "snow," and if you try to add a possible subject (e.g., "the rain" or "the snow") you fall into a tautology: "the rain rains,"[204] or even worse, you introduce a factor of confusion by suggesting that anything else except rain could "rain." The idea is interesting, but it rests, I believe, on an erroneous concept of so-called "impersonal"[205] verbs. Furthermore, Fränkel appears to

---

200 In note 194 we saw that Verdenius had said exactly the opposite.

201 **Calogero** (1936), 155.

202 **Mourelatos** (1970), 56 ff. Later, Mourelatos made his position a little more flexible: the copula is really a "conveyor" toward the predicate, which is approached as a "character-power" ("Heraclitus, Parmenides, and the Naive Metaphysics of Things," *Phronesis,* Supp. I, *Exegesis and Argument,* Studies in Greek Philosophy presented to G. Vlastos, ed. Lee, E. N., Mourelatos, A. P. D., and Rorty, R. M. [Assen: 1973], 43).

203 His influence is detectable in W. Kranz's translation, "dass IST ist" (in **Diels**, H., and **Kranz**, W., *Die Fragmente der Vorsokratiker,* Vol. I [Zürich-Berlin: Weidmannsche Verlagsbuchhandlung, 1956], 231). However, Calogero criticized Kranz's version, stating that he "to disguise such eccentricities has to resort to typographical ploys" (**Calogero** [1936], 155, note 1).

204 **Fränkel** (1951), 403, note 13.

205 I will set out my position on this point *infra.*

apply his position to the whole of the Poem, and not just to the passages in which the verb appears without a subject, since, according to him, any identification of a subject "would determine being in an inadmissible way."[206] This is not true. In 6.1 Parmenides says tautologically that "that which is being, is" (*eón émmenai*), and in other passages the verb "to be" is used in an undoubtedly predicative way, which requires a subject; this would not be possible if, as Fränkel says, impersonal verbs cannot have a subject, even a conceptual or psychological one.[207]

Halfway between the positions of Calogero and Fränkel, we find L. Tarán. He states that 2.3a and 2.5a do not have any subject and that the verb *éstin,* in the third person, signifies the notion of existence in these passages.[208] In other passages, the same notion is expressed by a participle or by an infinitive. That is, like Calogero and Fränkel, Tarán considers that *éstin* "is used in an impersonal manner," but, contrary to Fränkel, he limits this use to fragment 2, and contrary to Calogero, he gives the verb an existential value and not just a predicative one. In contrast, the rest of his interpretation floats on a highly hypothetical plane, because he bases it solely on the fact that "Greek, unlike English, admits the existential as well as the copulative impersonal without an expressed subject."

I adopt explanation (4). It cannot be denied that Parmenides' *éstin* has a subject, because it appears explicitly in various passages of the Poem. I have already cited 6.1, "*eón émmenai,*" and 8.19; we may add 8.36–37: "nothing *éstin* or *éstai* [is or will be] apart from *tò eón.*" But the fact that there is a subject does not mean that this must be already postulated in 2.3a and 2.5a. Parmenides' starting point is *éstin* because the philosopher wants to give pride of place to an undeniable certainty (the malign genius of Descartes had not yet been born): now, in the present, at this very moment, "is." It does not matter who or what "is," but no one, much less a future philosopher, can be unaware that "is being." Parmenides will draw a series of consequences from this sort of intuition, but the best way of giving pride of place to the imperious and present character of this "fact" consists in presenting it on its own. In any predicative sentence, the predicate clarifies, informs about, or characterizes the subject, and the subject is the central nucleus of meaning. "Write" remains empty of meaning if we do not know who is writing, and when we add the subject, for example, Borges, we know something . . . about Borges. If Parmenides had made a subject explicit from the beginning of his philosophy course, it would have been said

206 **Fränkel** (1951), 403.

207 For the difference between a conceptual or psychological subject and a grammatical subject, cf. **Brugmann**, K., *Griechische Grammatik* (Munich: C. H. Beck, 1913), 656, note 1.

208 **Tarán** (1965), 37.

about this subject that it "is." Parmenides starts from "is" and shows that that "is" hides a broader, richer notion within itself, which will be reached only after having grasped the present and undeniable force of "is." For Kahn, partisan of the "veridical" meaning of *eînai* in Parmenides, the *éstin* is just a point of departure, from which Parmenides develops "other aspects of the ontological claim entailed by this assertion," and among these aspects, fundamentally, we find the "existential" nuance, according to which "what is must be something rather than nothing."[209] That broader notion will be "the subject" of "is," the only possible subject, that is, a sort of product *extracted analytically* from the predicate. As B. Cassin luminously writes, "the verb has no other possible subject than itself, which unfolds, segregates itself as subject: 'that which is, is being.'"[210]

Indeed, what else can "be" unless it is the fact of being? The fact of being (which, as I shall show, is expressed in Parmenides both by the participle *eón*—very rarely, *tò eón*—and by the infinitive *eînai*) is the only notion whose reality is defined by stating it through the conjugated form "is." That "is" also grammatically only denotes "being" in the present tense, just as "is writing" denotes that someone is writing now, that at this moment, the fact of writing "is happening," even though when we say "is writing" we do not yet know who embodies that fact. But the fact is undeniable from the moment that we say "is writing." Exactly the same occurs with the fact of being: we are saying "is being" when we say "is." And we are saying "is being" even in a tautological way, in "that which is" (*eón*), which is that which is being *par excellence. No one can deny that that which is, is being: "eón éstin."*

The Spanish expression "se es"—translated either as plain "is" or "it is"—that I have often used, may suggest that in our interpretation the *éstin* in 2.3a is considered to be an impersonal verb. Yes and no. *Estin* is not impersonal, but it is used by Parmenides as if it were. To clarify this point, we must look, very briefly, at the question of verbs called "impersonal." As I have already said, I do not share the viewpoint of H. Fränkel about the decidedly impersonal character of *éstin* in 2.3a,[211] because, I believe, his interpretation confuses two levels: on the one hand, there is the psychological aspect of impersonal verbs, which he brings up, and on the other, the meaning content of his examples. For a Greek of the classical epoch, the psychological subject of verbs called impersonal was probably the divinity.[212] But it is obvious that the meaning content of "is raining" is not "Zeus

---

209 **Kahn**, C. H., "Being in Parmenides and Plato," *La parola del passato* 43 (1988) 247.

210 **Cassin**, B., *Si Parménide* (Lille: Presses Universitaires de Lille, 1980), 55.

211 Cf. note 204.

212 This is the opinion of **Schwyzer**, E., *Griechische Grammatik*, Vol. II (Munich: C. H. Beck, 1950), 362; **Kühner**, R., *Ausfürliche Grammatik der griechischen Sprache*, 2nd ed., Vol. II(1)

is raining";[213] at most, we might think, "Zeus is making it rain." In fact, when we say in any kind of language that "it is raining" or "it is snowing," we are alluding to the *effective presence* of something (rain, snow) in the corresponding verb tense ("it rained" if it happened in the past, and "it will rain" if we are talking about the future). That is, semantically, "it is raining" means "at this moment the fact of raining is happening." We do not know whether the origin of the notion "raining" preceded the formation of the term "rain," or vice versa (personally, I think, without being able to prove it, that the formation of the verbs preceded the nouns). However that may be, it cannot be denied that the third person singular of the present tense of the verb "to rain" is "it rains," and when we say "it rains" we are asserting the presence of rain now in the present. The verb in question is called "impersonal" because there is no "person" to be the subject. "It is raining positively states a process taking place outside the 'I-you,' the only pronouns referring to persons," E. Benveniste wrote.[214] If we take this interpretation of impersonal verbs into account, I have no doubt in stating that in 2.3a and 2.5a the two instances of *éstin,* as autonomous elements up until now, are used in an impersonal way. Then, just as "it rains" means "the fact of raining is happening now," "raining is present now," "it is" means "the fact of being is happening now," "the fact of being is present now."

In summary, let us say that the two instances of *éstin* do not have a subject at first because, for reasons of method or didactic reasons, Parmenides preferred to expound his "thesis" by means of an affirmation that implies, itself, the *only* possible conceptual "subject" (just as "rain" is the only possible "subject" of the phrase "it rains"). For this reason, my position with regard to Parmenides' *éstin* is a little different from the classical conceptions: I do not deny that there is a subject, but I do not believe that this subject must be extrapolated from the passages in which it is found. The subject must be analytically extracted from the meaning of *éstin* as Parmenides' fundamental thesis.

As a result of everything I have said, and provisionally (because I have not yet adopted a position with respect to the value of the verb "to be" in Parmenides), we may propose "is" as a translation of 2.3a and "is not" as a translation of 2.5a, with the proviso that the "subject" of both expressions,

---

(Hannover: Hansche Buchhandlung, 1870), 33; **Hölscher** (1969), 78, note 30; **Brugmann**, K., *Griechische Grammatik* (Munich: C. H. Beck, 1913), 656, note 1.

213 *Contra* C. H. Kahn, who thinks this belief exists even in modern Greek, where the subject "god" is added to "is raining" to say "*theós brékhei*" (**Kahn**, C. H., *The Verb "Be" in Ancient Greek* [Dordrecht/Boston: D. Reidel Publishing Company, 1973], 174). Benveniste had already said that this expression was a rationalization backwards (**Benveniste**, E., *Problèmes de linguistique générale,* Vol. I [Paris: Gallimard, 1966], 230).

214 **Benveniste**, *Problèmes de linguistique.*

which will appear at the opportune moment, is "*eón*" or "*einai,*" "that which is," "the fact of being," "[that which is] being."

(2) The Modal Complement of *éstin* on Its Own and Its Negation

The content that each way proposes to think is constituted, as I said, by two coordinated phrases. Or, if you prefer, there is a double content. According to our symbolization, we have already looked at "A" and "not-A." Now we must decipher the meaning of the second hemistiches of each formulation, that is, "B" (*ouk esti mḕ eînai,* fr. 2.3b) and "not-B" (*khreṓn esti mḕ eînai,* fr. 2.5b). From the syntactic viewpoint, unlike what happened with the first hemistiches, both "B" and "not-B" are complete sentences: there is an infinitive (*eînai*) negated (*mḗ*), which acts as the subject of the two "impersonal" expressions, *ouk* ***esti*** and *khreṓn* ***esti***. If the scheme is valid, it assumes that the value of the two *esti* is different from that in the first hemistiches of each formula. Is that possible? There can be no doubt about it. Even in Homer, the verb "*eînai*" ("to be") has multiple[215] values, and among these, as well as a "strong" sense ("exist"), we find copulative or "impersonal"[216] meanings. The same thing happens in Parmenides, who draws his inspiration from Homer.

Nevertheless, there are scholars, who without being able to deny the evidence that the *esti* in 2.5b is linked to *khreôn,* and together they form a cliché,[217] deny that *ouk esti* in 2.3b has an impersonal character. This is the case with O. Gigon, who translates 2.3b as "non-being, is not";[218] H. Fränkel, "Nicht-Sein ist nicht";[219] and Ruggiu, "il non-essere non è."[220] From the viewpoint of the passage's content, all these translations are correct (in fr. 6.2 Parmenides says exactly the same thing: "*mēdèn, d'ouk éstin,*" "nothing is not"). I have adopted an "impersonal" version since I believe that Parmenides took care with all the details of his thesis' presentational structure, especially in this fragment 2, which introduces it. So it would be difficult

215 Ebeling finds nineteen different meanings of *eînai* already in Homer (**Ebeling**, H., *Lexicon Homericum* [Leipzig: B. G. Teubner, 1885]).

216 *Il.* 13.114: "it is not possible [*ouk estin*] for us to abandon the fight"; 21.191: "it is not possible [*ouk estin*] to fight against the son of Kronos."

217 In this cliché, each of the two terms has had to abandon its own specificity: *esti* does not have existential value, and *khreṓn* has abandoned (if indeed, it ever had) its participial aspect (since, according to some scholars, the term originates from the combination of *khréō* and *ón:* cf. **Wackernagel**, J., *Vermischte Beiträge zur griechischen Sprachkunde* [Basel: 1897], 62; and **Redard**, G., *Recherches sur khrê, khresthai* [París: H. Champion, 1953], 73).

218 **Gigon**, O., *Der Ursprung der Griechischen Philosophie von Hesiod bis Parmenides* (Basel: Schwabe & Co., 1945), 251.

219 **Fränkel** (1951), 403.

220 **Ruggiu** (1975), 251.

to admit that in this structure, one of the second hemistiches definitely has an "impersonal" value (2.5b, *khreó̱n esti*), whereas the other (2.3b, *ouk éstin*) does not. My hypothesis is the following: in the double presentation (*te kaí,* "and") of each way, the second hemistiches have a *modal value;* the first hemistich alludes to possibility and the second to necessity. In the first case the possibility is denied ("it is im-possible"), as it concerns the *negation* of the reality of "is" (indeed, it is impossible to deny that one is); in the second case the necessity is asserted, as it also concerns the negation of "is," but in this case the negation of it would make this way a wrong one: to assert necessarily that one is not being is an aberration.

Hence we adopt a "modal" version of the second hemistiches, but in this case as well, there are two possibilities, since both *ouk esti* (2.3b) and *khreó̱n esti* (2.5b) are related to the negative infinitive *"mè eînai."* Note that it is *the same* idea occurring in both ways that are considered to be opposites. This confirms that those who assume a change of subject in the first hemistiches of the two ways (cf. *supra*) are mistaken. The two possibilities are based on the fact that, from a syntactic viewpoint, "impersonal" expressions have a "subject," and this may be (1) a verb in the infinitive or (2) a complete phrase. For example, (1) "it is necessary *to die,*" "it is possible *to survive*"; or (2) "it is necessary *that human beings die,*" "it is possible *that we may survive.*" The phrase called the "subject complement" (example [2]) has a subject and a conjugated verb (in our examples, "human beings"/"we" and "die"/"may survive," respectively). Matters become complicated in Greek because in the complement phrases, the verb (conjugated in Spanish) is in the infinitive. [Translator's note: English may use either a conjugated verb or an infinitive.] It is worth pointing out that the infinitive *ouk esti* ("not to be") is open to both possibilities: it could be the subject infinitive of the impersonal phrases, or it could be the conjugated verb—for which Greek uses the infinitive—that follows them. The difference in our case is **vital.** In our examples, it is "to die" that is necessary, it is "to survive" that is possible. There is no subject, but once the possibility or necessity of the fact is admitted, then candidates may appear to fulfill the action of "dying" or "surviving," and these candidates are plentiful. In contrast, in the second case, where the verbs are conjugated, they are predicated *of a subject,* and the necessity of dying is asserted about *human beings,* and the possibility of surviving is asserted about *us.* As can be seen, the difference between one case and the other is vast: in one case, the weight of modality falls upon an action, denoted by a verb; in the other case, it falls upon a subject, whatever that might be. As regards Parmenides, the choice between one or the other of these brings back the thorny problem of the subject of *éstin.*

Let us see what solutions have been proposed. Let us begin with the second possibility. Its partisans assume that there is a tacit subject in the second hemistiches as well. They consider that the verb "*mē̱ eînai*" corresponds to this subject, and as these second hemistiches are linked to the two first ones, and a change of subject in the same line would be inadmissible, they assume that "*mē̱ eînai*" has the same subject that they assumed for "*éstin*." Thus they arrive at translations corresponding to this scheme: "[being] is, and it is not possible that [being] should not be" ("should not be" is "*mē̱ eînai*" transposed into conjugated form); and "[being] is not, and it is necessary that [being] should not be." This is how F. M Cornford translates: "[that which is] is, and it is impossible *for it* not to be," "it is not, and must needs not be";[221] D. Gallop, "that [it] is, and that [it] cannot not be" and "that [it] is not, and that [it] needs must not be";[222] J. Beaufret and J. J. Riniéri, "comment il est et qu'il ne soit possible qu'il ne soit pas,"[223] among others.

As I favor postulating a subject *already* in 2.3b and 2.5b, I adopt the possibility that considers only the infinitive "*mē̱ eînai*" to be the "subject" of the modal expressions. If this is so, the second hemistiches have a pleasant surprise for us: retroactively, they provide a possible "conceptual" subject for the first hemistiches. I say "conceptual," since the notion of "being," around which the whole Poem revolves, is polysemic: it appears represented by "*ésti*" on its own, the infinitive "*eînai*" (and synonyms), and the participle "[*tò*] *eón*." Indeed, if the two hemistiches are linked by *te kaí* ("and"), they must refer to the same notion, and that of which "is" is said in 2.3a must logically reappear in 2.3b, although negated, since the verb is also negated:[224] "it is not [possible]." So I propose this translation scheme for the second hemistiches, which I will develop throughout this work: "and it is not possible (*ouk ésti*) not to be (*mē̱ eînai*)";[225] "and it is necessary (*khreō̱n esti*) not to be (*mē̱ eînai*)."

---

221 **Cornford** (1939), 3. The sametranslation can be found in **Guthrie** (1965), 13; in **Austin** (1986), 159; and in **Kirk-Raven-Schofield** (1983), 245.

222 **Gallop** (1984), 55.

223 **Beaufret- Riniéri** (1955), 79.

224 Hölscher, who does not heed this negation, criticizes those who hold that the subject of 2.3b is "*mē̱ eînai,*" since then, given that the phrases are linked, the same would have to go for 2.3a. Parmenides presents two linked "phrases," each with its own structure, one in the affirmative and the other in the negative; it is logical that, if the phrases do not contradict one another, *the same* subject should also appear, once in the affirmative and once in the negative. (**Hölscher**, U., "Grammatisches zu Parmenides," *Hermes* 84 [1956] 393).

225 In the 1997 edition of my *Deux Chemins de Parménide,* this hemistich was translated in the following way: "ne pas être n'est pas possible" (p. 27), that is, in function of the potential value of "*ouk esti.*" Although his article is extremely subtle, **Constantineau** is mistaken when he says that my translation is "heterodox." He must have misread me: I had translated the passage in the same way as him. Moreover, he accuses me (after paying homage to my "impressive erudition": thanks!) of confusing *mè eînai* and *tó mè eón* ("op. cit. in note 11," 227). This is not the case. Both formulas mean the same, but their syntactic

Before leaving this passage, we may note that various scholars are against considering "*mē̱ eînai*" to be the subject of 2.3b and 2.5b. For example, G. Calogero says that if this were so, there would be a "nominalization" of the infinitive—making it into a noun—and this would go against Greek syntax, which requires an infinitive and not a noun as the subject of *khreṓ̱n esti.*[226] This criticism can be applied to scholars who introduce the notion of "the non-being" here. But this is not the case with me: I always think of the fact of being or not being.[227] With respect to these passages, we may say that Parmenides does not hesitate to turn an infinitive into a noun (cf. *tò pélein,* 6.8), but this does not mean a "reification" ("thingifying") of the notion: from Homer onward, "the infinitive, with or without the article, means the development of an action."[228]

function is totally different, since *mè eînai* can be the subject of a potential impersonal, and *tó mè eón* cannot.

226 **Calogero** (1936), 157.

227 I share Mansfeld's opinion: "In frs. 2 and 3 the infinitives have their usual meaning, they are not turned into nouns" (**Mansfeld** [1964], 81).

228 **Falus** (1960) 279.

Chapter IV: The Meaning of Parmenides' Thesis (and of Its Negation)

Now that we have looked at the structure of the presentation of the only two ways for investigation presented by the Goddess, we must try to grasp the meaning of the true thesis they transmit. As I have already said, Parmenides presents his thesis in positive form and then reinforces this position by negating it. In the first way we find the statement of the thesis; in the second, its negation. The syntactic structure of the two ways (that is, the body of terms that configure both formulations, since each way has the form of a *lógos,* i.e., a discursive phrase and not an isolated term) has displayed an abusive presence of the verb "to be" in both formulations, found in lines 2.3 and 2.5. If we leave aside conjunctions, connecting terms, adverbs and the impersonal *khreō̱n,* all the terms used are persons or modes of the verb "to be" (and some scholars say that forms of this verb are also assumed as the subject).

(a) The Grammar of "To Be"

There can be no doubt that Parmenides' Goddess's philosophy course is concerned with "being." *But saying this is not saying anything.* In Greek, as in Spanish [or English], "to be" is a verb and, like any verb it can be used as a noun, and then we can speak of "being" (used as a noun). But this verbal noun is essentially different in Greek than it is in other languages, and so we cannot ignore the problem. This specificity is one of the results of the flexibility of the Greek language, which permits all kinds of juggling. E. Benveniste wrote that "the linguistic structure of Greek created the predisposition for the notion 'to be' to have a philosophical vocation."[229] Indeed, the use of the verb "to be" as a noun **absolutely does not mean what philosophers call "being"** (the noun). To use an infinitive as a noun in Spanish it must be preceded by an article, in this case "el" ["the"]. Then the infinitive "ser" ["to be"] becomes "el ser" ["the being"] used as a noun, in Greek "*tò eînai.*" However, this formula never figured among the concerns of the Greek philosophers. No Greek philosopher who inquired into

229 **Benveniste**, *Problèmes de linguistique,* 73.

what today we might call "the being of things," or even "certain types of beings," including the supreme being, ever asked "what is *tò eînai?*" literally "what is being?"[230] As we know, especially since the Aristotelian systemization, the formula used by all Greek philosophers to ask the question of being is *tí esti tò ón* (*tó eón* in Parmenides), "What is being?" "*Tò eón*" is the present participle of the verb to be, used as a noun. The difficulty of grasping the scope of this neuter present participle (since there is also a masculine and a feminine present participle) has always given rise to all kinds of misunderstandings, since its use as a noun, represented by the neuter article "*tó*," is deceptive, and so Parmenides avoids it whenever he can. Indeed, just as verbal-noun infinitives always have a dynamic character,[231] something similar occurs with the participle *tò ón,* which as a *present* participle means "that which is being," that which engages in the act of being *now.* In all that I have said up till now, philosophy is absent: I have only summarized, perhaps too superficially, what Benveniste calls "un fait de langue,"[232] a fact about Greek simply as a language.

It is upon this linguistic fact that Parmenides reflects. In Greek the word for "things" is *ónta.* Even in current everyday language, things are "beings," "something(s) that is (are)," "that which is being." Philosophy has not yet come into it: that's the way the Greek language is. But why do we call something that is a "being"? Because the fact of being manifests itself in that which is; if there is that which is, then the fact of being is *assumed.* **Without the fact of being, there would not be things that are.** This sort of platitude will constitute the nucleus of Parmenides' philosophy. And that is the reason why his thinking starts from an analysis of the notion of the fact of being, arrived at from the evidence that "is" is occurring. If there is something undeniable for anyone who is, it is "is." If Greek syntax allowed the formula, we could say, with R. Regvald, that the basic question would be "*tí esti ésti,*" "What is 'is'?"[233]

(b) The Meaning of "Being" and Returning to the Question of the Subject of éstin *in 2.3a*

Let us return to the abusive presence of the verb "to be" in the presentation of the two ways of investigation. At the beginning of this work, I said that

230 Only the overactive imagination of Heidegger could think that "*tò eînai*" was an object of reflection in Greece. Cf. **Heidegger**, M., *Einführung in die Metaphysik,* 4th ed. (Frankfurt am Main: Max Niemayer, 1976), 73.

231 Cf. **Falus** (1960), 279: "the infinitive, whether with or without article, signifies the development of an action."

232 **Benveniste**, *Problèmes de linguistique,* 71, note 1.

233 **Regvald**, R., "Parménide: Le trajet de la non-coïncidence," *La revue philosophique* 176 (1986) 18.

Parmenides takes his inspiration from Hesiodic and Homeric models, which may aim to make his Poem sound like an archaic, "classical" text. And I also said that the presentation of the two possibilities for investigation, called "ways" by Parmenides, revolve around forms of the verb "to be." It would not be exaggerating to think that Parmenides is also taking his inspiration from classical models in his use of the verb "to be." So we may inquire what the value or meaning of "to be" is in the Homeric poems, for example. It goes without saying that my analysis will be impertinently brief, since it might well require several volumes to do justice to the question.[234]

Already in Homer, the verb "to be" has very different meanings, but it is interesting to note that the Homeric poems still contain vestiges of the original concrete meaning of the verb, synonymous with "live," "breathe," "possess the breath of life."[235] However, in most cases, the verb has a more abstract value, called "strong" by linguists. For E. Schwyzer, this is equivalent to "exist (*existieren*), be present (*vorhanden sein*),"[236] and P. Chantraine stresses that this means "existing in the strong sense of the term."[237]

As he wants to give his philosophy an epic-didactic atmosphere, Parmenides retakes the original meaning of "to be"[238] and *gives it an absolute and necessary character,* to the point of making it the central concept of his system. In the passages of the Poem where the verb appears on its own, or at most accompanied by a subject, the meaning "be present," "exist," "possess effective reality" prevails. For convenience, in translations or paraphrases, I shall continue to speak of "to be," but when this term is used, it must be interpreted in this work according to the above-listed meanings.

From what I have said, we can now return to the question of the subject of "*éstin*" in 2.3a and 2.5a. The reply to this question must now be sought in the meaning of *éstin* as the basic thesis of Parmenides' teaching. When Parmenides simply says "*éstin*" on its own, he is stating (or proposing) a fact: that "there is," that "exists," "that is," "that is being," "that there is [a] presence." So, what is it that there is, what is it that exists, what is it that is present? *For the moment*—that is to say, as the starting point of his system—Parmenides does not tell us, and he does not tell us because he wants

234 We need only mention the excellent—and much discussed—work of **Kahn**, *The Verb "Be,"* 486.

235 Cf. **Curtius**, G., *Grundzüge der griechischen Etymologie* (Leipzig: B. G. Teubner, 1858–62), 350 ; and **Müller**, M., *Nouvelles leçons sur la science du langage* (Paris: 1868), 69. Cf. *Il.* 2.641: "the children of Aeneas were already dead" (literally, "no longer were"), as well as the epithet usually attributed to the gods: "the ever-living" (literally, "those who always are").

236 **Schwyzer**, *Griechische Grammatik,* 624.

237 **Chantraine**, P., *Dictionnaire étymologique de la langue grecque* (Paris: Klincksieck, 1968), 137.

238 On the verb "to be" in texts before Parmenides, cf. **Cordero** (1997), Appendix I, 215–33, "La signification du verbe *einai* dans la littérature pré-parménidienne."

to stress the fact of being present and not a possible "subject" to take on this role. By leaving the verb without a subject, for the moment, with a hint of provocation (since, as I said above, in Greek too the phrase is unusual), Parmenides wants to draw attention to a fact: it is not his intention to present a traditional type of formula (at that point) in which such and such a principle or element would deserve to be considered as "the being" of things. In a traditional formula of the type "S is P" or "S is," something is predicated of a subject by means of the verb, or, if there is no predicate, the verb gives information about the subject. In formulas of the type "Socrates is Athenian" or "Socrates is," the verb adds an attribute to the subject or states the subject's existence. But in both cases, the subject, "Socrates" in our examples, is the term to stress. The subject is what something is said *about:* that he exists, or is Athenian.

If Parmenides had put forward a subject, his *éstin* on its own would have related to that subject. But Parmenides avoids this schema on purpose, by presenting his verb at the beginning, without a subject. Thanks to this syntactic anomaly, Parmenides proposes a genuine *thesis* (etymologically, this is the term that corresponds best to what Parmenides wants to do: establish, set forth, and maintain an assertion): the presence, the existence, the effectiveness of the fact of being. Parmenides expresses this idea in multiple ways, thanks to the flexibility of the verb "to be" in Greek, through infinitives (*eînai, pélein*), through the participle ([*tó*] *eón*), and fundamentally through the verb standing on its own in the third person singular, *éstin,* as in 2.3a and in 2.5a. Clearly Parmenides feels that this latter form of the verb is the one that best expresses his thought, because not only does it appear at the beginning of what he has to say, but it also reappears in the recapitulations (cf. 8.2) and in the key moments of the Poem (cf. 8.16).

This preference for the conjugated verb (in the *present* tense) is perhaps because it avoids any kind of "reification" ("thingifying") of the notion.[239] There can be no doubt that the participle and the infinitive, even when they are used as nouns, always keep their verbal character, as Parmenides wants to stress, but according to the original meaning of *eînai,* it is clearly the *present*[240] tense that respects Parmenides' thesis best—his postulation of *presence*[241]—because, as B. Cassin also saw, that is when the term "has its

239 This is the case with a term absent from Parmenides, *ousía,* which expresses the notion of being as an already effective reality. It is interesting to point out that Kahn calls Parmenides' use of the verb "to be" "veridical"; in it, "the infinitive and participle serve merely as a convenient nominalization of the indicative *ésti*" (**Kahn**, *The Verb "Be,"* 191).

240 As we shall see, this certainty prevents Parmenides from referring the verb positively to the past or the future. Homer, who was ostensibly not a philosopher, did not have this problem: cf. *Il.* 1.70.

241 Cf. 8.5: "it neither was nor will be, but is *now* . . ."

full force as a conjugated verb."[242] Contrary to what is usually said, Parmenides' *éstin,* at least at the beginning of the Goddess's speech, is not non-temporal. Albeit a platitude, we must remember, with L. Tarán, that "'is' is the present of the verb 'to be.'"[243] We may add that the reference to the present is reinforced by the adverb "*nûn*" ("now") of line 8.5, which "assumes the 'punctual,' that is, temporal meaning of the verb."[244] This "presence" value of the verb *eînai,* whose Homeric roots were strongly stressed by E. Heitsch,[245] is the key, for this scholar, to Parmenides' thought: "Sein ist Gegenwärtigsein."

Despite what I have said, there are passages in the Poem in which the third person of the verb does not appear on its own, but is accompanied by a subject. In the first case, after the presentation of the two ways, in 6.1 we find "*eòn émmenai*"[246] ("[that which] is being, exists," or better still, "by being, it is."[247] Another example can be found in 8.46, "that which is not being (*ouk*[248] *eón*) does not exist (*out' . . . éstin*)," where, in virtue of the double negative, the same thing is being said as in 6.1. Finally, to go on to a rather complicated syntactic structure, we may say the same about 8.36–37, "since what else exists (*éstin*) or will exist (*éstai*), except that which is being (*toû eóntos*)?"

So I am not denying that Parmenides' *éstin* has a subject (cf. *supra,* where I comment on line 2.3a, for my position on this), but we must respect Parmenides' wish not to have put it in where he did not think it was appropriate to do so. If *éstin* appears without a subject in the decisive passages of the Poem, it is because Parmenides wants to make clear that it is enough to admit "exists" in order to "deduce" from that, automatically (even tautologically) that there is existence. *Indeed, what else could be except that which is being (eón)? And that which is being, is being because the fact of being is possible and manifesting itself now (éstin).* In order to say this, it is enough to say *éstin* and give this verb its original meaning, now confirmed as a philosophical thesis. Only an *a posteriori* analysis can distinguish a "subject" and a "predicate" in such a notion, and Parmenides does so as his text progresses. A

---

242 **Cassin**, *Si Parménide,* 51.

243 **Tarán**, L., "Perpetual Duration and Temporal Eternity in Parmenides and Plato," *The Monist* 62 (1979) 49.

244 **O'Brien**, D., "Temps et intemporalité chez Parménide," *Les études philosophiques* 3 (1980) 258.

245 Cf. **Heitsch**, E., "Sein und Gegenwart im frühgriechischen Denken," *Gymnasium* 18 (1971) 427.

246 "*Émmenai*" is the epic form of *eînai* and is in the infinitive because it is the verb belonging to a complement phrase; in direct speech it would be "*éstin.*"

247 This formula could have other possible translations. I will justify my choice later on.

248 I follow the text of the Aldina edition (cf. the summary critical apparatus that accompanies my version of the Poem). The Simplicius manuscripts propose "*oute.*"

symptomatic case is the long text preserved thanks to Simplicius and known today as fragment 8, which begins with the same formula as 2.3a: "*ho̱s éstin*" ("that exists") and then expounds the "characteristics" or "proofs" of this "exists," proofs that all revolve round a "subject": *eón* (the first of these is: "[that which is] being [*eón*] is unbegotten . . ." (8.3). As I said above about my interpretation of verbs called "impersonal," these attest *the real and effective presence* (in the corresponding verb tense) of the activity related to the formation of the verb. As *éstin* is related with the activity of *eînai* (just as "raining" is related to the activity of "to rain"), "is" on its own means "there is being" (just as "it is raining" means "there is rain—now"), that is to say, "the fact of being is *present*."

(c) The Absolutization of the Fact of Being, the Negation of the Thesis and the Ways of Investigation

However, the first way of investigation is a way to think, as well as the enigmatic *éstin*, that *ouk esti mè̱ eînai* (2.3b). This second statement, linked to the first, confers an *absolute and unique* value upon the first statement. I mean that in a twofold logic like that of Parmenides, "it is not possible (*ouk esti*) not to be (*mè̱ eînai*)" necessarily means that "only being is possible." This statement, which could be deduced from the elimination of the two negatives in 2.3b, and which will appear literally in 6.1, "*esti gàr eînai*" ("since it is possible to be") is summed up in the *éstin* standing on its own in 2.3a. Insofar as only existence exists, insofar as there is only the fact of being, this term implies in itself both the "subject" and the "predicate" of Parmenides' thesis.

The *absolutization* of the concept of being is achieved by the negation of the contradictory concept of not-being. Thus we arrive at a crucial point in Parmenides' thought, which, I believe, has not been analyzed to date with the attention it deserves. This involves an analysis of non-being, the fact of not existing, together as the other side of the coin with the fact of being.[249] When we set the statement of the two ways side by side, we will tackle this point more precisely. For now, we may say that Parmenides not only re-

249 One of the few scholars to take an interest in the question, Zucchi has a very radical opinion on it. For him, "Parmenides' ontology is preceded by a *medenology*" (**Zucchi**, H., *Estudios de filosofía antigua y moderna,* [Tucumán: Universidad Nacional de Tucumán, Instituto de Filosofia, 1956], 9–19, chapter "El problema de la Nada en Parménides"). In a slightly exaggerated way, Colombo (**Colombo**, A., *Il primato del nulla e le origini della metafisica* [Milan: Publicazioni della Universita Cattolica Sacro Cuore, 1972]) shows no doubt in stating that Parmenides' starting point is the thesis "il nulla è nulla" (12) and that being "non è altro che non-nulla" (37).

lates the impossibility of non-existence to the necessity of existence,[250] but he puts the radical statement about being ("there is being") together *in the same way* with the only thing that can be said about non-being: "it is not possible not to be" (really a double negative). *These two formulas constitute Parmenides' thesis.*

This brief incursion into the domain of the first way (which, as I have said, contains a "thesis") offers us decisive elements for understanding the negation of the thesis expounded in the second way, formulated in 2.5. Each of the hemistiches in this second formulation is set against[251] those in 2.3 and, as I have already pointed out, in order to keep the opposite values ascribed to each way, we have to presume that the tacit "subject" of both ways is the same. So the first hemistich of the second way (2.5a) (which we have called "not-A") denies what the other way (which we have called "A") states—the absolute reality of existence—and therefore proclaims that the fact of being does not exist, that there is no being, that it is not being. And the second hemistich, which is presented in modal form, reinforces this thesis by stating that *it is necessary* that there should be no being. Thanks to this game of oppositions, this second way establishes a thesis diametrically opposite to that of the first way (that is, it is its negation), since it has to be said of the fact of being that it does not exist, and the necessity of the fact of its not existing must be proclaimed. *These two statements constitute the negation of Parmenides' thesis.*

So now let us look in a bit more detail at the content of the thesis and its negation. I may say at once that, unlike various interpreters, I do not consider that the statements in 2.3 and 2.5 are simply empty formulas, abstract statements applicable to any content. This interpretation, which goes back to G. Calogero, finds its most distinguished representatives among Anglo-Saxon scholars, including A. P. D. Mourelatos,[252] M. Furth,[253] and J. Barnes.[254] This position is not very far from those scholars who see in 2.3

---

250 Basson says that 2.3 is really the conclusion of a reasoning that will appear later in 2.7–8, a reasoning that establishes the impossibility of nonexistence (**Basson**, A. H., "The Way of Truth," *Proceedings of the Aristotelian Society* 61 [1960–61] 75). I believe, vice versa, that it can be deduced from the impossibility of not being, stated in 2.3b, that it is not possible to say or to express that which is not (2.7–8).

251 Kahn has observed that there is an opposition between "contraries" in the first hemistiches and a "contradictory" opposition in the second hemistiches. (**Kahn** [1968/69], 707.)

252 **Mourelatos** (1970), Chapter I.

253 "Whatever Parmenides is saying will apply equally well to ascertain whether there is animal life on Mars, or a rational root to a certain equation, or an amount of tribute that will satisfy the Persians, or whether Socrates can fly, etc." (**Furth**, M., "Elements of Eleatic Ontology," *Journal of the History of Philosophy* 6 [1968] 117.)

254 According to Barnes, "*éstin*" has to be translated into English as "it is," but "it" does not mean anything: the term only has an "ordinary anaphoric role," indicating that "if something is inquired into, then either it exists . . . or . . ." (**Barnes**, J., "Parmenides and the Eleatic One," *Archiv für Geschichte der Philosophie* 61 [1979] 19).

and 2.5 simply the operative premises on the basis of which Parmenides' philosophy will be expounded. It is probable that this interpretation contains an echo of the desire to insert Parmenides' philosophy into formal schemes, or, directly, into syllogisms, as first proposed by W. J. Verdenius[255] and then by A. H. Basson,[256] J. Mansfeld,[257] U. Hölscher,[258] and D. Gallop.[259] It is obvious that the success or failure, the luminosity or obscurity of these attempts, are imputable to their authors and not to Parmenides, who did not have any idea that at some later date Aristotle would propose certain rules to follow in a scientific demonstration and praise the virtues of the syllogism. This mania for formalizing Parmenides' thought led certain interpreters to try to "complete"[260] his original ideas.[261] The fact that we can detect in Parmenides the implicit presence of the principles of identity ("that which is, is," 6.1) and of non-contradiction ("it is or it is not," 8.16) and of the excluded middle ("it is necessary to be absolutely or not to be at all," 8.11), as well as arguments from the absurd (cf. fr. 8), does not authorize these excesses.

Both Parmenides' thesis and its negation are presented as "ways of investigation." According to Mourelatos, when the verb "to be" is given an existential value, this fails to respect the character of being a "way," possessed by both possibilities, since "existential propositions can be the starting point of a route, or they could be the goal of the route, or they could be stations along the route" but they are not "themselves a route."[262] This criticism by Mourelatos can be refuted. But this refutation leads us into greater depth in the presentation of the two ways. As I have already said, Parmenides sets out "the only ways of investigation there are to think" and the statement of both ways begins with two pairs of declarative conjunctions: *hópo̱s-ho̱s*" (2.3) and "*ho̱s-ho̱s*" (2.5). Little has been said in general about these conjunctions, except in the particular case of M. Untersteiner,

255 Cf. **Verdenius** (1942), passim.

256 Cf. **Basson**, "Way of Truth," passim.

257 Cf. **Mansfeld** (1964), Chapter II.

258 Cf. **Hölscher** (1969), 83.

259 Cf. **Gallop** (1984), 69.

260 For example, Manchester imagined a dialogue between the Goddess and the "missing interlocutor" in order to *explain* the obscure stages of Parmenides' argument (**Manchester**, P. B., "Parmenides and the Need of Eternity," *The Monist* 62 [1979] 87 ff.).

261 This is the case with Calogero, who suggested placing the current fragment 3 as a complement to line 2.8 and then reading "as much as you think to say" (**Calogero** [1932]. 16). For his part, Mansfeld suggests this conclusion to fragment 2, as a link with fragment 3: "since only that which is, is for thinking and saying" (**Mansfeld** [1964], 82). The most coherent and well-founded position among these is that of Wiesner, who places the current fragment 3 ("since it is the same to think and to be") after 2.8a and before fragment 6, which, according to him, follows on from it (**Wiesner** [1996], 139 ff.).

262 **Mourelatos** (1970), 275.

who gives them an interrogative value, and thus arrives at a very special position on the "subject" of *éstin*.[263] As we have already seen, most scholars translate them as a complemental "that," or state the implicit existence of a verb that needs a "that" of this type. I do not think it is necessary to introduce a new verb to explain these declaratory links, since line 2.2 already offers us "*noē̂sai*," whose value is complemented in 2.3 and 2.5. Indeed, the content of the only ways of investigation there are *to think* is given in what follows. On the one hand, there is a way to think *that* it exists and it is not possible not to be (2.3) and, on the other hand, a way to think *that* it does not exist and that it is necessary not to be (2.5).[264]

Our version of 2.3 and 2.5 enables us to explain the four declarative conjunctions coherently and confirms that the nucleus (in 1.29 the Goddess called it "the heart") of the thesis, which will be true, is the statement of the effectiveness of the fact of being. The way and its content fuse, since the way is correlative with a way of thinking. As Heitsch states, "the way is the content of thinking."[265]

In this respect we can say that, although it would be dubious to seek a theory of "language levels" already in Parmenides, there are certain expressions in the Poem that operate on a plane that, with J. Jantzen, we might call "metasprachlich."[266] In particular, this is the case with judgments *about* the thesis and its negation that state the content of each way. Given that this content is expressed by expository phrases (statements or negations), the judgment stands on a higher, or at least different, level. This allows us to justify certain apparent contradictions in Parmenides' exposition: for example, the statement of positive references with respect to the fact of not-being, even though this fact is denied. We know that thinking must move away from not-being, but the expression "it is not possible not to be" (2.3b) is *true* (2.4). Anything that is not being is "inexpressible" (2.7–8), but the Goddess *mentions* (2.6) that the way that states the existence of something that is not is absolutely unknowable.[267] As we shall see, these—perhaps

263 **Untersteiner** (1958), lxxxv. Robinson proposes a compromise solution: for him the four terms are deliberately ambiguous, since Parmenides wishes to indicate both existence and a type of existence (**Robinson**, T. M., "Parmenides on the Real in Its Totality," *The Monist* 62 [1979] 54).

264 The fact that *further on*, in 2.7–8, it is stated that the content of this way cannot be thought or stated does not deny that, *a priori*, as a possibility, this way must be taken into account.

265 **Heitsch**, "Sein und Gegenwart," 429, and *Gegenwart und Evidenz bei Parmenides* (Wiesbaden: Franz Steiner Verlag, 1970), 15.

266 Cf. **Jantzen**, *Parmenides zum Verhältnis*, 118.

267 Heitsch, who does not take these nuances into account, maintains that the ways are mere metaphors for the "principal alternative ('being or not being')" and that, therefore, Parmenides can say the same about the way of being that he says directly about being (cf. **Heitsch**, "Sein und Gegenwart," 430, note 37). But this scholar does not explain how this "principal alternative" can be reached before the values of *éstin* and *ouk éstin* have been

spontaneous—nuances of language justify the possibility of being abreast of "everything" (*pánta*), even if this everything implies, in addition to a positive content, a theory about something that is wrong or false. *Knowing what the falseness of the false entails, is true.*

If this is possible, it is because the first way of investigation is a **thesis**, and the second way is **its negation**. I do not share Mourelatos's criticisms about this assimilation (way = thesis). The thesis, which like any thesis, is made more explicit further on, is completed, reinforced; it is a road to travel. The thesis in itself is not the object that the Goddess proposes for study. On this point I agree with Mourelatos, for whom in any "investigation" (*dízesis*) information is gathered about the object of study.[268] "Investigate" does not have a special meaning in Parmenides. As we can see from 8.6 "what origin will you seek for it (*dizéseai*)?"—"*dízemai*" means "seek," "investigate," and the same happens with the noun "*dízesis*" ("investigation"), apparently invented by Parmenides.[269]

So each "way of investigation" is a way for investigation to follow,[270] to develop[271] the supposed or suggested content of the respective thesis.[272] Consequently, both the thesis expounded in 2.3 and its negation, contained in 2.5 are possibilities for "directing" investigation, one of which will be eliminated because of its contradictory content, whereas the other will unfold in a long series of characteristics or properties or proofs (*sémata*), which will form part of fragment 8.

The way in which both the thesis and its negation propose to direct thinking consists in presenting a specific message. The thesis, expounded in 2.3, states or proposes the fact of being, of being present now. Additionally, as we have already seen, it confers a necessary and absolute character

---

fixed, especially when in 8.16, after having set forth this alternative, Parmenides recalls that the choice "has already been decided" (*kékritai*, "perfect"). This decision has been made in fragment 2, where the theoretical impossibility of one way has been shown, and in fragments 6 and 7, in which the practical impossibility of following that same way was demonstrated.

268 **Mourelatos** (1970), 67.

269 Cf. **Mourelatos** (1970), 67. The verb indicates a thorough search. Heraclitus used it for seekers of gold (fr. 22), and the famous fragment 101 ("I sought for myself") refers to the deep nature of the self (cf. **Guthrie**, W. K. C., *A History of Greek Philosophy*, Vol. I [Cambridge, England: Cambridge University Press, 1965], 418), which, like every "nature," "loves to conceal itself" (cf. fr. 123).

270 Note that "*dizésios*" ("*of* investigation") is a *subjective* genitive. The same occurs with the other genitives related with the notion of "way": "the ways of night and day" (1.11), "the way of persuasion" (2.4), and "the way of all" (6.9). This means that the ways in the fragment are ways that investigation (subject) has at its disposal.

271 I prefer to avoid the term "deduce" or "assume" in order not to involve Parmenides in logical procedures that will be systematized later.

272 When we analyze fragment 6 we shall see that this development, *from* the original thesis, will be represented by the preposition "*apó*."

upon the fact of being. These two aspects reappear, in an explicit way, in 8.11, where the *khreo̱n esti* of 2.5b is repeated, referring to the fact of being: "*pámpan pelénai*[273] *khreó̱n esti,*" "it is necessary to exist wholly." Here the adverb "*pámpan*" characterizes the fact of being wholly, absolutely and the necessity of this is indicated by *khreó̱n esti.* In fact, the same thing had already been said in 2.5b, although negatively, and if we admit that 2.3 and 2.5 are opposites, we can assume that in the first way *éstin* on its own already implied the necessity of the fact of being. In all cases, the necessity refers to the predicate, but I believe that it can be extended to the possible subject. This is how the matter was considered, for example, by G. Buroni (for whom 2.3 means that "essere è necessariamente"[274]) and R. Falus (who sets the "absolute necessity of being" against not being).[275]

(d) The Opposition Between the Thesis and Its Negation

If we admit the "unique" character of the fact of being, on the basis not only of the maltreated "*hén*" ("one") of 8.6,[276] but also of expressions such as "*oûlon mounogenés*" ("total, only-begotten") (8.4) and "no other thing is or will be, apart from that which is being" (8.36–37), we can maintain that Parmenides' thesis states the effectiveness of *necessary, absolute and unique* existence. This existence, this fact of being, this presence is first stated in positive form, that is, inasmuch as it fulfills its role of being present, almost tautologically, and then in a sort of *reductio ad absurdum* in 2.3b, through a double negative that denies the possibility of its nonexistence. The purpose of this double negative is to reinforce the previous statement,[277] the absolute assertion of the fact of being. On the one hand, Parmenides states that by being, it is (*eón éstin*); this is his fundamental idea, his thesis, the statement

273 *Pelénai* and *eînai* are synonyms: cf. the interchange of these verbs in 6.8 and in 8.44–45.

274 **Buroni**, B., "Dell'essere e del cognoscere: Studii su Parmenide, Platone e Rosmini," *Memorie della Reale Accademia delle Scienze di Torino,* Serie II (Scienze morali, storiche e filologiche) 29 (1878) 334, note 1.

275 **Falus** (1960), 273. Cf. also Guazzoni Foà: "In line 2.3 there is not only the explicit assertion of the existence of being, but also that of the necessary existence of being" (**Guazzoni Foà**, V., *Attualità dell'ontologia eleatica* [Turin: Società Editrice Internazionale, 1961], 39).

276 The thesis of Untersteiner, according to which "Parmenides' being is not one, but all (*oûlon*)," (**Untersteiner** [1958], Chapter I, passim) won few followers. Even so, it is clear that Parmenides said nothing about "the One" (cf. **Barnes**, J., "Parmenides and the Eleatic One," *Archiv für Geschichte der Philosophie* 61 [1979] passim, especially 20–21).

277 The double negative is "a long way round in relation to the simple statement, but this long way round can often be very useful. Its purpose is to confirm and reinforce the conviction: I consolidate the value of a statement by negating its negation." (**Morot-Sir**, E., *La pensée négative* [Paris: Aubier, 1947], 369.) Cf. also **Sigwart**, C., *Logik,* 5th ed. (Tübingen: Mohr, 1924), 200 ff.

that of itself justifies Parmenides' eminent place in the history of philosophy. But if Parmenides' thesis had been limited to this statement, it could have been held that, hypothetically (since the rest of the Poem refutes it), as well as that which is being, something else could also have "existed." So, to rule out this possibility, Parmenides also states his first thesis in negative form. Nothing except the fact of being can exist, since "it is not possible not to be" (2.3b). With this second statement, which is simply a consequence of the previous statement,[278] the whole conceptual field is covered, as the summary of the alternative in 8.16 shows: "exists or does not exist" (*éstin ḛ ouk éstin*). For Parmenides, any exhaustive study of reality must take into account as possible "objects" of investigation (that is, as *a priori* possibilities) existence and that which is not existence and which, therefore, deserves to be called "not being."[279] Everything corresponding to the terms of the alternative that Parmenides takes as his starting point (the reality of existence, of the fact of being) is excluded from the opposite term, and there is no intermediate possibility. Parmenides considers that the conceptual field is constituted, *a priori,* by only two terms or spheres, and because of the basic opposition within these, there can be no intermediate states. This is the scope of the thesis presented in 2.3: on the one hand, it determines the positive aspect of the doctrine and immediately denies anything that does not respect the postulation of the fact of being stated in 2.3a. If the starting point had been "white," Parmenides would have denied not only "black," but also "red" or "green," that is, everything that, by not being white, belongs to the sphere of the "non-white." The notions of being and not being are not contrary, but contradictory.[280]

This incursion into the dichotomous structure of Parmenides' thought enables us to pose a thorny problem that we have not yet given the attention it deserves. This is the relationship that exists between the thesis in fragment 2 and its negation. There are scholars who state that 2.3a and 2.5a are contradictory expressions, whereas 2.3b and 2.5b are contrary expres-

278 According to Ralfs (**Ralfs**, G., "Der Satz von Widerspruch bei Parmenides," in *Lebensformen des Geistes,* ed. Glockner, H. [*Kant-Studien,* Ergänzungsheft 86] [1964] 12), the value of the conjunction *te kaí* in 2.3 is only understood when we get to 6.1–2, where the correlation "*gàr . . . d'*" ("since . . . whereas") reinforces the complementarity existing between the two hemistiches. Cf. also **Tarán** (1965), 191, note 44: "existence implies the impossibility of nonexistence."

279 Cf. **Simplicius**, *Phys.* 116.23: "[For Parmenides] it is obvious that what remains besides that which is (*tò parà tò ón*), does not exist, and that which does not exist is nothing."

280 If this is so, "the other" than being, discovered by Plato in the *Sophist* as the substitute for non-being, would have been assimilated by Parmenides into his notion of not-being and the parricide would not have taken place. If the crime was committed it was because for merely "chronological" reasons, Parmenides could not defend himself.

sions. This is the viewpoint of Kahn,[281] Mourelatos,[282] and Lloyd.[283] From this, Lloyd deduces that the alternative between 2.3 and 2.5 is not exhaustive (but his analysis, as J. Klowski[284] aptly points out, does not take into account the non-modal expressions, which are obviously contradictory). Even so, it occurs to us that Aristotelian logic would demonstrate that the statements in 2.3b and 2.5b are also "contradictory." The impossibility represented by "*ouk ésti*" ("it is not possible") is contradictory to the notion of possibility, but in order for something to be necessary, as postulated by "*khreo̱n esti*" ("it is necessary"), it must first be "possible" (something impossible cannot be necessary). If we admit that "*adúnaton*" ("impossible") is a synonym of "*ouk éstin*" ("it is not possible") and "*anagkaîon*" of "necessary," Aristotle comes to our aid when he states that "*tò anagkaîon* (the necessary) *kaì tò adúaton* (the impossible), *antestremménos* (contradictory)" (*De int.* 22b8). As P. Aubenque points out, Parmenides "merely applies *avant la lettre,* Aristotle's definition of necessity, which is the impossibility of its contrary,"[285] and therefore, "with respect to the first way, he could have said that 'it is and it is necessary that it should be.'"[286] For E. Heitsch, "it is not possible not . . ." ("es ist nicht möglich nicht . . .") signifies necessity ("die Notwendigkeit")[287] and J. Wiesner shares this view, since, for him "cannot not be" ("kann nicht nicht sein") is synonymous with "must be" (muss sein").[288] When Parmenides expresses himself through exclusive alternatives, whether these are modal or non-modal, he wants to show that he is thinking in terms of contradictory notions. A symptomatic example occurs in 8.11, "*e̱ pámpan pelénai khreo̱n ésti, e̱ oukhí*" ("it is necessary either to exist wholly, or not"): the adverb "*pámpan*" confers a modal character upon the verb "exist," and its negation is "not," that is, its contradiction.

In the negation of Parmenides' thesis we find once more the absolute systemization that we already found in the thesis itself. This negation of the absolute systemization, as in the previous case, broadens the scope of the thesis to cover the whole conceptual field and prevents the appearance

---

281 **Kahn** (1968/69), 707.

282 **Mourelatos** (1970), 71: "The modal clauses in the statement of the two routes in B2 are opposed not as contradictories but as contraries."

283 **Lloyd**, G. E. R., *Polarity and Analogy* (Cambridge, England: Cambridge University Press, 1966), 104.

284 **Klowski**, J., review of Lloyd, *Archiv für Geschichte der Philosophie* 51 (1969) 196.

285 **Aubenque**, *Études,* 109. The author bases his point on the text of *Met.* V.5.1015a34 and b2–3.

286 **Aubenque**, *Études.*

287 **Heitsch**, H., *Parmenides: Die Anfänge der Ontologie, Logik und Naturwissenschaft* (Munich: Tusculum, 1974), 143.

288 **Wiesner** (1996), 116.

of any new element. The negation of the thesis tries to affirm that "*ouk éstin* [*eînai* or *eón*]" ("it does not exist, there is no being"), but it immediately goes on to maintain that at the same time "*khreó̱n esti mé̱ eînai*" ("it is necessary not to be"). What is said in the first hemistich acquires the quality of necessity in the second.

(e) Structural Difference Between Statement and Negation

Nevertheless, there is *an essential difference* between the structure of the thesis and the structure of its negation. In the thesis there is a statement, reinforced by a double negative. In the negation of the thesis there is a rejection of a term, reinforced (with the addition of necessity) by the statement of a negative term. This *strongly* didactic dissymmetry leads us to study the meaning of Parmenides' thesis, as well as the scope of its negation.

The two ways of investigation, which contain Parmenides' thesis and its negation, are concerned with both being and not-being.[289] In the first (that is, the one the Goddess states first, in 2.3, which is the original thesis), it is stated that there is being and that it is impossible not to be. In the second (2.5, which is the negation of the thesis) it is stated that there is no being and that it is necessary not to be. Consequently, I hold that it makes no sense to speak of a "way of being" as opposed to a "way of not-being," since both ways speak of being and not-being;[290] the difference between the two is that in one case the fact of being is stated and non-existence is denied, and in the other, the fact of being is denied and the fact of not-being is stated. To persist in speaking of the ways of being and of not-being, we would have to call the first way the "way of being that is" and the second the "way of not being that is" (or "of being that is not"). It is worth pointing out that the difference between both ways does not lie in the terms of which they are composed (which are practically the same), but in the way in which they are related, that is, in the type of predication established between being and not being. In the case of the first way, we have a statement ([*eón* or *eînai*] *éstin*) and a double negative (*ouk esti mè̱ eînai*), which, in my analysis, is equivalent to a positive statement.[291] But, as we saw above, we

---

289 I use the terms "being" and "not-being" for the sake of convenience. The patient reader who has followed my text to this point knows that by these terms I am alluding to the fact of being, of existence, the effective reality of a presence, and to their negations.

290 That is why I prefer to speak of the "first thesis" and the "negation of the thesis" or, as we shall see later, of the "way of Truth" and of "opinions."

291 "For a double negative to be equivalent to a positive statement, it is necessary that between the true and the false there should be no possible third solution, and thus the principle of the excluded middle should be explicitly admitted." (**Morot-Sir**, *La pensée négative,* 371.) This is the case with Parmenides.

construed the expression *éstin eón* (or *eînai*) through an analysis of *éstin* standing on its own, which produced *itself* as its only possible "subject."

In contrast, in the second hemistich (2.3b), the formula *mḛ eînai* is the direct "subject" of the impersonal "it is necessary." It is worth pointing out that the first way, as a whole, asserts that *of* ***eón*** *(or* ***eînai****), we can only say that it "is," and of* ***mḛ eón*** *(or* ***mḛ eînai****), we can only say that it "is not."* The way that supports this thesis accompanies the truth (2.4). *So the primary structure of the way of truth consists in stating or predicating a notion regarding itself:* it establishes the being of being and the non-being of not-being.[292] There can be no doubt: we have here a tautology, or if you like, the principle of identity, but without the postulation of this tautology, any type of thinking is impossible.

In contrast, in the second way, exactly the opposite occurs, since it is the negation of this thesis. In the second way, we find the rejection of a positive term (*ouk éstin* [*eón* or *eînai*]) and the assertion of a negative notion (*khreo̱n esti mḛ eînai*). In this second way, *of* ***eînai*** *(or* ***eón****), it is said that it "is not," and of* ***mḛ eînai*** *it is said that it "is necessary."* This way is unknowable (2.6): it is the way of error. *The primary structure of the way of error consists in the assertion or predication of a concept with respect to its own negation:* it establishes the non-being of being and the being of not-being.[293] This dissymmetry between the conceptual structure of the thesis and its negation covers a much more profound difference, essential for the understanding of Parmenides' thought.

The thesis expounded by the first way is formulated, we might say, on a single level: both the statement and the double negation operate between similar notions (cf. the schemes in footnote 292). In both cases there is a notion that splits into two and that is predicated or attributed to itself (the reason why I have spoken, formally, of a tautology). Being is attributed to being and it is said: there is being; not being is attributed to non-being and it is said: it is not possible not to be. The thesis operates on one basic, fundamental level. I call it "basic" because this level will act as a basis for further reasoning. We could say that this thesis is **the** thesis of Parmenides, his only thesis.

Therefore, its negation, represented by the second way, is, in contrast, *secondary* to it. Parmenides' Poem is an eminent example of the *secondary and derivative character of any negation in relation to the positive statement.* This hierarchy can be explained in the following way.

292 If, didactically, we give the "positive" terms the symbol X (*eînai, éstin, eón, khreo̱n esti*) and the "negative" terms the symbol Y (*ouk éstin, mḛ eînai, mḛ eón*), the first way follows the scheme "XX and YY."

293 According to the symbolization assigned in the previous note, the structure of the second way would be "YX and XY."

In a system like that of Parmenides, there is a primordial concept: the fact of being, existence, presented at first by *éstin* standing on its own and later clarified. Everything that does not correspond to this presence does not exist.[294] The only "existence" of that which does not exist (provisional existence, we might say) consists in its presence in formulas such as "nothing," "non-being," and so forth, within the body of the argument: its only reality resides in the negation of the only real; it is a mere empty name. This scheme belongs preeminently to Parmenides' thought. It is not the case with other philosophical systems, in which nothing or negation have had a positive role. In Hegel's philosophy, for example, "being" is the thesis and "nothing[ness]" the antithesis, but despite this opposition that makes nothing[ness] something secondary with respect to being[295] (it is anti-being, since it is an antithesis): "the intuition or thought of nothing[ness] has a meaning; the two are different and, consequently, nothing[ness] exists in our thinking and our intuition."[296]

The philosophy of existence also recognizes the positive nature of both principles, although they are radically opposed; human existence is suspended in nothing[ness] and it is in this rootlessness that it finds the possibility of an authentic philosophy.[297] Therefore, this primacy of nothing[ness] confers autonomy upon negation, which does not have to be the negative aspect of a positive statement, but is itself an independent expression: "the necessary condition for it to be possible to say 'no' is that not being should be a perpetual presence in us and outside us, and that nothingness besieges being."[298]

Everything is different in Parmenides, whose absolutization of the fact of being (which is the only thing that can be grasped whose reality cannot be questioned) is expressed both by a statement and by a double negation.

---

294 Parmenides' "extremism" is such that he does not dare formulate the negation of being in an affirmative way, which would have been possible: "non-being *is* non-being." However, fragment 8 presents some examples of negations referring to terms, which, in their term, imply a negation: "[that which is being] is not divisible" (8.22); "[that which is being] is not deficient" (8.33). Even so, Parmenides would never have subscribed to the phrase with which **Plato** paraphrases his thinking: "that which is not (*tó mḕ ón*) is really (*óntōs*) non-being (*mḕ ón*)" (*Soph.* 254d).

295 As Sartre wrote, "nothingness is logically posterior [to being], since it presupposes being in order to negate it" (**Sartre**, J. P., *L'être et el Néant* [Paris: Gallimard, 1943], 51).

296 **Hegel**, G. F., *Wissenschaft der Logik,* 3rd ed. (Leipzig: Felix Meiner, 1929), 67.

297 Cf. **Heidegger**, M., *Was ist Metaphysik?* (Bonn: Cohen, 1929), 20.

298 **Sartre**, *L'être,* 47. Certain philosophers of the analytic tendency, generally situated at the antipodes of the philosophy of existence, agree with it on this point and even admit the existence of "negative facts." Cf. Ryle: "there really are negative facts" (**Ryle**, G., in *Knowledge, Experience and Realism,* ed. The Aristotelian Society, Vol. Supp. 9 [1929] 80). Cf., *contra,* notes 303 and 304.

In Parmenides *the negation is the* ***rejection*** *of the statement.* Various scholars followed his example, although none of them went as far as Parmenides. Below, I mention certain cases that have treated the negation as secondary to the statement. For H. Bergson, for example, "that which is perceived is the presence of one thing or another, and never the absence of what might have been,"[299] and consequently, as H. Höffding had already noted,[300] "negating always consists in setting aside a possible positive statement."[301] This position found its most enthusiastic supporters in two eminent logicians: W. T. Krug and C. Sigwart. The former stated the problem thus: "there is no negation conceivable without the concomitant conception of an affirmation, for we cannot deny a thing to exist, without having a notion of the existence which is denied."[302] This reliance of negation *on* the corresponding positive statement was also indicated by C. Sigwart, for whom "the object of negation is always a formulated or attempted judgment."[303] This position is a consequence of the thesis according to which, in reality, nothing can be based on a negative judgment,[304] and that is why negation is relegated to a subjective or psychological plane. Thus, according to J. Thiede—who appears to base himself on Trendelenburg[305]—"being in which we find ourselves, given reality, is composed of simple positive facts;[306] negation derives its origin from thought and does not exist without thought."[307] Finally, as a curiosity, I may add that similar positions can be found in some thinkers from India. Prabhakara, for example, does not admit the metaphysical reality of negation, and for this reason, the problem does not exist from the epistemological viewpoint either.[308] In this system, negation is nothing but

---

299 **Bergson**, H., *L'évolution créatrice,* 3rd ed. [Paris: Alcan, 1907], 305.

300 "The negative judgment always presupposes the corresponding positive judgment" (**Höffding**, H., "La base psychologique des jugements logiques," *La revue philosophique* 26 [1901] 374).

301 **Bergson**, *L'évolution,* 311.

302 **Krug**, W. T., *System der theoretischen Philosophie,* Vol. I: "Denklehre oder Logik" (Königsberg: Goebbels und Unzer, 1806), 118.

303 **Sigwart**, *Logik,* 155. Mabbott shares this opinion: "The *real* foundation of the negative judgment is the corresponding affirmative judgment [. . .]; therefore negation is subjective" (**Mabbott**, J. D., in *Knowledge,* 72).

304 "In the complete grasp of experience of truth, no negative judgment would remain" (**Mabbott**, in *Knowledge,* 73).

305 **Trendelenburg**, F. A., *Logische Untersuchungen,* Vol. I, 3rd ed. (Leipzig: S. Hirzel, 1870), 44.

306 Cf. Hobbes: "Sunt autem positiva negativis priora" (**Hobbes**, T., *Elementorum philosophiae,* Vol. II [London: A. Crook, 1655], 7).

307 **Thiede**, J., *Über die Negation, den Widerspruch und den Gegensatz,* dissertation, (Berlin, 1883), 6. Cf. also § 4.0621 of the *Tractatus* of Wittgenstein: "the sign '-' does not correspond to anything in reality" (**Wittgenstein**, L., *Tractatus* [Frankfurt/Main: Suhrkamp, 1989]).

308 Cf. **Mookerjee**, S., *The Buddhist Philosophy of Universal Flux* (Calcutta: University of Calcutta, 1935), 409.

the absence of a knowable fact, and consequently, the negation of a negation "must assume that which must be negated."[309]

Parmenides' reasoning evolves in a similar atmosphere. The assertion of *éstin,* as J. Jantzen stresses, "states a fact (*Tatsache,* 'a state of things')."[310] The statement is primordial and the negation relies *on* (that is "sup-poses") the corresponding statement. That is why I maintain that whereas the thesis—that is, the first way—operates on a single level, the negated thesis—the second way—assumes *two* levels: the statement and its negation. It is precisely this fact that leads to Parmenides' second way being condemned because of its *internal contradiction.* To grasp the scope of this contradiction we have to take into account the fact that Parmenides' thesis, precisely because it is a *thesis,* is a statement. But because of its object, it is a privileged, exceptional, unique, statement: "the word 'be' assumes the implicit assertion that the object designated by it exists; if any word uttered expresses a reality, then, we could say, the word 'be' expresses a reality squared."[311]

I think this statement by Verdenius is apt, so I can state that simple "*éstin*" is not a neutral term. It is a "stated" term, whose "strong" value is shown throughout the rest of the Poem. We may also adduce the viewpoint of Kahn: *estín* "calls for no argument, and in fact Parmenides offers none. He merely asserts that his thesis is true."[312] In Parmenides, *éstin* is the exclusive content of the first way, and as such, reappears with the recapitulation of the only *múthos* that remains, once the wrong way has been eliminated. This *múthos* is a word that is also a statement "*ho̱s éstin*" ("that there is"). So, *éstin* standing on its own, as a statement, can be true or false, but Parmenides cannot fail to state that it is true, since its negation is impossible, and for this reason *éstin* becomes the basis of his system. The subsequent unpacking of the term into a "subject" and a "predicate" enables him to give "proofs" (*sé̱mata*) of its necessary and absolute character in the extensive fragment 8. But it must not be forgotten that "predicate" and "subject" are indissociable, since there is only that which is being, and only that which is being is. As A. Baumann states, "the predicate is that which is thought with the subject."[313] *For Parmenides, both plain **éstin** and plain **eînai** mean "there is being," "the fact of being exists," "it is being."*

---

309 **Das**, A. C., *Negative Fact, Negation and Truth* (Calcutta: University of Calcutta, 1942), 134.

310 **Jantzen**, *Parmenides zum Verhältnis,* 115.

311 **Verdenius**, W. J., "Der Logosbegriff bei Heraklit und Parmenides," II, *Phronesis* 12 (1967) 112.

312 **Kahn** (1968/69), 711.

313 **Baumann**, A., *Formen der Argumentation bei den vorsokratischen Philosophen,* dissertation (Würzburg, 1906), 41.

If we take this analysis into account, we see immediately that the negation of Parmenides' thesis (=*ouk éstin* [*eón*]) is a *combination of statement and negation:* it negates a statement (*eón*). If my above analysis is correct, saying "*éstin*" assumes the statement of the fact of being. Therefore, by stating—as the negation of the thesis does—"*ouk éstin* [*eón*]," we are stating that *being that exists does not exist,* since the notion of existence is inseparable from *eón,* and *we are postulating non-existence of this* ***eón*** *that exists.* To put it another way: in the negation of the thesis there is a mixture of positive and negative notions (cf. the symbolization proposed in note 292), of being and not-being, since when we say "there is no being," we are saying that being exists *and* does not exist.

The scope of this second thesis was wonderfully grasped by Parmenides' fiercest enemy, the only philosopher who decided polemically to set out on the second way: Gorgias. According to him, "if non-being exists, it will exist and at the same time, it will not exist, since insofar as we think it does not exist, it does not exist; but as it is non-being, it will exist" (Sextus, *Adv. Math.* VII.64).[314] In this intrinsic contradiction lies the error of the negation of the thesis, which does not respect the principle postulated by the thesis itself: *the concept of being can only be stated or predicated with regard to itself.*

But everything gets worse when the negation of the thesis also says that "it is *necessary* not to be." Now we not only have the statement of a negative notion, but of the necessity of the existence of that notion, the postulation of the effective reality of non-being, as against its impossibility pointed out in 2.3b. From this, as I have argued up till now, it must be recognized that in Parmenides the existence of a negative term regarding the fact of being already represents a contradiction, since the fact of being is affirmative and cannot be negated. F. M. Cornford is right when he says that "the words 'the non-existent' (absolute nonentity) cannot be uttered at all without self-contradiction."[315] In the best Parmenidean tradition, H. Bergson states that "by the mere fact of saying 'the object A,' I already attribute a sort of existence to it."[316] Consequently, "thinking of the object A as inexistent is to think, from the start, of the object, and consequently to think of it as existing,"[317] and then replacing it with another object, which is its nega-

314 According to Guthrie, in this passage Gorgias argues "in ultraparmenidean terms" (**Guthrie**, W. K. C., *A History of Greek Philosophy,* Vol. III [Cambridge, England: Cambridge University Press, 1965], 196).

315 **Cornford**, F. M., *Plato's Theory of Knowledge* (London-New York: K. Paul-Harcourt, 1935), 208.

316 **Bergson**, *L'évolution,* 314.

317 **Bergson**, *L'évolution,* 309.

tion. This shows us that "every negative object possesses a positive moment," as G. Kahl-Furthmann[318] says: that in which the object in question is considered and the particle "not" is associated with it to obtain the corresponding negation.

However, according to Parmenidean postulates, it is not possible negatively to state a term referring to the fact of being (because it is not possible not to be), and 2.5b falls into this contradiction. A negation referring to the fact of being can only be negated, as is seen in 2.3b. Even in fragment 8, where Parmenides is concerned with the "proofs" or "properties" of the fact of being, there is a long series of negative terms, but these terms originally assume a negation.[319] The two negatives cancel each other out and Parmenides does not violate his own principle, which consists of stating positive terms and negating the negative ones when talking about being.

This already implicit contradiction in the negative terms referring to being is reinforced—with the modal nuance of necessity—in the second hemistich of the second way (2.5b). Here we find again the mixture of being and non-being in 2.5a, and we state "it is necessary not to be." So, as a whole, this second way combines, mixes, and interchanges notions of being and not-being, predicating one of the other, attributing to each concept the contrary concept ("there is no [being]," 2.5a; "it is necessary not to be," 2.5b). In order to do this, the negation of the thesis has to assume the thesis itself, which had postulated the two concepts (but at the same time had set out the rules of the game: predicating each notion of itself).

For this reason I say that the second way is secondary in relation to the first: every negation of the fact of being **presupposes** the fact of being and decides to negate [deny] it. In the same way that someone who denies the white must know what white is (indeed, what meaning would the expression "non-white" have for someone who did not know what "white" is?), and as an atheist is someone who denies that that which is considered or called "god" can exist, any attempted negation of the fact of being must start from an understanding of the notion of the fact of being. But the analogy and the temptation to find already in Parmenides a sort of "ontological

---

318 **Kahl-Furthmann**, G., *Das Problem des Nicht*, 2nd ed. (Meisenheim/Glan: A. Haim, 1968), 129.

319 For example, "unbegotten" (*agéne̱ton*, 8.3): in "begotten" the idea of generation is implicit, which, for absolute being, implies originating from non-being. The prefix "*a*" ("un") of "*agéne̱ton*" denies this generation, which would be against the everlastingness of the fact of being. So Parmenides can say that that which is, is unbegotten, since this means that it is "un-un-everlasting"; ergo, that which is, is everlasting. The same occurs with *anó̱lethron:* in-destructible = un-un-solid; therefore, the fact of being is solid. *Atremés* and *akíneton:* im-mobile = un-un-fixed; therefore, being is fixed. *Anarkhon* and *ápauston:* non-temporal = un-un-everlasting; ergo, that which is, is everlasting. According to Fränkel, even there it is a case of double negatives. (**Fränkel** [1951], 402, note 12).

argument" ends here, given that any type of negation could be legitimate if the notion negated does not exist (for many people, for example, god does not exist, and it could be imagined that white did not exist); in the case of the fact of being, that is impossible: *denying that it is is denying itself.* That "anything should be, by not being"—according to G. Imbraguglia's[320] subtle formula—makes no sense.

(f) Why Is the Negation of the Thesis Impossible?

After expounding the thesis and its negation (and expressing various value judgments that the first "accompanies the truth," whereas the second is "completely unknowable"), Parmenides tries to justify why one way must be adopted as a valid way and the other must be rejected. We should not be surprised that Parmenides begins by expounding the reasons for condemning the negation of the thesis, since it is precisely these elements that justify the necessity of the thesis itself. Indeed, it is the impossibility of not-being (the necessity of which attempts to be the negation of the thesis) that will make the fact of being necessarily evident. If you like, Parmenides invents arguing from the absurd: the impossibility of the negation of the thesis proves the validity of the original thesis.

Line 7 of fragment 2, which immediately follows the negative judgment the Goddess expresses about the second way, begins with the formula "*gár* . . ." ("since . . ."). This particle usually has a causal meaning; indeed, in line 8 it begins the exposition of the reasons that make the second thesis completely unknowable, unknown:[321] "since (*gár*) you will not know (*gnoíe̱s*) or utter (*phrásais*) that which is not (*tó ge mè̱ eón*) (since it is not possible)."[322] The nucleus of the expression is the formula "*tó ge mè̱ eón,*"[323] the direct object of the verbs "know" and "utter" and antecedent of the parenthetic phrase (". . . it is not possible.") In this formula *mè̱ eón* sums up the content of the negation of the thesis: it is the negation (*mè̱*) of that which is (*eón*), whose content is synonymous with *mè̱ eînai* ("not to be") and whose necessity is postulated in 2.5b. In other passages of the Poem, Parmenides always

320 **Imbraguglia**, C., *Teoria e mito in Parmenide* (Genoa: Studio Editoriale di Cultura, 1979), 99.

321 The Greek term is *panapeuthéa,* from the verb *punthánomai* ("be abreast of," "inform oneself about," "know"). In 8.21, Parmenides uses *ápustos* in the same sense: "unknowable," referring to the possible corruption of that which is. In Homer, these terms also have an active value: "ignorant" (*Od.* 1.242; 3.88; 3.184). In the case of Parmenides, stating that the second thesis is completely ignorant would open up a worrying perspective.

322 **Wiesner** (1996), 165–66, strongly stresses the value of *gár* in this passage.

323 The particle "*ge*" cannot be translated, but as we shall see (cf. *infra*), perhaps it plays an important part in this passage.

uses "*ouk eón*" ("that which is not") and "*me̱dén*" ("nothing")[324] as synonyms. As the contradictory notion to *eón, me̱ eón* has the same characteristics as it, but negated: instead of being possible, it is impossible; instead of being absolutely, it is absolutely not. In other words: these are two contradictory ways: in fragment 2 "there is absolute statement or absolute negation."[325] As O. Becker remarks, the negation of the thesis "is the absolute [*bloss*] negative complement" of the first way.[326] Non-being, in Parmenides, is absolute non-being; but as there is no intermediate term between being and non-being, any type of "relative" non-being is also excluded (if this were not so, Plato would not have written the *Sophist* in order to invent it).[327] As there is only being, any negation of the fact of being (relative, absolute, provisional) is impossible. *Me̱ eón* is the term that contradicts *eón* and, as with any *contradictory* opposition, there are no intermediate terms. The conceptual field is divided into two areas: being and the negation of being, and as the latter is impossible, only the former remains.

Despite Parmenides' insistence on presenting his thought in *a priori* dichotomous schemes (which then become monadic, as one element is eliminated), there are scholars who believe they have discovered "nuances" within each part of the alternative. This is the case with Verdenius, who sees a difference between "absolute Nothingness" (*me̱dén*) and "that which is not" (*me̱ eón*).[328] Likewise, Loenen is opposed to *me̱ eînai* representing absolute non-being, since, according to him, the expression refers to the phenomenal, concrete, non-necessary world.[329] I think that to refute these attempted subtleties, we need only examine the interchange of the terms in question in different passages of the Poem; this shows that Parmenides says exactly the same about *me̱dén, me̱ eón* and *me̱ eînai*.[330] As we shall see below,

324 The exhaustive reasoning in 8.7–10 clearly shows that all these terms are synonyms. Cf. also Mondolfo: "the antithesis between *eón* and *me̱dén, me̱ eón,* even *ouk eón* . . ." (**Mondolfo**, R., "Discussioni su un testo parmenideo [fr. 8.5–6]," *Rivista critica di storia della filosofia* 19 (1964) 313).

325 **Schwabl**, H., "Sein und Doxa bei Parmenides," *Wiener Studien* 66 (1953), reprinted in *Um die Begriffswelt der Vorsokratiker,* ed. Gadamer, H. G. (Darmstadt: Wissenschaftliche Buchgesellschaft,1968), 412.

326 **Becker**, O. "Das Bild des Weges und verwandte Vorstellungen im frühgriechischen Denken," *Hermes,* Einzelschriften 4 (1937) 142.

327 Plato is a subtle reader of Parmenides. Indeed, when in the *Sophist,* he begins the criticism of Parmenides' position, Plato starts from the notion of "absolute non-being" (*tò me̱damôs on,* 237b), but a few lines later he suppresses the adverb and simply attacks "non-being," since he knows that, for Parmenides, any possible non-being is absolute.

328 Cf. **Verdenius** (1942), 42.

329 **Loenen** (1959), 24.

330 That *me̱ eón* and *me̱dén* are synonyms can be seen from 8.7–10: that which is being cannot arise from "that which is not" (*me̱ eón*), since it cannot begin "from nothing (*me̱dén*)." With respect to *me̱ eînai* and *me̱dén,* cf. the equivalence between 2.3b, "it is not possible not to be (*me̱ eînai*)" and 6.2a, "nothingness (*me̱dén*) does not exist."

nothing can be said of any possible Parmenidean theory about the phenomenal world. Either this problem did not interest him, or he left to his readers/listeners the difficult task of propounding a coherent theory about it (that is, one that respects the only possible way).

I said that in the expression *tó mȩ̄ eón* in 2.7 we find the mixture of being and not being belonging to the negation of the thesis, but I must add that the neuter article "*tó*" accentuates the contradiction. Parmenides rarely uses the article to turn the notion of "that which is being" or "that which is not being" into noun form, and probably there is a sort of assimilation in Parmenides' mind between the article and a possible "*ti,*" or "something." For example, R. J. Ketchum suggests translating *tó mȩ̄ eón* as "what is not anything,"[331] as if the article particularized certain existence. Furthermore, the important position the article occupies in the phrase, reinforced by the particle "*ge,*" which to an extent separates the article from the participle it "turned into a noun," has also attracted the attention of some scholars. For example, W. Bröcker says the article has a demonstrative character and roundly maintains that here it is synonymous with "*toûto,*" "this,"[332] and Hölscher says that "the article, with the participle does not mean it is turned into a noun, but it emphasizes the generality of the predicate: 'a thing' or 'something' (that is not)."[333] The same author discovers this generalization in fragment 4.2, but in relation to the opposite concept: "you cannot force that which is being to be separate from that which is." Finally, for J. Klowski, the particle "*ge*" absolutizes "*mȩ̄ eón,*" which thus become "absolute non-being."[334]

It is true that in Parmenides we find examples of the archaic use of the article as a demonstrative,[335] but this does not mean that the same thing has happened here. Certainly, there are passages in which it is impossible to decide whether we have an article or a demonstrative or relative pronoun.[336] In 8.37, for example, "*tó ge Moir'epédēsen*" ("fate [Moira] forced it"),

---

331 **Ketchum**, R. J., "Parmenides on What There Is," *Canadian Journal of Philosophy* 20 (1990) 172.

332 Cf. **Bröcker**, W., *Die Geschichte der griechischen Philosophie vor Sokrates* (Frankfurt: Klostermann, 1965), 57.

333 **Hölscher** (1969), 80, note 37.

334 **Klowski** (1977), 113. For Ruggiu, too, *mȩ̄ eón* is equivalent to "absolute nothingness" (**Ruggiu** [1975], 215).

335 According to Kranz, "the article has a 'deiktische'" (demonstrative) force, for example in 8.60: "this" ("*tón*") (**Kranz** [1916], 1172).

336 The typical case is 8.58, "*tō̧i d'heterō̧i.*" In 6.1, the *tó* preceding *légein* is a relative, according to Diels (**Diels**, *Vors.*, 3rd ed., 143) and according to Gomperz (**Gomperz**, H., "Psychologische Beobachtungen an griechischen Philosophen," *Imago* 10 [1924] 7). Since I reestablished a second *tó* in the same line, this opinion has become unsustainable (cf. **Cordero**, N. L., "Les deux chemins de Parménide dans les fragments 6 et 7," *Phronesis* 24 [1979] 24–25).

where the particle "*ge*" recalls our passage, obviously a relative. Despite everything, the case that concerns us, 2.7, is more problematical,[337] since "*tó*" could be the neuter article of the participle. Nevertheless, whether it is an article or pronoun, "*tó*" *individualizes* the concept to which it refers, and if we apply to Parmenides the analysis in Plato's *Sophist*[338] (which does, indeed, refer to Parmenides), we see that the singular article implies the unity of that to which it refers (just as the plural article refers to multiplicity), that is to say, that the article "indicates" something as "one thing" or as "several things." Be that as it may, if the formula "*mḕ eón*" is a contradiction in itself (combining, as it does, affirmation and negation), the addition of "*tó ge*" does no more than reinforce this.

337 Some scholars, like Calogero, translate this "*tó*" as if it were a relative, without saying anything about it: "you could not know *that which* is not" (**Calogero** [1932], 16).

338 Cf. the passage 238d–e.

Chapter V: Parmenides' Thesis, Thinking, and Speaking

Parmenides' thesis states that that which is being is, that there is being. Presenting this certainty as a way, a road to travel, suggests that a well-directed and methodical argument will unfold its richness, deduce the final consequences arising from accepting it, and possibly even justify it. Already in fragment 2 the presentation of the thesis announced that it was a way of thinking, and as we saw, the content of that thinking was expressed through an utterance (or, if you prefer, in an attributive phrase) in which the truth resulted from the type of predication that was established between the terms. It is worth pointing out that already in fragment 2 (and even in the allegorical presentation of the thesis at the end of fragment 1) Parmenides establishes a relationship between an "object," thinking about that object, and expressing it by means of speech.

So lines 3 and 5 of fragment 2 showed that this "object" had an absolute and necessary character, since its negation was impossible. This then leads to a consequence: thinking and speaking cannot dispense with this object. Further, it is *necessary* to think and to say that by being, it is; that there is being; that that which exists, exists. Part of fragment 8 and the first two lines of fragment 6 set out to demonstrate this necessity.[339] Indeed, if nothing existed, there would be nothing to think about. "Without that which is being (*eón*)," says Parmenides, "you will not find thinking" (8.35–36). "Why?" the pupil might ask his master. "Because it is the same to think and that by [because of] which there is thinking" (8.34). Thinking and being are inseparable. Thinking recognizes one single cause (and it is by virtue of this that there is thinking): the fact of being, which is its single object. It is thanks to this that thinking is "found." Let us now analyze that passage of

339 Wiesner has demonstrated with certainty that fragment 3, "it is the same to be and to think," plays an essential role in this argument (**Wiesner** [1996], passim), and that this phrase is "the premise of the theory of knowledge in B 2.7–8 and 6.1a" (162). We take the value of this fragment as relative, and Wiesner is right when he says that "the role of B3 in the argument is left in complete obscurity by Cordero" (**Wiesner** [1996], 200). The reason for my mistrust is simple: this brief text has come down to us isolated from any context. Cf. also Tarán's opinion in agreement, where he hesitates to accept a literal interpretation of the phrase (**Tarán** [1965], 42 and 198). I have only taken it into account when its terms reappear together in (and, in my judgment, clarified) other passages, especially in 8.34. Cf. *infra* the commentary on this passage.

the Poem in detail, because in it we have the foundations of Parmenides' theory of knowledge.

(a) Thinking Is Expressed Thanks to *Being*

The Greek text of lines 34 and 36 in fragment 8 is not as uniform as the critical apparatus of the classical edition of H. Diels claims. For this reason, direct consultation of the manuscript tradition has led me to modify in one respect the version unanimously accepted to date. The two single sources of the passage are Simplicius (the whole of the passage in *Phys.* 86, 87, and 143) and Proclus (lines 35 and 36a in *In Parm.* 1152). Line 34 does not present major problems and can be translated in the following way: "thinking and that because of which [*hoúneken*][340] there is thinking [*esti nóēma*] are the same." In contrast, in line 35 there is a minor variation in the manuscript tradition,[341] but there is also an important difference between the versions of Proclus and Simplicius, radically changing the meaning of the passage and, I believe, solving various problems. Let us look at this point. In line 35, interpreters have unanimously accepted the preposition "in"[342] as accompanying the relative (*hói*) and have translated, with slight variations, "since without that which is being, *in which* it is expressed." I incline toward "*eph,*" (= "*epí*")[343] and translate "*thanks* to which." The rest of the passage (lines 36 and 37) presents us with major problems. Let us now look at this crucial passage in detail.

---

340 Cf. *infra* the justification for this translation.

341 "*Pephōtisménon*" ("illuminated," "clarified") instead of "*pephatisménon*" ("expressed"). Like all the other interpreters I follow the second option.

342 This reading is only found in **Simplicius**.

343 This version is in all the Greek manuscripts deriving from Proclus, though in very different families (cf. **Klibansky**, R., and **Labowsky**, L., eds., *Plato Latinus,* Vol. III: "Parmenides nec non Procli Commentarium in Parmenides" [London-Leide: In Aedibus Instituti Warburgiane-Brill, 1953], xxxvi), which suggests that it was already in the original. It also appears in the Latin translation of **de Moerbeke**, G., which is itself based on a very ancient text (cf. *Plato Latinus,* xxv). Dillon holds that this version "has the advantage of enabling one to discern fairly clearly the original Greek from which he was working" (**Morrow**, G. R., and **Dillon**, J. M., eds., *Proclus' Commentary on Plato's Parmenides* [Princeton, NJ: Princeton University Press, 1987], xliv). The most important codex among those containing this Latin translation (*Ambrosianus* A 167 sup.) keeps the quotations from Parmenides in Greek, and the reading "*eph' hôi*" clearly appears in folio 189 v° (cf. **Proclus**, *Commentaire sur le "Parménide" de Platon,* trans. **de Moerbeke**, G., critical edition of **Steel**, C., Vol. II [Louvain: Presses Universitaires de Louvain, 1985], 426). On the value of this manuscript, cf. **Klibansky** and **Labowsky**, *Plato Latinus,* xii, and **Steel**, *Commentaire sur le "Parménide,"* 3*, for whom "the *Ambrosianus* is the most important witness to the tradition, since it is the one closest to the archetype." This scholar also states, "The terms in Greek must have been found in the model" (*Commentaire sur le "Parménide,"* 4*).

We saw that in these lines there is a relationship among the fact of being, the expression of being, and thinking about it. In line 34, the term "*hoúneken*" may have two different meanings: as a synonym of "*hoû héneka*" ("that by [because of] which") it has an adverbial-causal meaning; but, as a synonym of "*hóti,*" it can have the two normal uses of this term: complemental ("that") and causal ("because"). In Homer there are various examples of the adverbial-causal use[344] and the simple causal value.[345] In contrast, the complemental meaning only occurs with verbs that expect a complement clause (*Od.* 5.216, *oîda,* "know"; *Od.* 7.300, *noeîn,* "think"), but never with a noun. As this is the case in 8.34, it is very probable that here *hoúneken* does not have a complemental value, even though some authors have held that it does.[346]

The previous use of the same term in line 8.32 with a clearly causal value (*hoúneken ouk ateleúteton,* "because it is not infinite") and even before, in 8.13, of its synonym *toû heíneken* with the same value,[347] allows us to state that the meaning of the term in 8.34, as H. Diels,[348] K. von Fritz[349] and J. Wiesner[350] have maintained, is "it is the same to think and that by [because of] which there is thinking." This meaning could also be deduced from Simplicius' commentary on the passage 8.34–37 ("if that exists by virtue of which thought exists, it is clear that it must be something intelligible, since it is by reason of the intelligible that thinking and the intellect exist" [*Phys.* 144.22–24]),[351] and it would offer a plausible explanation of the causal nexus *gár,* which completes the passage. "That because of which there is thinking" is, clearly, a paraphrase of *eón* (or of *eînai*).

The following lines offer the reasons for this statement: "since without that which is being (*eón*) [. . .] you will not find thinking." The unknown has revealed itself: "that which is being" is synonymous with "that because of which there is thinking." Without that which is, thinking has no foundation, since (*gár,* 8.36), as Parmenides observes as a conclusion to this argument, *there is only that which is being* (indeed, "there is not and there will

344 For example, *Od.* 3.61: "allow us to accomplish that by [because of] which (*hoúneka*) we are here."

345 For example, *Il.* 9.505: "Ate has light feet; that is why (*hoúneka*) she arrives before all of them."

346 This is the case with Conche, who translates: ". . . the thought that there is" (**Conche** [1996], 128); Cassin: ". . . and the thought that 'is'" (**Cassin** [1998], 89); and Gómez-Lobo: ". . . and the thought of what is" (**Gómez-Lobo** [1985], 113).

347 Cf. **Tarán** (1965), 103: "*toû heíneken* means 'because of which.'"

348 **Diels** (1897), 85.

349 **von Fritz**, K., "*Noûs, noeîn* and Its Derivatives in Presocratic Philosophy (Excluding Anaxagoras)," [I: From the Beginnings to Parmenides] *Classical Philology* 40 (1945) 237.

350 **Wiesner** (1996), 151.

351 On the quotations from Parmenides to be found in Simplicius, cf. **Stevens**, A., *Postérite de l'être: Simplicius interprète de Parmenide* (Brussels: Ousia, 1990).

not be anything apart from that which is being [*eón*]," 8.36–37). Thinking is condemned to be thinking about that which is: "Denken heisst: Seiendes denken."[352] Nothing remains apart from that which is being.

We may add, in parentheses, that these lines 8.34–37 offer us the only context in which to set any possible interpretation of the succinct fragment 3,[353] since "it is the same to think [*noeîn*] and to be [*eînai*]."[354] If we compare this enigmatic text, word for word, with 8.34, we can state that "since it is the same to think" (*tò gàr autò noeîn estin*) in fragment 3 is equivalent to "it is the same to think" (*tautón d'esti noeîn*) (8.34), and "and to be" (*te kaì eînai*) is echoed in "and that by [because of] which there is thinking" (*te kaì hoúneken esti nóe̱ma*). "Being" is "that because of which there is thinking."[355] There is identity between thinking and being, but any idealist interpretation is excluded, since it is being that has priority. The fact of being is the cause of thinking[356] and therefore all thinking is necessarily thinking of being. In the formula "thinking of being" the genitive is obviously objective, since the fact of being is the object of thinking. If this were not so, we would share the extravagant idea of Phillips, according to whom "the totality of being thinks of its own totality."[357] Being and thinking are very closely related, but in another sense: "I only perceive that which is present, and that which is present is the only thing I perceive."[358]

At the heart of this clear and precise reasoning, the relative phrase containing the pronoun "*hô̱i*" ("which" in the dative) plays an essential part, but the phrase's whole structure has given rise to fierce polemics. W. Leszl shows no doubt in stating that "whereas the rest [of the passage] is clear, the meaning of the interpolation '*en hô̱i pephatisménon esti*' is not."[359] Let us start from the unanimously accepted version (a version which, as I said, I do not share: cf. *infra*): "*en hô̱i pephatisménon esti*" (8.35). The interpretation closest to Parmenides' thought holds that that which is, is expressed (*pephatisménon,* from *phatízo*) in thinking. If this is so, "*en hô̱i*" refers to thinking

---

352 **Hoffmann** E., *Die Sprache und die archaische Logik* (Tübingen: 1925), 8.

353 On fragment 3, cf. *supra,* note 339.

354 Vuia even proposed setting the line that constitutes fragment 3 between 8.33 and 8.34, as the premise of 8.34 ff. (**Vuia**, O., *Remontée aux sources de la pensée occidentale: Héraclite, Parménide, Anaxagore* [Paris: Centre Roumain de Recherches, 1961], 82).

355 Wiesner rejects the apparent similarity between fragments 3 and 8.34 since, according to him, the first case refers to the gnoseological aspect of the theory, and the second to the ontological aspect (**Wiesner** [1996], 162).

356 "*Eón* is the *conditio* of *noeîn*" (**von Fritz**, "*Noûs, noeîn* and ts Derivatives," 238). "Thinking implies that by [because of] which there is thinking" (**Mansfeld** [1964], 85).

357 **Phillips**, E. D., "Parmenides on Thought and Being," *Philosophical Review* 64 (1955) 558.

358 **Heitsch**, E., "Sein und Gegenwart im frühgriechischen Denken," *Gymnasium* 18 (1971) 428.

359 **Leszl**, W., "Approccio epistemologico all'ontologia parmenidea," *La parola del passato* 43 (1988) 309, note 40.

and the subject of the participle is *tò eón:* "without that which is being, you will not find thinking, *in which* that which is being (*tò eón*) is expressed." Despite its coherence with Parmenides' thought,[360] this version has attracted practically no adherents. Perhaps the "contorted" syntax—as Verdenius[361] calls it—of this version caused it to be set aside, seeing that the relative precedes its antecedent.

So let us try to respect the order of the terms (that is, put the antecedent first and then the relative) and consider, somewhat imaginatively, that the participle "expressed" alludes to thinking and that the relative picks up "that which is being." This is the classic position of Diels,[362] which has had many supporters. The general scheme of this structure of the terms is as follows: "Without being, in which it is expressed, you will not find thinking." This is how Verdenius, among others, translated it: "you will not find knowing apart from that which is, in which is utterly";[363] Tarán has it as "without Being, in what has been expressed, you will not find thought".[364] Bormann adopts this view as "knowledge of being is communicated or expressed in being,"[365] and in his turn, P. A. Meijer justifies this translation as, according to him, "thinking is in being."[366] Looking at these possibilities, I have to say that the relationship between that which is being and thought or thinking does not emerge clearly from the relative phrase in 8.35. Indeed, how could thinking or a thought be expressed, expounded, or communicated in that which is? Being is the cause of thinking, and the effect cannot be expounded or expressed in the cause. That which is cannot include thought; if it did, the risk of idealism would be enormous, since that which is thought would be, when in reality Parmenides, who is not Gorgias,[367] says the opposite: that which is being, is thought.

As the traditional version led us down a blind alley (since the structure most adapted to Parmenides' thought was "contorted," and that which appeared impeccable from the syntactic point of view did not agree with what Parmenides was proposing), I have adopted the text unanimously transmit-

---

360 Indeed, this version maintains that, as thinking and the cause of thinking are the same, without that which is (that is, without the cause of thinking) there can be no thinking, in which, precisely, that which is, is expressed. Moreover, the priority of being over thinking is reinforced, since if that which is were not, nothing could be expressed in thinking, since thinking is the expression of that which is.

361 Cf. **Verdenius** (1942), 39.

362 **Diels** (1897), 37.

363 **Verdenius** (1942), 40.

364 **Tarán** (1965), 86.

365 **Bormann** (1971), 84.

366 **Meijer** (1997), 83.

367 As we know, Gorgias decides to set out polemically along the way prohibited by Parmenides and says that if being and thought are the same, everything that is thought, is (cf. fr. 3 § 77–82).

ted by all of Proclus' manuscripts, "*eph'* [and not *en*] *hō̂i*." There are various reasons supporting this choice. The relative phrase refers to a statement, the expression of something, and when something is named in Greek the formula *epí* (*eph'* in our case) plus dative is used. When we want to say in Greek that "X applies the name B to A," we use this formula: "X *names* (that is, puts the name) B *upon [epí]* A."[368] The complement in the dative expresses the object receiving the name, or with a phrase in the passive voice, the name by which the object is called.[369] This is the causal use of the preposition *epí* (the Liddell, Scott, and Jones *Lexicon* gathers various examples; see *epí* in section III: "various causal senses," especially § 5 "on names"), since the object is considered as *the cause* of the name applied to it, and this name is *borne* or *carried* like something carried or supported on your back, like a label (*epí* also means "carry upon," "sup-port"). Parmenides himself gives us a clear example in fragment 9: things which have their own characteristics "are named [*onomástai*] thanks [*epí*] to these or those." According to Woodbury, this proposed interpretation arises naturally from Simplicius' paraphrase (*Phys.* 180.8): "cold is [so] called thanks (*epí*) to density"; "the construction *onomázein* (or *kaleîn*) *epí tiní* ('put a name upon something') is used of the relationship between names and reality."[370]

This same value of *epì* + dative is present in the text I propose to adopt in 8.35. The participle *pephatisménon* alludes to the fact of thinking (thought is that which is expressed), and the relative picks up the notion of *eón*. Intellectual activity is possible thanks to that which is, which serves as its basis and which is exhibited through expression. Expression or utterance (*légein, phatízein, phrázein*) makes thinking become concrete in "thoughts" (*noḗmata*), but the support of thinking is that which is being, which is the "matter" of all thought. Line 8.35 brings out this fact: thinking is expressed (becomes concrete) *ep' ónti*, "thanks to" (or "because of": *epí* never loses its causal force[371]) *that which is*. This idea is expressed in the relative phrase "*eph'hō̂i*," which is the reading I am proposing to adopt. Without that which is being (*aneû toû eóntos*, 8.35, to which the relative *hō̂i* refers), thinking does not exist.[372] This is the meaning of 8.34–36: "Thinking and that because of

368 Cf. **Mourelatos** (1970), 184.

369 Cf. **Plato**, *Parm.* 147d: "you pronounce each of the names *upon* something (*epí tini*)"; *Soph.* 218c: "the fact *upon* which (*eph'hṓi*) we are speaking."

370 **Woodbury**, L., "Parmenides on Names," *Harvard Studies in Classical Philology* 63 (1958) 149. In the case of a person, this construction expresses the name given to someone, or the "thing" that is named in (*epí*) the person: the name or the "thing" fits the person (160).

371 About my reading, Stevens says that "this causal value of *epí* was already found in the *hoúneken* of 8.32 and the *toû heíneken* of 8.13" (**Stevens**, A., *Postérité de l'être: Simplicius interprète de Paeménide* [Brussels: Ousia, 1990], 48–49).

372 Without alluding to my reading of the text, Wiesner arrives at a fairly similar version to mine: "Thinking is expressed within [that is how this scholar interprets the preposition

which there is thinking are the same, since without that which is being, *thanks to* which [*eph'hôi*] it is expressed, you will not find thinking." In other terms: thinking does not exist except when it expresses something about that which is being. And as "there is not and there will not be anything else apart from that which is being" (8.36–37), thinking only has one single correlative: that which is. When being is absent from what is thought or said, there are only empty words, deceptive "names" (8.52), which belong to opinions.

This necessary relationship between that which is being and thought or thinking, to which utterance will be added in lines 6.1–2, appears again in negative form in 8.8–9: "It is not sayable [*phatón*] or thinkable [*noetón*] that it is not [*hos ouk éstin*]." Once again Parmenides leaves out the subject, which should not surprise us: at this point in the Poem we already know that the only thing that exists is that which is being, and that therefore it is necessary to think it and express it. The negation of the thesis, which tried to assert that that which is being does not exist, must *necessarily* be abandoned: "It has been decided, through necessity, that one remains unthinkable and unnamable (since it is not the true way) and that the other exists and is genuine" (8.17–18). The notion of necessity picks up on the impossibility denied in fragment 2. Necessity presupposes an *a priori* possibility. This necessity to say and think that that which is being is, is formulated at the beginning of fragment 6.

Lines 34 and 36 of fragment 8 have established the indissoluble relationship among that which is being, the fact of thinking it, and the possibility of expressing it in speech. We can say without exaggeration that philosophy finds its justification in this passage. Any philosophical system tries to express a thought about reality in speech. Parmenides shows, for the first time (if there was anyone before him, no texts remain to prove it), that thinking and speaking must grasp and express that which is; if they do not, they are condemned to stray, wander off, and reproduce illusions, wishes, and opinions. And for Parmenides, "that which is," "that which is being" (*eón*), is inseparable from its existence, since there is only that which is being. Parmenides says nothing about possible later developments in philosophical thought; he lays the foundations for all possible reflection: nothing can be investigated if it does not start from the basis that that which is being is, that the fact of being characterizes (how? each philosopher will give his or her own reply) that which is being. And this is so for a very simple reason: because there is being and nothing[ness] does not exist. The first lines of fragment 6 expound this obvious fact.

'*en*'] thought," since there is nothing outside being (**Wiesner**, J., "Überlegungen zu Parmenides, fr. VIII, 34," in *Études sur Parménide,* Vol. II, ed. **Aubenque**, P. [Paris: Vrin, 1987], 187).

(b) It Has to be Said and Thought That That Which Is Being, Is

Parmenides' text known today as fragment 6 completes the formulations in fragment 2 and relates them to two special ways of grasping that which is being: thinking and speaking. The trilogy be-think-say we found in lines 34 to 36 of fragment 8 had already been given their foundation in this fragment 6.[373] The content of this fragment 6 provides a series of essential elements for the understanding of Parmenides' thought and, as was the case with fragment 2, it is odd that over more than a millennium, no classical author has seen fit to quote any passages from it (unless possible quotations have not come down to us). Indeed, this fragment 6—which, as we shall see, has been the cause of all kinds of misunderstandings—has come down to us exclusively from Simplicius. If this commentator on Aristotle had not had the brilliant idea of quoting these bare nine lines of the Poem, today we would not know why Parmenides justifies the necessity of saying and thinking that there is being and why, at the same time, he fears that any future philosopher might be tempted to follow a wrong way (or method) that is unaware of this necessity. Simplicius cites the complete passage (the whole nine lines) just once. The quotation is to be found in his commentary on Aristotle's *Physics,* page 117, lines 4–13. Part of the passage (the beginning of the fragment, lines 6.1a–2a) also appears in the same work, on page 86.27–28; and a fragment from the end of the text, lines 6.8–9a, is quoted on page 78.3–4.

The text begins by expounding in a direct, clear, and distinct way the need to say and to think that that which is being, is. The first term in the passage is an impersonal *khrę̄,* "it is necessary." There is nothing against the infinitives "to say" and "to think" being the subjects of "it is necessary." To reach this conclusion, first we must reestablish Simplicius' original text (which, we may suppose, faithfully transcribed Parmenides' original), since from 1835 to date[374] a modified version of this text has been used, in which *only one* of the infinitives, "to say" is preceded by the article *tó* ("the"), which led a considerable number of scholars to think that that *tó* was not

373 Although we shall never know the order in which the nineteen quotations today called "fragments" were set in Parmenides' original, given the methodological nature of the presentation of his philosophy, there are texts that have to come before or after others (cf. the chapter "Introduction to Parmenides"). There can therefore be no doubt that the text called "fragment 6" today precedes fragment 7, and that the latter continues directly in fragment 8.

374 I presented this original text in 1979 (cf. **Cordero**, "Les deux chemins"), but few scholars took any notice.

an article, but a demonstrative, and caused them to construe the phrase as if it were saying: "*this* [*tó*] is necessary to say and to think . . ."[375] In Parmenides' original text, as cited by Simplicius, each infinitive is preceded by an article, and then it makes no sense to speak of two demonstratives; each *tó* is simply the article that precedes the infinitives that are used as nouns: *khrḕ tò légein tò noeîn*, that is, "it is necessary *the* saying [Greek: to say] and *the* thinking [Greek: to think]." The story of the disappearance of the second article from 1835 onwards is an odd one and deserves to be told, since it shows us that understanding of classical texts usually depends on "details" foreign to their authors. Indeed, it was S. Karsten and C. A. Brandis who proposed replacing the "*tó*" before "*noeîn*" with a "*te*," despite the fact that this *tó* had been transmitted unanimously in all Simplicius' manuscripts.[376] Karsten considered that the "reduplication" of the articles (since there was already a "*tó*" before the infinitive "*légein*") was "vulgar,"[377] and changed the second "*tó*" to "*te*."[378] For his part, C. A. Brandis suggested—in a work also published in 1835[379]—not only changing the "*tó*" before "*noeîn*" to "*te*," but also changing the "*tó*" in "*tò légein*" to "se" (according to Professor Grauert). From then onward, this Karsten-Brandis conjecture has been accepted, and it reappears in fundamental works, such as those by Riaux,[380] Mullach,[381] and Stein,[382] until H. Diels finished off the job of disinformation by inverting the terms in the critical apparatus of his 1882 edition: "*te noeîn libri* [that is, the original manuscripts], *tò noeîn Karsten*." Diels should have written the opposite: "*te noeîn Karsten, tò noeîn libri*."[383] As P. A. Meijer lu-

375 A single example will be enough: "Questo bisogna dire et pensare . . ." (**Giannantoni**, G., "Le due 'vie' di Parmenide," *La parola del passato* 43 [1988] 211, note 7). The same construction was already to be found in **Diels-Kranz**, *Fragmente* I, 153; and in **Cornford**, F. M., "Parmenides' Two Ways," *Classical Quarterly* 27 (1933) 99.

376 I owe this information to Leonardo Tarán, who some years ago now told me about the true text of line 6a. Later consultation of all the Simplicius manuscripts containing this text enabled me to confirm the correctness of Tarán's information.

377 **Karsten**, S., *Philosophorum graecorum veterum praesertim qui ante Platonen floruerunt operum reliquiae,* Vol. I, "Pars Altera: Parmenidis" (Amsterdam: J. Müller & Soc., 1835), 77.

378 Kahn shares Karsten's viewpoint: he believes the second *tó* to be the result of a copyist's error, repeating the first *tó* where Parmenides had written *te* (**Kahn**, C. H., "Being in Parmenides and Plato," *La parola del passato* 43 [1988] 261). The application of this kind of intuition to other passages in the Poem would produce very odd results.

379 **Brandis**, C. A., *Handbuch der griechisch-römischen Philosophie* (Berlin: G. Reiner, 1835).

380 **Riaux** (1840), 210.

381 **Mullach**, F. G. A., *Aristotelis, De Melisso, Xenophane et Gorgia disputationes, cum Eleaticorum Philosophorum fragmentis* (Berlin: 1845), 114.

382 **Stein**, H., "Die Fragmente des Parmenides *perí physeos,*" in *Symbola Philologorum Bonnensium in Honorem F. Ritschelii* (Leipzig: Teubner, 1864/67), 783.

383 A detailed explanation of this philological tragedy can be found in **Cordero**, "L'histoire du texte," in **Aubenque**, *Études,* 19–20.

cidly pointed out, this error caused "a little philological tragedy." Since I restored the second *tó,* as Meijer says, "the problem is resolved,"[384] as any hope of considering the term as a demonstrative now makes no sense.[385]

Tò légein and *tò noeîn* ("[the] to say and [the] to think") are therefore the subjects of the impersonal "it is necessary" (*khrḗ*),[386] but both infinitives have a content. It is necessary to say and to think something. What? That that which is being is; that by being, it is: *eòn émmenai.* This necessary content of thinking and speaking is Parmenides' thesis. *Émmenai* is the Aeolian form of the epic infinitive of *eînai,*[387] that is, the phrase *eòn émmenai,* in direct speech, would take this form: *eòn éstin.* As we have already said, plain *éstin* standing on its own appears, in this fragment 6, accompanied by its subject *eón,* "that which is," "that which is being," "by being." This is nothing new. We have already seen that the *only* indubitable possible subject of "is" is "that which is being," since this speaks for itself, once we have grasped the scope of "is" as the basic and fundamental thesis of any attempt to do philosophy. But Parmenides does not confine himself to presenting his thesis, he also states that thinking and speaking must *necessarily* admit it. Why? Because the negation of the thesis is inconceivable, unimaginable, inexpressible. It is the impossibility of admitting the negation of the thesis that gives it its absolute and necessary character. As that which is not being is impossible, unthinkable, and inexpressible, it is necessary to say and to think that only that which is in being, is. Parmenides expounds the impossibility of following the negative way in lines 7 and 8 of fragment 2.

(c) Impossibility of Thinking and Saying That Which Is Not Being

In 2.7–8 we see the first appearance in Parmenides of the relationship we analyzed at the beginning of fragment 6, which will reappear in various

384 **Meijer** (1997), 118–21. Inexplicably, a year before this optimistic statement by Meijer, Wiesner, who knew about my restoration of the original text (cf. **Wiesner** [1996], 10), continued to support the demonstrative nature of *tó* (**Wiesner** [1996], 8–18).

385 Cassin said that Bollack and Wismann were tempted by this possibility. Both "suggested giving the article its full demonstrative meaning" (**Cassin**, *Si Parménide,* 54). This suggestion was dropped, and today Cassin kindly admits that "convinced by Néstor Luis Cordero, I abjure the *te* that I retained in *Si Parménide*" (**Cassin**, B., *L'effet Sophistique* [Paris: Gallimard, 1995], 557, note 9).

386 It is true that it is more common to find infinitives without articles as subjects of impersonal verbs, but in Parmenides we also find the use of infinitives *with* article as subjects: cf. fr. 6.8, *tò pélein,* which is undoubtedly a subject, related to *ouk eînai* ("being and not being").

387 Cf. *Il.* 2.249.

passages of the Poem: that between the fact of being (or, negatively, between the notion of not being) and different modes of verbal or conceptual reference to the fact of being. Lines 7 and 8 of fragment 2 state that the way that expounds the negative thesis is completely unknowable "since you will not know that which is not (as it is not possible) or utter it (*oúte gàr án gnoíe̱s tó ge mè̱ eón [ou gàr anustón] oúte phrásais*)." This passage is concerned with "that which is not," "knowing" (*gignóskein*), and "expressing" (*phrázein*). If we take into account other synonyms of these notions, we have seen that this trilogy has already appeared in 6.1 ("*eón, noeîn, légein*"; "that which is being, thinking, saying") and that we shall meet it again in 8.7–9 ("*eón, éstin, noeîn, phánai*"; "that which is being, is, think, say"), in 8.17 ("*hodós [ho̱s éstin], noeîn [anóeton], onomázein [anónumon]*"; "way [that is], think [unthinkable], name [unnamable]"), and in 8.34–36 ("*áneu toû eóntos, noeîn, phatízein*"; "without that which is, think, say"). In all of these expressions there are no significant differences in the terms referring to the act of "thinking" or those referring to the act of "expressing." For "think" we only find "*noeîn*" and "*gignóskein*," which are equivalents in Parmenides. Verdenius,[388] Tarán,[389] and Mansfeld[390] agree on this point. M. Untersteiner is of the same opinion, but the reasons he gives to explain the presence in Parmenides of the verb "*gignóskein*" ("know") do not seem to me to be relevant.[391]

As for the expression of the fact of being, the five verbs I have listed (*phrázein, légein, phánai, onomázein, phatízein*) certainly are not synonymous, but they denote similar nuances of the possibility of referring orally, by means of speech, to that which is being. "*Phrázein*" stresses the possibility of "indicating," "showing"[392]—especially in words—whereas "*onomázein*" refers to giving a "name," which is the reason Parmenides reserves this verb for the way of error, in which reality is supplanted by empty words. "*Légein*" has no special meaning in Parmenides; as for any Greek, the word means "say" something significant, whereas "*phánai*" and "*phatízo*" allude to "saying" in the sense of uttering words.

So Parmenides forbids "indicating and knowing that which is not," "that which is not being." There are various ways of explaining this prohibition, but the first way had already stated that it is not possible not to be. *Therefore,* it is also impossible to indicate, utter, know, think, etc. that which

---

388 Cf. **Verdenius** (1942), 35.

389 Cf. **Tarán**, L., "El significado de *noeîn* en Parménides," *Anales de filología clásica* 7 (1959) 135.

390 Cf. **Mansfeld** (1964), 57, note 1.

391 According to this scholar, Parmenides should have written "*nooíe̱s*" ("you will think"), but to respect the meter, he used "*gnoíes*" ("you will know") (**Untersteiner** [1958], cviii, note 28).

392 Cf. **Mourelatos**, A. P. D., "*Phrázo̱* and Its Derivatives in Parmenides," *Classical Philology* 60 (1965) 261.

is not. This relationship between the double negation of the first way (2.3b) and the impossibility of referring (verbally or mentally) to that which is not reappears in the parenthetic expression "since it is not possible."[393] A. P. D. Mourelatos considers that this expression in fragment 2.7 (by means of *gár*) offers the explanation of the impossibility of knowing that which is not, not the impossibility of that which is not.[394] Other authors who share the same position translate the expression as "non e fattibile"[395] or as "it cannot be consummated."[396] There is no doubt that "*anustón*" can have this meaning of "realizable,"[397] but in the philosophical terminology of the fifth and fourth centuries it is the meaning "possible" that predominates. In fragment 2 of Melissus we find the expression "*ou gàr aeì eînai anustón,*" which Albertelli translates as "it is not indeed *possible* that it should always be"[398] and W. Kranz has it as "denn *unmöglich* kann immerdar sein."[399] The same meaning reappears in fragment 7 (3): "*all'oudè metakosmeth̲ê̲nai anustón*" ("neither is it *possible* that it should change structure";[400] "neither is it *possible* that it should change organization").[401] In Diogenes of Apollonia we find the expression "*ho̲s anustòn kállista*" (fr. 3), with the meaning of "in the best possible way,"[402] and in Democritus (fr. 279) the formula "*málista tô̲n anustô̲n*" means "as far as *possible*"[403] or "with the greatest *possible* generosity."[404] Finally, in Anaxagoras, an expression appears that is identical to that of Parmenides: "*ou gàr anustòn pánto̲n pleío̲ eînai*" (fr. 5), whose meaning is "it is not *possible* that there should be something more than the whole."[405] The same occurs in Parmenides. In 2.7 "*ou*[*k*] *anustón*" returns to the impossibility of not-being formulated in 2.3b. The "subject" of the expression is "*tó ge mè̲ eón*"; it is "that which is not" that is not possible, and therefore it cannot be uttered or known.

Anything attributed to that which is not being remains bereft of any reference. Parmenides reasons thus: the way that tries to state non-being is

393 We follow Simplicius' reading instead of *ephiktón* ("accessible"), transmitted by Proclus. On this preference, cf. **Diels** (1897), 67.

394 **Mourelatos** (1970), 23, note 36.

395 **Untersteiner** (1958), 131.

396 **Mourelatos**, A. P. D., "Some Alternatives in Interpreting Parmenides," *The Monist* 62 (1979) 9.

397 Cf., for example, **Xenophon**, *Anab.* I.8.11.

398 **Albertelli** (1939), 230.

399 In **Diels–Kranz**, *Fragmente,* I, 271.

400 **Albertelli** (1939), 235.

401 **Bernabé**, A., *De Tales a Demócrito* (Madrid: Alianza, 1988), 186.

402 "In the best possible way," **Kirk–Raven–Schofield** (1983), 440.

403 **Solovine**, M., *Démocrite* (Paris: Alcan, 1928), 153.

404 **Bernabé**, *De Tales,* 325, note 63.

405 Bernabé translates: "it is impossible that there should be something greater than all things" (**Bernabé**, *De Tales,* 262).

completely unknowable (*panapeuthéa,* 2.6). Why? *Because* it is impossible to refer mentally or verbally to that which is not. Why? *Because* there is no non-being. The causal particle *gár* in 2.7 explains the cause of the impossibility of following the second way of investigation, that is, of adopting the negation of the thesis.[406] But it had already been postulated in the first thesis that there is no non-being. Therefore, it can be stated without taking any risk that Parmenides' reasoning is circular, even though his circle has nothing vicious about it. He himself says so: "it is common for me that where I begin, there I shall return again" (fr. 5).

Line 6.1a states the *necessity* of saying and thinking that that which is being, exists: that by being, it is. This necessity is a novelty since what we know up until now is that non-being is not *possible;* necessity had been postulated about the erroneous content of the second way: "not-being is necessary." Now this necessity belongs to the first thesis, which is thereby enriched. We have moved on from possibility ("it is [not] possible [not] to be," 2.3b) to necessity. Now we know that the thesis "*éstin*" is necessary, since, as I said, *éstin* standing on its own develops into "*éstin eón,*" literally, "by being, [it] is." But this first thesis has been enriched in another way too. Whereas in fragment 2 its presentation unfolded on what we could call an "ontological" level, the beginning of fragment 6 extracts a first consequence on what we could call the "gnoseological" or "referential" level: as only X exists, it is necessary to think and to express that X.[407] Speaking and thinking have a privileged position in Parmenides' system, but they depend on an ontological content, determined by the way of truth. Only that which exists is thinkable and expressible by a *lógos.* And as the presence of that which is being is absolute and necessary, all thinking and speaking must refer necessarily and absolutely to that which is.

It is worth pointing out that the beginning of fragment 6 returns, in affirmative form, to the relationship between that which is being, and saying and thinking, but the negative proof presented in 2.7–8 ("you will not know or utter that which is not being") adds a basic positive foundation: it is necessary to say and think that by being, it is, "since it is possible to be, whereas nothing[ness] does not exist." This new formulation of the thesis, in its affirmative and its doubly negative aspect (that is, newly affirmative) appears in the second hemistich of 6.1 and in the first hemistich of 6.2. Let us see how Parmenides presents his thesis again in fragment 6.

---

406 **Wiesner** (1996), 165, stresses the force of the term *gár* in this passage.

407 This way of presenting things excludes any kind of idealist interpretation that might be encouraged by an isolated reading of the problematic fragment 3, "being and thinking are the same." As Levi observes, Parmenides "does not say that only the thinkable exists, but that only that which exists is thinkable" (**Levi**, A., "Sulla dottrina di Parmenide e sulla teoria della *doxa,*" *Athenaeum* 5 [1927] 270).

Chapter VI: Presentation of the Thesis and Its Negation in Fragments 6 and 7

In the previous chapters we saw that Parmenides' thesis and its negation are represented by two ways of investigation, one of which, corresponding to the thesis, is valid, that is, a way that can be taken, whereas the other, corresponding to the negation of the thesis, is a blind alley leading nowhere. After presenting both ways in fragment 2, Parmenides takes up his formulation again in fragment 6. This time the presentation of both ways is a bit different, because they have already been proposed as possibilities, worth considering *a priori*. Now it is a question of showing that one of the ways necessarily must prevail, because it offers the basis of all thought and all speech, whereas the other way must be abandoned because it contains an internal contradiction.

Fragment 6 sets out this new formulation, but scholars differ appreciably in their interpretations of it. *All* the interpreters agree that fragment 6 begins by expressing the necessity of thinking and saying that that which is being, is (fragment 6.1a), then goes on to expound the thesis and its negation again, that is, the two ways of investigation already presented in fragment 2. But interpretations begin to differ when it comes to specifying *which lines each of the ways is described in*. An analysis of the huge bibliography devoted to this subject enables me to state that, in fact, there are two possible interpretations. The great majority of scholars find the formulation of the thesis (i.e., the first way) in the second hemistich of line 1 of fragment 6 (i.e., in 6.1b) and the formulation of the negation of the thesis (i.e., the second way) in the first hemistich of line 2 of fragment 6 (i.e., 6.2a). That position is mainly based on the presence of the term "nothing" (*mḗdén*) in 6.2a, which—according to that view—demonstrates that this way is concerned with "not-being." *So this means that, according to these interpreters, there is* ***already*** *a formulation of two ways in the first two lines of fragment 6.* A secondary consequence of this interpretation has devastating effects for the understanding of Parmenides' philosophy, because from line 6.3 onward, there can be no doubt that another way of investigation is presented, and as these interpreters have already found two ways at the beginning of fragment 6, a "third way" naturally appears.

A few interpreters (including myself) also find the formulation of two ways of investigation in fragment 6 (i.e., the thesis and its negation), but now the presentation of the first way takes place in *the whole of* 6.1b–2a, that is, at the end of line 1 and the beginning of line 2 of fragment 6. This would mean that in the first two lines of fragment 6 only one way is being presented. Therefore, the presence of the term "*me̱dén*" in line 6.2a is reintroducing the formula "*mè̱ eînai*" from line 2.3b, in which Parmenides stated that "it is not possible *not to be.*" Here, as it is said of "nothing[ness]" that it "does not exist," line 6.2a is reformulating the double negation of the positive thesis, that is, the first way. For this position, *the beginning of fragment 6 presents one single way,* the true one. So the new way that Parmenides presents immediately afterward is the *second* way. There is no room for a "third way," either theoretically or practically. So let us look in detail at lines 6.1b and 6.2a, because it is this passage that determines the number of "ways" that we find in Parmenides.[408]

(a) 6.1b–2a Reintroduces the First Way of Investigation

The formula that concludes the first line of fragment 6 (second hemistich of 6.1 = 6.1b) continues naturally (. . . *gár* . . . "since," "because") in the first part of the following line (first hemistich of 6.2 = 6.2a) (. . . *d'* . . .). It is a single formula, split into two lines for the sake of the meter "*esti gàr eînai/ me̱dèn d'ouk éstin.*" The variations to be found in the manuscript tradition are not important. I have already mentioned that the only source for the passage is Simplicius, but, as we know, various manuscripts of Simplicius' text have come down to us. In 6.1a, the codices *Laurentianus* 85.1 (B) and *Riccadianus* 18 (C) have "*esti **tò** eînai.*" In 6.2a, instead of "*me̱dén d'*" some codices have the corrupt text "*me̱deoid',*" which does not mean anything (but which stimulated the imagination of R. Vitali, who proposed the reading "*mè̱ d' oîd',*" "ma non vedo").[409] However, this can be explained by a lowercase transliteration, at a given moment, of the primitive manuscripts, which, as we know, were written only in capital letters.

Before pronouncing on the thesis (or theses) formulated in this passage, we must analyze the syntactic structure of 6.1b–2a. Essentially, the interpretations differ according to the value that they place on the conjugated verbs

408 An impartial observer would say that this question is irrelevant, since when Parmenides presents the two possibilities in fragment 2, he says that they represent the "only" (*moû-nai*) ways of investigation. The "only" ways are just two.

409 **Vitali** (1977), 35.

"esti" and *"ouk éstin,"* whose subjects are *"eînai"* and *"me̱dén."* The main question is this: does the verb *ésti* have the same value in 6.1b and 6.2a? In 6.1b, as the subject of *esti* is an infinitive, *eînai,* the verb must have potential value: "It is possible . . ."; in 6.2a, on the other hand, the subject, *me̱dén,* is not an infinitive, and given that it has no attribute, in such a case the verb generally has an existential meaning. Therefore, on the basis of this difference, some authors have translated the verb in a different form in each case (position A), whereas other authors do not take these nuances into account (position B) and consider that the translation should be the same in both lines.

Position B already emerges clearly in the first translations of the Poem: "namque est ens, nihil vero non esse" (S. Karsten);[410] "car l'être existe et le non-être n'est rien" (F. M. Riaux);[411] "denn das Sein existiert, das Nichts existiert nicht" (H. Diels).[412] It also reappears in more modern translations: "There is Being, Nothing is not" (L. Tarán);[413] "denn das Vorhandensein ist vorhanden, Nichts aber ist nicht vorhanden" (J. Klowski);[414] "car il y a être, et rien il n'y a pas" (M. Conche);[415] "denn Sein gibt es, Nichts aber gibt es nicht" (J. Wiesner).[416] However, some of these authors have interpreted 6.1a differently than I have and made "that which is being" (*eón*) the object of "think" and "say": it is necessary to say and to think that which is being.[417] For that reason, these authors find in 6.1b the cause of the necessity of thinking that which is: it is possible "because there is being (or because 'being exists') and nothing[ness] is not."[418]

There can be no doubt that position B offers an excellent reading of the passage, but in nearly all the examples *eînai* is regarded as a noun, whereas it is not clear that this is so.[419] As I have said several times, Parmenides expresses the central idea of his system in very different ways: by means of an infinitive (*eînai*), a conjugated verb (*éstin*), a participle (*eón*), and even

---

410 **Karsten** (1835), 35.

411 **Riaux** (1840), 211.

412 **Diels** (1897), 35.

413 **Tarán** (1965), 54.

414 **Klowski**, J., "Die Konstitution der Begriffe Sein und Nichts durch Parmenides," *Kant-Studien* 60 (1969) 414.

415 **Conche** (1996), 100.

416 **Wiesner** (1996), 252.

417 These scholars considered that *émmenai* was related to *khré̱*. This was the case with Tarán (**Tarán** [1965], 58).

418 Untersteiner suggests a very personal version of the passage. He states that in 6.2a, the same infinitives should be understood as in 6.1a: "on the other hand, [thinking and speaking] nothing[ness] does not exist" (**Untersteiner** [1958], 135).

419 Unless we adopt the version given in some Simplicius manuscripts (cf. above), *tò eînai,* a hypothesis that no one has held.

an infinitive used as a verbal noun (*tò pélein*).[420] All these terms are synonymous, *from the semantic point of view*.[421] However, with regard to the *syntax*, each term must be analyzed in function of the value that Parmenides gives it, and in that case an infinitive is an infinitive and not a noun. Bear in mind that this syntactic specificity of the terms forms part of the Parmenidean method, which aims to bring out the wealth of nuances in the verb "to be."

In 6.1b, as in fragment 3, *eînai* is an *infinitive*.[422] If this is so, the expression "*esti gàr eînai*" is made up of the verb "to be" in the third person (*esti*), and "to be" (*eînai*) as the subject. In this case, "*esti*" must be read as modal (as was the case in 2.3b, *ouk esti* ["it is not possible"] *mè̱ eînai* ["not to be"]) in 6.1b, but not in 6.2a, and therefore the translation of the verb must be different in each hemistich. This position offers a more coherent understanding of the text, because the necessity of saying and thinking that that which is being exists, proclaimed in 6.1a, is based on the causal statement made in 6.1b: "that which is exists necessarily *because* it is possible to be."[423] But above all, this position takes into account the fact that the subject of the verb *esti/ouk éstin* is syntactically different in 6.1b and 6.2a: an infinitive in one case, a noun in the other. In fact, *esti* can only have modal value (as in 2.3b) when its subject is an infinitive, and therefore the only possible translation of *esti gàr eînai* is "since it is possible to be." On the other hand, this possibility does not exist when the subject is a noun, which prevents us translating *me̱dèn d'ouk éstin* as "nothing[ness] *is not possible.*" As G. Calogero observes, this formula simply means "and nothing[ness] does not exist."[424] Various scholars have translated the phrase thus: "Es ist nämlich möglich su sein, Nichts aber ist nicht" (K. Bormann);[425] "es muss sein; denn Nichtsein ist nicht" (K. Riezler);[426] and "denn das Sein kann sein; Nichts ist nicht" (U. Hölscher),[427] among others.[428] My position is as follows: 6.1b presents the "possibility" of being as the cause of the necessity of saying and thinking that that which is being, is (6.1a), and this possibility is confirmed

420 An extreme case could be 6.8, where *tò pélein* is coordinated with *ouk eînai*, and it could be said that, by hendiadys, the latter infinitive is also used as a noun.

421 That is why we do not hesitate to use the expressions "being," "that which is being," "present existence," etc. as synonyms here.

422 Just as the terms *mè̱ eînai* used in fragment 2 were infinitives, which we have always translated as "not to be" and never as a nonexistent "[the] non-being."

423 **Bormann** (1971), 75.

424 **Calogero** (1936), 159, note 3.

425 **Bormann** (1971), 37.

426 **Riezler**, K., *Parmenides* (Frankfurt am Main: Klosterman, 1934), 31.

427 **Hölscher** (1969), 17.

428 Cf. also **Cornford** (1939), 31; **Ranulf**, S., *Der eleatische Satz vom Widerspruch* (Copenhagen: Gyldendal, 1924), 161; **Mansfeld** (1964), 81; **Loew**, E., "Das Verhältnis von Logik und Leben bei Parmenides," *Wiener Studien* 53 (1935) 11.

because nothing[ness] does not exist (6.2a). Thus the translation of the passage is: "since it is possible to be, whereas nothing[ness] does not exist." Without any doubt, this refers to the expression of the thesis contained in line 3 of fragment 2, but because this evidence has not been accepted by a great many researchers, we must analyze this passage at length.

(b) Relation Between 6.1–2 and Fragment 2

The beginning of fragment 6 completes the reasoning begun in fragment 2. We saw that in line 2.3 Parmenides expounded his first thesis (broadly speaking, "being exists and it is not possible not to be"), and after having considered it as "the way of persuasion because it accompanies truth," he presented the formula for the second thesis (broadly speaking, "being does not exist and it is necessary not to be"). This thesis is rejected because "that which is not, which is impossible, is unthinkable and unsayable" (2.7–8). In fragment 6, Parmenides inverts the terms of this first refutation of the second thesis (other criticisms appear throughout the Poem, relating especially to its nonviability). In this way this criticism, now negated, becomes the *necessary* characteristic of the first way: "It is necessary to think and to say that that which is being exists" (6.1a). Why? "Since it is possible to be, whereas nothing[ness] does not exist" (6.1b–2a). This way of arguing follows the following pattern:

2.5:	statement of the second way
2.7–8:	basis of the error of the second way
6.1a:	basis of the possibility of the first way
6.1b–2a:	statement of the first way

The Goddess urges the proclamation of this statement of the first way, since, as we shall see, it is not enough merely to listen to it. Long habit (7.3) drives mortals into a blind alley with no way out. To understand the scope of this true command of the Goddess, we must briefly look at the Greek text of the formula "*phrázesthai áno̱ga,*" "I order to proclaim," which is really a Homeric and Hesiodic cliché.[429] In the case of Parmenides, the phrase contains a direct object "*ta,*" "these things" (plural: we will come back to this detail), and the sentence is completed by T. Bergk's unanimously adopted conjecture: "*s',*" a pronoun alluding to the hearer, "[I] order *you* [*s'*] to proclaim." This conjecture makes no sense. The critical apparatus presented by Diels offered other possibilities, "*tá g'egṓ̱*" (D), "*toû egṓ̱*" (E), and "*tá ge*" (F). If to these possibilities we add others, verified by me (and

429 Cf. **Homer**, *Od.* 1.269, 13.279, 16.312, 20.43, 23.122; **Hesiod**, *Works* 367.

ignored by Diels): "*tà egó̲*" (*Mut.* 184 [= III.F.6]), "*tà d'egó̲*" (T), and "*tá se*" (P), we see that the pronoun "*se*" only occurs in one instance, and that this one does not respect the meter. Doubtless, it was to correct this drawback that Bergk added the pronoun "*egó̲*," which occurs in various versions, and proposed a hybrid conjecture that fuses two different readings. However, the conjecture is also dangerous, because it restricts the exhortation to the hearer; he is the one who is to proclaim what he has just heard. We have followed the text of codex D, which most agree, even Diels, is the most important one in the basic DEF group.[430] It presents not only an acceptable text but one that is coherent with the meaning of the Poem. The Goddess orders, in general, that what she has just said should be proclaimed.

The content of the proclamation, referred to by the pronoun "*tá*," is the statement of the first way of investigation: "since it is possible to be, whereas nothing[ness] does not exist" (6.1b–2a, i.e., two statements, which is why the Goddess uses the plural, although, for convenience, the formula can be translated as "this").[431]

But this new formulation adds certain nuances exclusively concerning the syntactic value of the expressions. To put it another way, the presence of the "subject" *eînai* in 6.1b confers a potential character on the verb *esti,* which had an existential value in 2.3a, where it stood on its own; but, inversely, the use of the noun *me̲dén* in 6.2a takes away from *ouk éstin* the modal value that this verb had in 2.3b, where the infinitive *mè̲ eînai* was its subject. Thanks to this sort of interchange of terms, the new formulation of the Parmenidean thesis in 6.1b–2a is completely complementary, term for term, with its first formulation: each of the parts of the verbal statement (which is the basic one, since Parmenides starts from "is") gains the nuance that it lacked: the existential *éstin* of 2.3a gains a modal value in 6.1b, and the modal *ouk esti* of 2.3b gains an existential value in 6.2a. This double formulation *of Parmenides' first thesis* reinforces the identity it already possessed in its first formulation in the two hemistiches: 2.3a was confirmed by the double negation in 2.3b, just as 6.1b is confirmed by the negation (*ouk esti*) of a negative term (*me̲dén* = **mè̲** *dén*) in 6.2a. If we link the modal and nonmodal elements of both formulations of the thesis, its complete

430 **Diels**, H., "D doctior est," Preface to *Simplicius' Commentary on Aristotle's* Physics, 6.

431 The correlation "since (*gár*)," "whereas," can be interpreted as a coordination, "and." Cf. Denniston: "in such cases there is no substantial difference between "*de*" and "*kaí*" (**Denniston**, J. D., *The Greek Particles* [Oxford: Clarendon Press, 1934], 162. Cf. another example in Parmenides: 1.4–5. Wiesner has criticized my position in this respect (**Wiesner** [1996], 82, note 392). For me, even if the two parts of the formula are adversative, that is because they are concerned with opposing "objects," but both form part of the same thesis: it is said of being that it is, whereas (if we want to stress the adversative value) it is said of nothing[ness] that it is not. And that is true.

statement is as follows: *there is being because it is possible to be, and there is no not-being because non being is not possible.* Accepting this authentic apology for the fact of being makes the Goddess's hearer become "a man who knows" (1.3). And that is why the Goddess addresses her listener and tells him, "I order to proclaim this." "This" is the content of the first way, which, as was said in lines 2.4, is "the way of persuasion (*peítho̱*), since it accompanies the truth." That means that for Parmenides, truth "persuades," and this persuasion is strong enough to become an obligation. The Goddess orders the proclamation of a truth that becomes imperative because it is capable of persuading. So we must devote a few lines to the links, in Parmenides, between truth and persuasion, and given the disjunctive character of his thought, to the relationship between error and the notion of "deception" (*apáte̱*), which, as we shall see, is set against persuasion.

(c) Truth, Persuasion, and Deception

When we analyzed the allegorical presentation of the two ways in fragment 1, we saw that the Daughters of the Sun "persuaded" (*peîsan,* 1.16) Dike to open the heavy gates giving entry to the realm of truth. And we also saw that in order to persuade her, the maidens had to offer "enveloping arguments" (*lógoi*). Thus, from the beginning of the Poem, persuasion and *lógos* go together. In each case, persuasion will work, according to the type of reasoning that is presented on each occasion. To convince the Goddess, "enveloping arguments" were enough; to convince the future philosopher, the arguments must revolve around the truth. Let us recall the passage from fragment 8 in which the Goddess ends the first part of her philosophy course: "here I end for you my trustworthy reasoning (*lógos*) and thought (*nóe̱ma*) about the truth" (8.50–51). The *lógos* about the truth is trustworthy (*pistón*); it assumes a true "conviction" (*pístis,* 1.30, 8.28), capable of rejecting the possibility of either origin or destruction of that which is being: the "force of conviction (*pístios iskhùs,* 8.12) does not allow it either to be born or to die. A. Oguse demonstrated the close relationship between the verbs "*peíthomai*" ("allow oneself to be persuaded") and "*pistéuo̱*" ("trust"),[432] which are practically synonymous in Parmenides.

But even here Parmenides' thought is presented in the form of an alternative. So, as only truth persuades, non-truth (which in his dichotomous scheme is opinion) deceives. Let us recall that as soon as she has ended her true argument, the Goddess announces that now she will expound the

432 **Oguse**, A., "À propos de la syntaxe de *peítho̱* et de *pisteúo̱,*" *Revue des études grecques* 76 (1965) 31.

opinions of mortals, which will consist of a "deceitful order" (*apatelón*) of words (8.52). The alternative between persuasion and truth on the one hand and deception and opinion on the other corresponds to the Parmenidean double message, which, as I said, concerns both an account of the truth of the fact of being and a description of the error of opinions, and just as the former convinces, the latter can deceive. Therefore precautions must be taken: "I tell you of this probable cosmic order so that no viewpoint of mortals will prevail over you" (8.60–61). The power of conviction must prevail over the deceitfulness of opinion.

Several times I have already said that Parmenides inherits schemes from traditional epic. Persuasion and deception as ambivalent aspects of *lógos* are found in the Homeric poems, in which M. Untersteiner sees a legacy of ancient conceptions of the magic power of words.[433] In *Iliad* 9, for example, Achilles complains to Odysseus that Agamemnon deceived him (*apatése*) when he seized his female slave, and he lets his anger fly: "Don't let him now try to persuade me (*peísei*)!" (345). And in *Odyssey* 14, Odysseus tells how a Phoenician expert in deceit (*apatélia*) had persuaded him (*parpepithón*) to go to Phoenicia (288–90). The same pair appears in the Homeric *Hymn* to Zeus, in lines 7 and 33. The author of this work says that, despite her power, Aphrodite, who can prevail over both men and gods, is unable to persuade (*pepitheîn*) and deceive (*apatésai*) the trilogy made up of Athena, Artemis, and Hestia, the incorruptibles. J. P. Vernant, who looked at this passage in a famous article, wrote that Aphrodite possesses this power because she is accompanied by the goddesses Peitho and Apate.[434] Vernant's derivation of the verb *peítho* from the goddess Peitho is completely legitimate, because this goddess often appears together with Aphrodite, and her function is to exercise "erotic persuasion." R. G. A. Buxton observes that it is Peitho who in Hesiod (*Works* 73–74) offers Pandora the jewels that will awaken desire in men, especially in the naive Epimetheus.[435] Peitho's power of enchantment will be taken up again by the tragic authors and, after the Parmenidean interval, it will descend directly to Gorgias' *Helen*. If we look at the pre-Parmenidean literature, we can sum up, with Mourelatos, that in every context Peitho expresses the power residing in an agent, a power that is perceived as a sort of attraction exercised over a patient.[436] For M. Detienne, "Peitho is without doubt the power of the word as it is exercised over another, its magic, its seduction, as the other feels it."[437]

---

433 **Untersteiner**, M., *Les Sophistes,* (French translation), Vol. I, (Paris: Vrin, 1993), 164.

434 **Vernant**, J. P., "Hestia-Hermès," in *Mythe et pensée chez les Grecs,* Vol. 1 (Paris: Maspéro, 1971), 130.

435 **Buxton**, R. G. A., *Persuasion in Greek Tragedy. A Study of Peitho* (Cambridge, England: Cambridge University Press, 1982), 36–37.

436 **Mourelatos** (1970), 139.

437 **Detienne**, M., *Les maîtres de vérité,* 62.

As for Apate, we may say that as a goddess she is characterized by the *will* to deceive. Deception means the deliberate desire to pass one thing off as another, and in this sense, Apate, as M. Untersteiner remarks, has an even stronger significance than *pseûdos,* which originally only means *taking* one thing for another.[438]

The Parmenidean alternative is as follows: either persuasion or deception. It is the presence or absence of truth that decides whether the *lógos* convinces or, on the contrary, deceives. In order to convince, the *lógos* must offer proofs, evidence, arguments; thanks to these, long habit will be deprived of its deceiving power. Against "what is said" Parmenides sets "what must be said."

(d) The Exhortation to Proclaim That It Is Possible to Be and That Nothing[ness] Does Not Exist

If the Goddess urges the proclamation of the thought-content expounded in lines 6.1b–2a, it is, of course, because this is her thesis, that is, the first way of investigation. Although this is obvious, very few scholars have admitted that the way stated in 6.1b–2a is *the first way of investigation, or Parmenides' thesis.* The ones who have include, in particular, L. Tarán, who vigorously maintained this view; R. Kent Sprague; K. Bormann; and R. Vitali. The vast majority of scholars of Parmenides' thought distinguish between 6.1b, where they find a true thesis (which is more than obvious) and 6.2a, where, according to them, Parmenides suddenly goes on to talk about a wrong way, since they claim the formula "*me̱dèn d' ouk éstin*" ("nothing[ness] does not exist) is an expression of the *negation of the thesis,* that is, the second way. First of all, let me say that even if a strongly adversative content is ascribed to the particle "*dé*" in 6.2a and it is translated as "on the other hand," "however," "nevertheless," and so on, the formula "nothing[ness] does not exist" (or according to the scholars who mistakenly give this verb a modal value, "nothing[ness] is not possible")[439] is indubitably true, since it is merely a reformulation of "it is not possible not to be" (2.3b), a persuasive thesis, since it is accompanied by the truth (2.4).

So we may wonder why the interpreters almost unanimously follow this tendency to consider that in 6.2a Parmenides is alluding to the way of error? Doubtless it is because of the notion of "*me̱dén,*" "nothing[ness]." For this reason there are scholars who consider that here Parmenides is presenting the "way of non-being." This is the case with F. M. Cornford,[440] W.

---

438 **Untersteiner**, *Les Sophistes,* 166.

439 Later, perhaps on the basis of Parmenides, Aristotle writes: "that that which is, is, and that that which is not, is not, [is] true" (*Met.* G.7.1011b27).

440 **Cornford** (1939), 32.

Jaeger,[441] U. Hölscher,[442] W. R. Chalmers,[443] H. Fränkel,[444] Gómez-Lobo,[445] J. Wiesner,[446] and P. A. Meijer,[447] among others. According to these scholars, 6.2a is the way that states "the existence of nothing[ness]."[448] Or, as Überweg maintains, it is the way that holds that "besides being, there exists nothing[ness],"[449] but "*this* way [which one must take *ad sensum* to be the way of thinking that 'nothing' *can* exist] is the first to be avoided."[450] Doubtless all these arguments are valid, but applied to the wrong way, that is, the thesis stated in 2.5, which will reappear later in 7.1. They are also valid applied to the *notion* of not-being, or nothing[ness]. But in 6.2a there is no such notion: there is a phrase; something *is said* about nothing[ness]. What is said? It is said that *nothing[ness] does not exist* (*me̲dén d'**ouk éstin***). This formula states exactly the opposite of what we have just met in the arguments quoted above. It does not say "nothing[ness] can exist," or that "nothing[ness] exists" or that "there is nothing[ness]." It says the opposite. The copulative or existential verb appears negated: "nothing[ness] does *not* exist," "nothing[ness] is *not* possible," "there is **no** nothing[ness]." These latter phrases are not only *true* at first sight, but have already been proclaimed as true by the Goddess herself in line 2.4, since they are all simply reformulations of 2.3b, "there is no not-being," "it is not possible not to be," "non-being is not."[451] *It is because this is a true thesis that the Goddess orders these things are to be proclaimed.*"[452] If 6.2a had expressed the second way, that is, an erroneous thesis, the Goddess would not have been able to order that its content should be proclaimed, since she had already said that "that which is not" is not "utterable" or "proclaimable" (*oúte phrásais,* 2.8; the verb is the same: *phrázo̲*). The only thing that can be said, thought, and proclaimed is that there is being; that that which is being, exists; or, if you prefer, that nothing[ness] does not exist, that it is impossible not to be.

I have already said that I am against calling the first way the "way of

---

441 **Jaeger** (1947), 100.

442 **Hölscher** (1969), 85.

443 **Chalmers**, W. R., "Parmenides and the Belief of Mortals," *Phronesis* 5 (1960) 7.

444 **Fränkel** (1951), 404.

445 **Gómez-Lobo** (1985), 95.

446 **Wiesner** (1996), 86.

447 **Meijer** (1997), 153.

448 Cf. **Untersteiner** (1958), cxi.

449 **Überweg**, F., *Grundriss der Geschichte der Philosophie,* Vol. I, 12th ed. (Basel: Schwabe, 1953), 84.

450 **Guthrie** (1965), 22.

451 On the equivalence between "not-being" and "nothing[ness]" in Parmenides, cf. notes 324 and 330 in Chapter IV.

452 It tends to be forgotten that the Greek text has a neuter plural:"*tá*." As Tarán observes, the exhortation refers to *the two* preceding statements: "it is possible to be" (6.1b) and "whereas nothing[ness] does not exist" (6.2a) (**Tarán** [1965], 60).

being" and the second way "the way of not-being," since what characterizes each way is not a "notion" (being, not-being, or nothing[ness]) but what is said about it. For this reason the first way is a thesis, and the second is the negation of that thesis; and in each of the two ways (both in the thesis and its negation) the notions of being and not-being are present. It is the kind of relationship that Parmenides establishes between the notion in question and the fact of being that determines the truth or falsehood of the thesis in question. When it attributes a contradictory notion to a notion, the thesis is false; when an analogous notion is attributed to each notion, then the thesis is true. The first way is valid because it holds that there is being, *but also* because it states that it is not possible not to be. The negation of the thesis is erroneous because it states that there is no being, but also because it maintains that it is necessary not to be. As we can see, in the thesis, which is true, the notion of "not-being" is present, and in the negation of the thesis, which is erroneous, the notion of "being" is present. It is not the presence of a notion that characterizes each thesis but what is said about it. The notion of "nothing[ness]" is present in the first, the true thesis, because its existence is denied; *it is true to deny the existence of nothing[ness].* On the other hand, stating that nothing[ness] exists assumes that the second way is being followed and this way contradicts the first. This first way is clearly and distinctly expressed in 6.1b–2a.

I said that very few scholars admitted this evidence. R. Kent Sprague states that in 6.1a–2b there is "a recommendation of the way of being";[453] K. Bormann holds that contrary to what the second way states ("Das Nicht ist"), 6.2a belongs to the first way, which is the true one;[454] and we can deduce from R. Vitali's strange translation that this scholar also saw a formulation of the first way in 6.1–2 ("Vedo infatti essere l'è ma non il non è, ciò che io ti invito a considerare ovviamente di questa prima via di ricerca").[455] But it is L. Tarán who offers the most solid arguments in this respect: *tá* (6.2b) in the plural must allude to more than one phrase, and given that "all these clauses must refer to a single way, this has to be the first way of inquiry, because we have shown that *mẹdèn d'ouk éstin* may refer to it while it is impossible for *ésti gàr eînai* to be a part of this way."[456] If Parmenides urges the proclamation of this fundamental thesis, why, in the following line, does he tell his listener to "*withdraw*" from this way? This delicate question deserves special treatment.

---

453 **Kent Sprague**, R., "Parmenides: A Suggested Rearrangement of Fragments in the Way of Truth," *Classical Philology* 50 (1955) 125.

454 **Bormann** (1971), 97. This scholar adds that "the second way says the opposite of 6.1–2."

455 **Vitali** (1977), 35.

456 **Tarán** (1965), 60.

(e) Parmenides Does Not Recommend "Withdrawing" from the Thesis Expounded in 6.1b–2a

So in 6.1–2 we find a new formulation of the first way, that is, the true way, accompanied by an exhortation to proclaim or manifest this truth. The following line unequivocally alludes to this way by means of the demonstrative "this" (*taúte̱s*): "from *this* first way of investigation I <withdraw> you (*pró̱te̱s gár s'aph'hodoû taúte̱s dizé̱sios <eírgo̱>*)."[457] The manuscript tradition has transmitted this line in a mutilated form, and the verb "withdraw," which stands between angular brackets, was added by H. Diels as a conjecture. So according to the present state of the text, the Goddess exhorts the disciple she is addressing to withdraw from *this* way of investigation, that is, from the way that, as we have seen, is the true way. As Tarán observes, it is probable that this prohibition led the vast majority of scholars to consider that the condemned way was the second way, the way of error,[458] and then adapt the translation to fit its negative character. Nevertheless, there can be no doubt that "this" way, mentioned in the preceding line, is the way of truth. How can this obvious fact be harmonized with the Goddess's order to "withdraw" from it? The scholars who saw in 6.2a a formulation of the way of error did not ask themselves this question, but as we saw, this position is unsustainable. Given the clarity of the text, we must try to explain why the Goddess orders withdrawal from a true way. I believe there are four possible explanations, three of which have been proposed by scholars who were aware that this passage presents a serious problem: (1) the contradiction is eliminated if the passage is analyzed in a very free way, almost allegorically; (2) the lines in the passage could be rearranged; (3) it is possible to imagine a gap after line 6.2 so that the term "this" would not refer to the way of truth; and, finally, (4) it is possible to question Diels's conjecture, the source of all the problems.

(1) For K. Bormann, there is no problem whatever in the passage, whose spirit would be, "you have to follow the way of 'nothing[ness] is not'; if you do not, a first false way appears."[459] Doubtless, the first part of Bormann's argument can be found in Parmenides' text, but there are no

457 The reference to the previous way does not necessarily depend on the term "first" (*pró̱te̱s*), since Parmenides never calls the way mentioned first by the Goddess "the first way." It depends on the demonstrative "this," which refers to what has just been said immediately beforehand.

458 **Tarán** (1965), 59.

459 **Bormann** (1971), 98. For Heitsch, the prohibition refers to the phrase's negative term, "*ouk éstin,*" which is not even a way (**Heitsch** [1979], 87). We may answer that in 2.5a "*ouk éstin*" **is** a way, and although in the alternative in line 8.15 "*ouk estin*" has no subject, in 6.2a the subject is "*me̱dén,*" "nothing[ness]" and that, thanks to the double negative, the negative way "*ouk estin*" becomes positive: "*ouk éstin . . . me̱dén.*"

indications for the conditional phrase. The Goddess withdraws the disciple from that which she has just presented and not from a hypothetical disobedience of her order. W. Kranz had already offered a similar solution to Bormann's when he translated 6.3 thus: "dies (die Annahme von Nichtsein) ist nämlich der erste Weg der Forschung, von dem ich dich fernhalte."[460] Here, too, the solution is arbitrary, since the phrase in brackets does not exist in Parmenides' text and there is no right to imagine what the philosopher might have thought without venturing to say it. Finally, for A. P. D. Mourelatos, 6.1–2 presents both the first way of investigation and the doctrine that reinforces it by denying the second way.[461] But precisely this rejection of the second way (the negation of the negation of the thesis) is true, and Parmenides cannot withdraw us from the truth.

(2) The second possibility was attempted by R. Kent Sprague. Aware that the rejection expressed in 6.3 could not refer to a true way, this scholar proposed inserting between 6.2, where there is a true way, and 6.3, where there is the idea of rejection, a line alluding to a clearly wrong way: line 7.1, which states a way according to which "there are things that are not" (*eînai mē̱ eónta*). Immediately after the last line of fragment 6, Kent Sprague places fragment 7, but now with fragment 7 starting from line 3 (she has already set line 7.1 between 6.2 and 6.3, and she considers 7.2 to be inauthentic, a paraphrase composed by Plato).[462] In fact, Kent Sprague has inherited an old tradition that already envisaged the independence (even, in some cases, the doubtful character) of lines 7.1–2. G. G. Fülleborn had already eliminated 7.1 since, according to him, this line was "prosaica non nulla Parmenidis dicta,"[463] and consequently he placed 7.2–6 after fragment 1. S. Karsten did the same (he regarded 7.1 as "sententiam Parmenideam Platonis verbis expressam").[464] And so did F. M. Riaux (who states that the line is inauthentic).[465] On the other hand, H. Diels admits both the authenticity and autonomy of the group 7.1–2, and like Fülleborn, sets the rest of fragment 7 after fragment 1, according to the evidence of Sextus (VII.111).[466] This viewpoint was shared by J. Burnet[467] and later by G. Calogero, who proposed placing 7.1–2 before fragment 6.[468]

Kent Sprague takes her lead from these examples, but her originality lies in placing 7.1 between 6.2 and 6.3. It is true that then the passage ac-

---

460 **Kranz**, W., *Vorsokratische Denker*, 3rd ed. (Berlin: Weidmann, 1959), 95.
461 **Mourelatos** (1970), 77, note 7.
462 **Kent Sprague**, *Rearrangement*, 125.
463 **Fülleborn** (1795), 98.
464 **Karsten** (1835), 81.
465 **Riaux** (1840), 230.
466 **Diels** (1897), 34.
467 **Burnet**, J., *Early Greek Philosophy*, 4th ed. (London: A. & C. Black, 1930), 174.
468 **Calogero** (1932), 20.

quires a monolithic coherence: ". . . whereas nothing[ness] does not exist; I exhort you to proclaim it (6.2), since this can never be maintained: that there should be things that are not (7.1); I <withdraw> you from this first way of investigation (6.3)." But up to what point can we consider that Parmenides' Poem is a sort of puzzle that can be arranged as we like? Simplicius, who says himself that he has Parmenides' Poem in front of him, quotes the whole of fragment 6 *without interruption* (*Phys.* 117). Kent Sprague proposes inserting 7.1 into the middle of it. We could assume a gap in Simplicius' text.[469] But it is difficult to see how the content of this gap (viz. line 7.1) could have reappeared in three more passages of Simplicius (*Phys.* 135, 143, and 244) always accompanied by 7.2. But at the same time, we should not forget that Simplicius knows that Plato cites 7.1–2 (in *Soph.* 237a and 258a) and that perhaps, for that reason, he does not venture to separate these two lines to allow 7.1 to become independent, as Kent Sprague claims. Moreover, Simplicius' resistance to separating 7.1 from 7.2 is also doubtless due to the fact that the philosopher considers that 7.2 is authentic, contrary to the opinion of Kent Sprague. For all these reasons, I believe that Kent Sprague's solution could be taken into account only if the problem in question leads us down a blind alley with no way out. But, as we shall see, there is a possible way out.[470]

(3) In order to avoid the obvious contradiction between a true statement and the invitation to withdraw from it, some have assumed the existence of a gap after line 6.3. This hypothesis was proposed by O. Becker, for whom the whole passage 6.1–3, as it has come down to us, is incomprehensible.[471] According to Becker, the demonstrative "this" (*taútē̱s*) alludes to a "nearby" notion, but this nearness can be either before or after it, and he chooses the second possibility. If this is so, the Goddess would withdraw the disciple from the way stated after 6.3, in a passage now lost which would have begun with "I withdraw," a word miraculously added by Diels, and which would continue in a hypothetical line 6.3a, which might, for example, have this form: "in no way can this be said or thought: that

---

469 Tarán states that "if there is a gap, this must come after line 6.3 and not between 6.2 and 6.3" (**Tarán** [1965], 60). Nevertheless, this hypothesis does not refute Kent Sprague's thesis, since there could be a gap between 6.2 and 6.3 (and Tarán gives examples of fragmentary quotations by Simplicius) and another, perhaps smaller one, at the end of line 6.3.

470 Before abandoning this possibility (b), we may note that Bicknell proposed another rearrangement of the fragments, but his hypothesis does not concern our passage. This scholar maintains that 6.3–9 should be completed by fragment 4, and then fragment 8 should follow, but he does not say what kind of relationship there is between 6.1–2 and the new fragment made up of 6.3 ff. plus fragments 4 and 8 (**Bicknell**, P. J., "A New Arrangement of Some Parmenidean Verses," *Symbolae Osloensis* 42 [1968] passim).

471 **Becker**, O., "Drei Abhandlungen [but "Bemerkungen" in the contents] zum Lehrgedicht des Parmenides," *Kant-Studien* 55 (1964) 256.

there are things that are not" (that is, a mixture of 6.1 and 7.1). If this is so, this means that in 6.3 Parmenides would be saying: "I withdraw you from this first way of investigation (6.3); in no way can this be said or thought: that there are things that are not (6.3a); and then also . . . (6.4)." This idea of Becker's is ingenious, but I do not understand why his attempt at reconstruction is really an attempt to justify the notion of "withdrawal," which only arises from the hypothetical "*eírgo̱*" proposed by Diels. If Becker quarrels with the traditional text—as he does—he should begin by questioning Diels's conjecture, which forms part of the traditional version even though it does not belong to Parmenides.

A year after Becker but independently, L. Tarán also asserted the existence of a gap at the end of line 6.3, much larger than that imagined by Diels. According to Tarán, this gap resulted from Simplicius' habit of only retaining passages that were closely concerned with the topic he was analyzing. The object of study on page 117 of his Commentary on Aristotle's *Physics* is the identity of being and not-being, and in the lines he did not quote, according to Tarán, there would have been "a reference to the second way of inquiry or some word (e.g., 'now'), which coming after [*eírgo̱*] would qualify the temporary abandon of the first way."[472]

Tarán is aware of the fact that this is a possibility and, as such, cannot be rejected completely.[473] Nevertheless, it is highly improbable that Simplicius would have omitted a whole passage from Parmenides. If Simplicius only mentioned the lines closely linked to the topic he was expounding, his quotation in our case should have begun with line 6.3, since 6.1–2 says nothing about those who consider being and not-being to be identical. Moreover, Simplicius himself says that he intends to quote the greatest possible quantity of passages from Parmenides, given the "rarity of the book" (*Phys.* 144), and he keeps his word, since he goes on to quote a block of fifty lines from fragment 8. Finally, we may say that both *aph'hodoû* (6.3) and *apò tê̱s* (6.4) depend on the same verb, whether we accept Diels's conjecture or any other, and with or without a gap, the meaning of 6.3 is picked up again in 6.4. And in 6.4 the wrong way is presented. So the problem subsists, since how can the same verb be applied to two contradictory ways, especially if it refers to a rejection?

---

472 **Tarán** (1965), 61.

473 Brumbaugh accepts the hypothesis (**Brumbaugh**, R. S., "Review of Tarán," *International Philosophical Quarterly* 4 [1966] 496); Long rejects it (**Long**, A. A., "Review of Tarán," *Journal of the Hellenic Studies* 86 [1966] 223). According to Mourelatos, the verb *eírgo̱*, accepted by Tarán, has too strong a meaning to assume that it could apply to a merely "temporary" abandonment of a way (**Mourelatos** [1970], 77, note 7). Finally, Heitsch accepts the gap and adds other quotations from Simplicius in support of Tarán's hypothesis (**Heitsch**, E., *Gegenwart und Evidenz bei Parmenides: Aus der Problemgeschichte der Aequivokation* [Wiesbaden: Franz Steiner Verlag, 1970], 42 ff.).

It cannot be denied that the Tarán-Becker hypothesis is ingenious, but it has to be admitted that these are desperate, even dangerous, measures. Indeed, we can postulate a gap with respect to any passage in the Poem, a providential gap that would give the text its (true?) meaning, that is, the one desired by whomever is making the conjecture. My position in this matter is as follows: the text must speak for itself, and if at any given moment there is a silence (corresponding to a gap), elements affecting the continuity of the argument, like the "withdraw" conjectured by Diels, should not be introduced into it.

(4) The last possibility consists of critically analyzing the hypothesis proposed by Diels. Everything I have said in the previous pages offers us a firm starting point. In 6.1–2 there is an unequivocal statement of the first way, and line 6.3, by virtue of a conjecture by Diels, states that it is necessary to withdraw from this way. We are facing a contradiction, but Parmenides is innocent; the suggestion to "withdraw" from a true way does not belong to him. It belongs to Diels.

(f) The Origin of the Notion of "Withdrawing" as a Conjecture in 6.3

So why did Diels resort to the notion of "withdrawing" as a conjecture, and what reasons did he offer in defense of his choice? Let us begin with the first point. A conjecture is necessary in this case because *all* the manuscripts of Simplicius' Commentary on Aristotle's *Physics,* the only source of the passage, present a mutilated text. I have personally consulted *all* these manuscripts, and I have verified that in every case line 6.3 ends with the word "*dizē̱sios*" ("of investigation"), followed immediately by the beginning of line 6.4, "*autàr épeit'* . . ." In line 6.3, the last half of the hexameter is missing, but the fact that the text is transcribed in a continuous manner in all the manuscripts leads us to suppose that the gap must go back at least to the archetype of Simplicius' text, or perhaps to the Parmenides text that Simplicius had in his library. So it is obvious that all the copyists who reproduced this passage found themselves with a text that was *already incomplete.*[474] Therefore, no attempt to restore the lost word can be based on efforts to decipher a content that has become hidden or distorted by material defects in the manuscripts (for example, a word erased but recoverable thanks to restoration techniques, a damaged folio, etc.). The terrain is free and the last word lies with the interpreter.

474 Cf. **Cordero** (1997), Appendix II, the list of currently existing Simplicius manuscripts that contain Parmenides' line 6.3.

Diels was not the first to try to offer a coherent version of the passage. Everything began when Simplicius' text containing fragment 6 of Parmenides passed from being in manuscript to being *printed.* Indeed, once printing was used to "reproduce" an identical text in hundreds and later thousands of copies, manual copying of ancient texts was abandoned. Simplicius' book was printed for the first time by the publishing house of Aldo Manuzio in Venice in 1526. As may be imagined, a printed edition must offer a comprehensible text, especially in the case of the "Aldine editions" (named for the first name of the publisher, Aldo), already famous in their time for the precision and rigor of their editing. That is how, when it came to printing the mutilated Parmenides' text, the editor responsible "completed" the phrase thus: "*withdraw thought* (*eírge nóēma*) from this first way of investigation." *That is, the paternity of the verb "withdraw" does not belong to Diels.* The text of the 1526 Aldine edition is of exceptional interest for our investigation into the origin of the lost term, and that is why I have studied it intensively over a number of years,[475] since the printed version depends on the manuscripts used by the publisher as a model. I have been able to establish that the copious bibliography dedicated to Manuzio's press, as well as the documents and correspondence of those in charge of it, give us extremely interesting data about most of the works carried out in 1526; unfortunately, nothing concrete can be found about the edition of Simplicius we are concerned with. The editor in charge appears to have been Francesco d'Asola ("Asulanus"), Aldo's son-in-law, since it is he who dedicates the edition to Cardinal Hercules Gonzaga in a sort of prologue. However, unlike what occurs in other cases, nothing is said in that prologue about the Greek manuscripts used in editing the work.

Today we know the manuscripts of Simplicius' Commentary on Aristotle's *Physics* were very plentiful at that time. Even now more than forty codices are preserved, containing at least the first book of the Commentary (in which Parmenides' text is to be found), either complete or in fragments. We may presume that these were even more numerous in Manuzio's time. A search through the repertories of existing manuscripts in the libraries of Italy at that time showed us that an editor did not usually use a large number of codices.[476] Today any researcher who wants to can examine the

---

475 Cf. **Cordero**, N. L., "Analyse de l'édition Aldine du Commentaire de Simplicius à la Physique d'Aristote," *Hermes* 105 (1977), and "Les sources vénitiennes de l'édition Aldine du Livre I du Commentaire de Simplicius de la Physique d'Aristote," *Scriptorium* 38(2) (1984).

476 With regard to the St Mark's Basilica library ("Biblioteca Marciana") in Venice, most of the manuscripts bequeathed to it by Cardinal Bessarion—including *all* those containing Simplicius' book—were stored away in chests until 1530, and loans outside the library were exceptional. Cf. **Cordero**, "Les sources vénitiennes."

forty-odd existing manuscripts, which would have been practically impossible during the period of Manuzio's successors (1526; Aldo had died in 1515). Be that as it may, I was able to draw up a list of sources *that theoretically could have been used* as a model for the 1526 edition, and in all of these the text of the line in question is cut short.[477]

So where does the expression "*eírge nóe̱ma*" ("withdraw thought") come from? We do not know. Clearly the editor, probably Francesco d'Asola, could have had at hand a manuscript in good condition, unknown today, but even leaving aside our passage, it would be suspicious that no traces remain of such an important manuscript. I do not think it likely that the editor could have consulted manuscripts more ancient than E, F, and D, from which all the others derive. If my hypothesis is correct, and on the basis of the documents I have analyzed, I will risk saying that the authorship of certain terms absent from the original belongs purely and simply to Francesco d'Asola. We know today that d'Asola did not always follow Aldo's motto—"non enim recipio emendaturum libros,"[478]—as we know that he corrected the texts he edited to a considerable extent. Although he did not know of the existence of Asola, H. Diels rightly wrote that in the case of Simplicius, "Aldini exempli *editor* haud pauca novavit, infeliciter plurima."[479] A clear example of this "emmendatio infelix" is his conjecture to complete line 6.3 of Parmenides, proposed to make a mutilated text comprehensible, but whose secondary consequences distorted the philosopher's thought for centuries.

After 1526 the version "*eírge nóe̱ma*" was accepted unanimously, and only minor corrections were proposed to adapt it to the requirements of the meter. That is how the unpublished version of the Poem made by J. J. Scaliger suppresses "*gár t'aph'hodoû*" ("for of the way") and proposes "from this first investigation withdraw thought."[480] For his part, G. G. Fülleborn eliminates "*taúte̱s*" and reads "for from the first way of investigation withdraw thought,"[481] a text also adopted by Brandis, since, according to him, the word "*taúte̱s*" was added by Simplicius "contrary to the meter" (a curious argument, since Brandis places more trust in Fülleborn than in Simplicius).[482] S. Karsten proposes his own version: "in the first place (*prô̱ton*) with-

477 In the works cited in note 475, I propose this list: Marc. Gr. 219 (G 1), Marc. Gr. 227 (F), Marc. Gr. 229 (E), Marc. Gr. Cl. IV.15 (G IV), Paris. Gr. 1908 (P), Laur. 85.1 (B), Laur. 85.2 (D), and Mut. 184 (III.F.6).

478 **Manuzio**, A., *Theocritus* (Venice: In Aedibus Aldi, 1496).

479 **Diels**, H., "Preface," in *Simplicii In Aristotelis Physicorum [. . .] Commentaria* (Berlin: G. Reimer, 1895).

480 Cf. **Cordero**, N. L., "La version de Joseph Scaliger du Poème de Parménide," *Hermes* 110 (1982) 117–22.

481 **Fülleborn** (1795), 59.

482 **Brandis** (1813), 104.

draw thought from this way of investigation,"[483] basing it on the fact that "*autár épeita*" ("but then") in 6.4 cannot be coordinated with "*prôtes*" in 6.3. F. G. A. Mullach restores "*taútes*" and takes up T. Bergk's version ("from this first way ["*prôt'aph'hodoû taútes*"] of investigation withdraw thought"[484]), and H. Stein simply changed the order of certain terms.[485] This is the state of the question until 1882, the year in which H. Diels published the second edition (three and a half centuries after the first) of Simplicius' Commentary. Between 1526 and 1882, the expression "withdraw thought" (*eírge nóema*) was always accepted, and line 6.3 of Parmenides was read in this way: "from this first way of investigation withdraw thought." The existing contradiction between the way of truth stated in 6.1–2 and this rejection in 6.3 does not seem to have bothered anyone.

As we know, the Simplicius edition published by Diels forms part of the series *Commentaria in Aristotelem Graeca,* and on page 117 of volume IX the quotation from line 6.3 of Parmenides reads thus: "for from this first way of investigation I withdraw you." There are three changes from the version in the Aldine edition. For one, *eírgo,* "I withdraw," is in the first person,[486] whereas in the Aldine edition it was in the second person, "withdraw." The complement "thought" (*nóema*) is absent: it is the disciple himself and not just his thought who must withdraw from "this" way. And the third change, as the Goddess addresses the disciple, is the appearance of the pronoun "you" (*s'*), which figured in most of the manuscripts but which had been left out of the Aldine edition: "I withdraw you." This version of 6.3 has been accepted almost unanimously from 1882 until a few years ago. I say "almost" because, before my rejection of it, I only found *one* author who did not accept this verb "withdraw," and after I published my view for the first time, two or three researchers agreed with my rejection. The only other author who rejected Diels's conjecture is Vitali. In a work published in 1977, this author presented a very special version of the text, since in order to complete the meter in line 6.3 he added a term from 6.4 and then introduced a conjecture into this line 6.4. Consequently, 6.3 acquired this form: ". . . which I invite you to consider obviously in this first way of

483 **Karsten** (1835), 77. Riaux accepted this version (**Riaux** [1840], 211).

484 **Mullach**, F. G. A., *Fragmenta philosophorum graecorum* (Paris: Didot, 1860), 131; **Bergk**, T., "Commentatio de Empedoclis Proemio," *Kleine philologische Schriften* II (Halle: Buchhandlung des Waisenhauses, 1886), 35.

485 **Stein**, H., "Die Fragmente des Parmenides *perí phúseos,*" *Symbola philologorum bonnensium in honorem F. Ristchelli* (Leipzig: Teubner, 1864–67), 804.

486 According to Patin, Diels's conjecture is preferable as it keeps the verb in the first person (which allows for the reintroduction of "*s*") and in the indicative (as in 6.2, *ánoga*) (**Patin**, A., "Parmenides im Kampfe gegen Heraklit," *Jahrbuch für klassische Philologie,* Supplementband 25 [1899], 516, note 1).

investigation, but which I reject in that one . . ." (6.4).[487] Finally, although my rejection of *eírgo̱* was first published in 1979 in an article in *Phronesis,*[488] after that—but clearly independently—A. García Calvo also contested the verb *eírgo̱* and proposed this version of 6.3: "for from this way of inquiry I first drove you back (*ô̱sa*)."[489] That is, this scholar does not accept the verb proposed by Diels, but keeps the idea of withdrawal now represented by the verb "*o̱théo̱*."

(g) Rejection of the Conjecture "I Withdraw You"

Let us return to Diels's text. Unlike the editor of the Aldine edition, Diels gives a reason for proposing the conjecture "I withdraw you." Indeed, in a footnote to his edition he says that this reading is based on a parallel expression found in a line belonging to the same context, 7.2: "but you, withdraw thought [*eírge nóe̱ma*] from this way of investigation."[490] Let us examine this argument from Diels. It is highly probable that the editor of the Aldine edition followed the same reasoning and that therefore he directly proposed the formula *eírge nóe̱ma* found in 7.1 for 6.3 as well. Diels keeps the meaning of withdrawal expressed by the verb *eírgo̱,* but adapts the text to the meter and suppresses the complement *nóe̱ma,* putting the verb in the first person, which leads him to add the pronoun "you": "[I, sc., the Goddess] withdraw you." The reasoning appears to be impeccable, since there can be no doubt that, as Diels says, 7.1 ("withdraw thought from this way of investigation") appears to be a parallel passage to 6.3 ("for from this first way of investigation I [. . .] you").

If it exists, this parallelism is deceptive: there are "parallel" passages in other parts of the Poem but, if words are missing in one of them these cannot be explained by terms provided by the other.[491] In the case concern-

487 **Vitali** (1977), 35. It is true that I published my criticism six years before the publication of Vitali's book in 1977 in my doctoral thesis *L'être et le non-être chez Parménide* (Paris IV, Sorbonne), but clearly Vitali did not know of this work. With respect to Vitali, let us say that it is not surprising that this writer rejects Diels's conjecture, since his book is characterized by acute hypercriticism. Although this scholar confesses to "rejecting corrections," he departs from the "orthodox" text of the Poem on *seventy-two* occasions, and some of his corrections are rather grotesque. For example, in 1.2, instead of "*pémpon*" ("they brought me"), Vitali adopts "*pémpton,*" which is found in codex N, and translates "at the fifth hour." And in 1.14, instead of accepting Scaliger's correction, "*dike̱,*" he keeps "*dikê̱n*" with an "adverbial accusative" meaning and translates "for the use of these [*sc.*, gates]."

488 **Cordero**, "Les deux chemins," 1–32.

489 **García Calvo**, A., *Lecturas Presocráticas* (Madrid: Lucina, 1981), 192.

490 Cf. also **Diels** (1897), 68.

491 The typical example is lines 2.3 and 2. 5. They are very similar (almost identical) but they maintain opposite theses. There is also an obvious parallelism between 1.1 ("the mares

ing us, by means of *taútēs* in 6.3 and *tēsd'* in 7.2, each line alludes to a way mentioned in the previous line, that is, in 6.2 and 7.1, respectively. For the parallelism to be complete, both lines must refer *to the same way,* from which the Goddess says, in one case, that it is necessary to withdraw, and in the other, that it is necessary to withdraw thought. However, we have already shown that the way presented in 6.1–2 is the way of truth (hence the difficulty of admitting that we must withdraw from it). But which way does the "this" (*tēsd'*) refer to in 7.2?

(h) The Thesis Expounded in Fragment 7

The Goddess's exhortation to "withdraw thought," which we find in line 7.2, refers to a way ("this") proclaimed immediately before, in line 7.1. Let us analyze this text. This line, first cited by Plato in the *Sophist* (in 237a and 258d) and then by Aristotle (*Met.* N.1089a4), by Pseudo-Alexander (*Met.* N.2 [805]), and by Simplicius (*Phys.* 135, 143, 244), consists of two parts. The first hemistich, which presents serious textual problems[492] (to the point where, as we saw, there are authors who consider it to be apocryphal: cf. *supra*), states "for this [*toûto*] shall never prevail [*damēi*]." The second hemistich makes the meaning of "this" explicit: "that there should be [*eînai; éstin* in direct speech] things that are not [*mē eónta*]."[493] However, *nobody ever stated that this formula might belong to the first way of investigation. All* authors admit that this is a presentation of the negative way (the false way, for those who think that Parmenides presents only two ways, or the second false way, for those who hold that there are three ways). If this is so, the parallelism between 6.3 and 7.2 collapses from the start, because even though it appears to exist, it is deceptive: each exhortation refers to a *different* way (6.3 would command withdrawing from the first way; in contrast, 7.2 orders the withdrawal of thought from a wrong way, that is, from the thesis "there are things that are not," "that which is not being, exists"). It is worth pointing out that it is not allowable to complete a mutilated text

that carry me as far as my spirit reaches") and 1.25 ("the mares that carry you to my home"), but if a word was lost from one of the passages, the other passage could not fill the gap.

492 The text generally accepted today is that proposed by several manuscripts of Aristotle (E and J) and Simplicius (E on pages 135 and 244, and D and E on page 134): "*toûto damēi.*" The verb is the epic form of the passive subjunctive.

493 The variant "*ónti,*" proposed by the Aldine editions and taken up by Estienne, has no manuscript authenticity (**Estienne**, H., *Poiesis philosophica* [Geneva: 1573], 42). A more "academic" translation would be "that non-beings exist," but the intelligent reader knows that when a Greek philosopher asks questions about "beings" (*tà ónta*), he wants to know what *things* are.

(6.3) with a term referring to a context that is not only different but contrary (7.2). It is clear that Diels made a wrong inference: *eírgo̱,* which makes sense when referring to a negative way (the one proclaimed in 7.1), is not appropriate for a positive way (that stated in 6.2).

Let us analyze this line 7.1 in detail. The expression *"esti mè̱ eónta" contradicts* the formula *"me̱dén d'ouk éstin"* ("nothing[ness] does not exist") in 6.2a[494] and is therefore a new way of formulating the second way of investigation, that is, the negation of the thesis.[495] This has been maintained, among others, by K. Reinhardt,[496] M. Untersteiner,[497] L. Tarán,[498] A. H. Coxon,[499] and G. Giannantoni.[500] Other scholars have seen in 7.1 the statement of a third[501] or even a fourth[502] way, but in both cases, once more, these are wrong ways, which are to be avoided. If we turn to Plato, there can be no doubt that the quotation from Parmenides in the *Sophist* refers to the impossibility of the existence of that which does not exist. Indeed, the first time that Plato quotes 7.1–2 he does so as an illustration of a *lógos* that "some have dared to suppose that that which is not exists [*tò mè̱ ón eînai*]," and when he is convinced he has refuted Parmenides, in 258d he says that, really, *the opposite* of Parmenides' statement is what must be said, that is, that *"tà̱ mè̱ ónta, ho̱s éstin,"*[503] since now that which is not has the right to be. Aristotle's case is similar: when he transcribes 7.1 he says that there Parmenides "shows that that which is not [*tò mè̱ ón*], is [*éstin*]" (*Met.* N.1089a). And, finally, for Simplicius there is in that passage an allusion to a way seeking that which is not [*tò mè̱ ón ze̱toúse̱s*]" (*Phys.* 78.5).

The opposition between the way indicated by the formula *eînai mè̱ ónta* and the true way is even more obvious if we take into account the expres-

---

494 We have already shown how, in Parmenides, "that which is not" and "nothing[ness]" are synonymous. The thesis in 7.1 states that nothing[ness] (the things that are not) exists and therefore is contradictory to 6.2a.

495 Like the vast majority of interpreters, I consider that "*mè̱ eónta*" is neuter plural. So I do not share Reich's exotic hypothesis, according to which the formula is an accusative singular alluding to "who no longer exists," that is, the dead. This viewpoint leads Reich to see in Parmenides an allusion to the Pythagoreans' metempsychosis (**Reich**, K., "Parmenides und die Pithagoreer," *Hermes* 82 [1954] 289).

496 **Reinhardt** (1916), 36.

497 **Untersteiner** (1958), cxxx.

498 **Tarán** (1965), 76.

499 **Coxon** (1986), 191. This scholar adds that Plato, Aristotle, and Simplicius had already understood that 7.1–2 rejected the negative way of 2.5, and that this opinion "is conclusive."

500 **Giannantoni**, G., "Le due 'vie' di Parmenide," *La parola del passato* 43 (1988) 216.

501 This is the case with **Gómez-Lobo** (1985), 101, and **Wiesner** (1996), 99.

502 This is the case with **Meijer** (1997), 147.

503 In the first case, Plato uses the singular, *mè̱ ón;* in the second, the plural, *mè̱ ónta;* and, clearly, in both cases he is speaking of the same thing. This shows that the "unusual" plural in 7.1 is completely irrelevant. It left even Plato indifferent.

sion "*ou mḗpote . . . damê̄i*" ("shall never prevail"), which as soon as an order or wish is assumed, is parallel to "is not possible . . ." in 2.3b. What is not possible, what shall never prevail, is nothing[ness], that which is not, considered already "impossible" in 2.7. Line 7.1 as a whole (hemistiches 1 and 2) is synonymous with 2.3b: it is an expression of the principle of non-contradiction, as S. Ranulf[504] and J. Moravcsik[505] have observed. The complement clause (hemistich 2) reintroduces the way of error. Indeed, in *eînai mḕ eónta* we have the assertion of a negative term, which, according to our analysis is equivalent to the assertion of a concept with respect to its contradiction, that is, the negation of the thesis. This contradiction must be avoided. Ruggiu stated that the Goddess wants to prevent "things being both *eónta* and *mḕ eónta* at once."[506] This internal contradiction (all in all, the non-respect of the principle of non-contradiction) is the principal characteristic of the negation of the thesis, the second way.

The Goddess orders the withdrawal of thought from *this* way of investigation (7.2). That is logical. On the other hand, there can be no obligation to withdraw from a way that is *the opposite* of this way. As this is the case with 6.1–2, we cannot admit the only reason adduced by Diels to propose his conjecture (viz. the "parallelism" between both ways). The ways referred to in 7.2 and 6.3 are not parallel: *they are opposite.* Therefore I shall try to solve the problem of the gap in line 6.3 in a different way.

(i) A Possible Solution for the Gap in Line 6.3

After having stated his thesis once more (and only his thesis: "it is possible to be, whereas nothing[ness] does not exist") in the first two lines of fragment 6, from line 4 onward in the same fragment (as I shall try to show), Parmenides expounds the negation of the thesis, according to the same procedure already used in fragment 2 (thesis: line 3; negation of the thesis, line 5). However, between the presentation of both possibilities, in line 6.4, the Goddess expresses "something" concerning both the thesis she has just expounded in 6.1–2 ("this first way of investigation . . .") and the one she will expound from 6.4 onward ("and then . . ."). As I have already shown, the phrase's verb is missing: we do not know what the Goddess says about the two possibilities. Be that as it may, we must not forget that in the original text *there was a verb* (although this has been lost in successive transcrip-

---

504 **Ranulf**, S., *Der eleatische Satz vom Widerspruch* (Copenhagen: Gyldendal, 1924), 160.

505 **Moravcsik**, J. M. E., "Being and Meaning in the *Sophist*," *Acta philosophica fennica* 14 (1962) 25.

506 **Ruggiu** (1975), 147.

tions of the Poem), and it is essential that this verb should have been *valid for the two formulas, both for that in 6.3 and that in 6.4, which express contrary contents.* The expressions *pró̱te̱s gár* . . . and *autàr épeita* . . . ("first . . ." and "then . . .") depend on this unknown verb. Therefore the missing verb must have had a meaning capable of being applied *to two contradictory ways,* since, as I have shown, 6.3 alludes to the thesis, that is, the first way, and 6.4 ff. to its negation, that is, the second way. This fact presents no difficulty at all. In various parallel passages Parmenides uses *the same verb* to refer to two contradictory ways. In 1.28–30, truth and opinions (that is, the two ways) must be the object of "inquiry" (*puthésthai*), and therefore they are lumped together in the notion of "*pánta,*" "everything." In 2.2–5 the expression "to think" (2.2) is valid for both the ways that will then be stated. Finally, in 8.17–18, the verb "*eân*" (allow) is valid both for the way of error (which has been "allowed" as unthinkable) and for the way of truth (which has been "allowed" as genuine).[507] This means that, regardless of each way's merit, the same verb (or similar verbs) can be applied to both ways: both must be the object of inquiry (1.28–30), both constitute the *múthos* that must be listened to (2.2), both are possibilities offered to thought (2.3, 2.5) and both merit precise assessment (8.17–18).

However, there is an essential nuance that must not be forgotten: both ways are stated or proclaimed by the Goddess and listened to or accepted by the traveling disciple. And once she has stated both ways, the Goddess explains their *content* to the disciple: truth corresponds to being, and opinion to human perception and the wandering intellect. The description of the way of truth will be the object of most of fragment 8, up to line 51. After that there will be an explanation of *dóxai,* an explanation that will take place even though there can be no *pístis ale̱thé̱s* ("real trust," 1.30) in them. This observation leads us to take into account one of the meanings of the preposition *apó,* which goes with the missing verb in the two lines and does not necessarily mean a rejection, as in Diels's conjecture ("*from* this . . . I withdraw you"). Here, in fragment 6, we have the use of *apó* with the meaning of "by," "with," and in particular, "from."[508] My hypothesis is as follows: in lines 6.3 ff. the Goddess alludes, as in 1.28–30, 2.3–5 and 8.50–52, to the *starting point* of the mental journey the disciple must undertake, the journey that covers the content of the Goddess's "course." This journey, like any other, has an end, clearly mentioned by the formula "*en*

507 In two other parallel passages there are different verbs, but their meaning is similar. 1.26–27 speaks of traveling the road of truth that *lies* near the Goddess, whereas the road of men *lies* far away. And in 8.50 the Goddess "concludes" (*paúo̱*) her explanation of one way and invites the disciple to "listen" to her account of the second way; so we may say that both ways are "heard about" from the Goddess by the disciple.

508 Cf. L. S. J., s.v. "*apó,*" I.

tôi soi paúo" ("here I end for you") (8.50–51). But there must also be a starting point for the teaching, and it occurs to me that the most appropriate verb to indicate this start is the verb whose meaning is the opposite of "end": "begin," "*árkhesthai,*" in the middle voice.

Parmenides uses this verb on two occasions: in fragment 5, *árxomai* ("I shall begin"), and in 8.10, *arxámenon* ("beginning"). We may suppose that he also used it in 6.3, but in this case it must not be forgotten that the preposition "*apó,*" which appears on two occasions (in 6.3 and in 6.4) stands in relation to this verb, just as it stood in relation to *eírgo* ("withdraw") in Diels's conjecture. So can *apó* stand in relation to *árkhesthai* ("begin")? There can be no doubt that it can. Furthermore, the combination "*árkhomai* (only in the middle voice)[509] + *apó*" is a real cliché in ancient Greek literature, and in line 2 of fragment 5 Parmenides himself uses *árxomai* accompanied by a synonym of the preposition "*apó*": "*hoppóthen*" ("where," "whence"). This combination alludes to the starting point of something, be it a list, a series, an account, a mental journey, even a philosophy "course."[510] There are no examples of this construction[511] in Homer. On a single occasion he uses a parallel form in which "*ek*" replaces "*apó*": "*ek de toû arkhómenos*" ("beginning by . . .") (*Od.* 23.199). However, Herodotus gives us three representative examples of the construction: "he gave an account consistent with the truth, beginning from the beginning" (*arkhómenos . . . apò arkhês*) (I.116.5); "the Egyptians shave their heads, beginning from childhood" (*apò paidiôn arxámenoi*) (III.12.10); and "he expounded Cyrus' paternal genealogy, beginning from Achaemenes" (*arxámenos de ap' . . .*) (III.75.2). In Plato we find a number of relevant examples: *Gorgias* 471c, "beginning with you" (*arxámenos apó sou*); *Phaedrus* 228d, "beginning with the first [of the gods]" (*arxámenos apò toû prôtou*); *Phaedo* 100b, "I begin with those" (*árkhomai ap'ekeínon*); *Parmenides* 137b, "I shall begin with you yourself" (*ap'hemautoû árxomai*) (137b); *Sophist* 218b, "beginning, in the first place, with the Sophist" (*arkhoménoi . . . apò toû sophistoû*);[512] *Sophist* 242d, "beginning from Xenophanes" (*apò . . . arxámenon*); *Timaeus* 28b, "beginning from some beginning" (*ap'arkhês tinos arxámenos*); *Laws* 771a, "beginning from the sacred" (*ap' hierôn ergméne*); and *Laws* 771c, "up to twelve, beginning from one" (*apò*

---

509 This fact invalidates A. **Nehamas**' conjecture (cf. *infra,* Chapter VII, note 619), who, after my work published in *Phronesis* (1979), adopted the same verb, but in the active voice.

510 Later, in grammar, *árkhesthai* + *apó* was used to mean the letter beginning a word. Cf. Dionysius of Thrace: "It begins with (*apò . . . arkhómenen*) a vowel, like 'érgon'"; "it begins with (*id.*) a consonant, like Nestor" (*Ars. gramm.* 6.33.26).

511 The only case to be found in Homer, "*kaproû apò tríkhas arxámenos*" (*Il.* 19.154), is a clear case of *tmesis: aperxámenos.*

512 Cf. the parallel passage, "what is the beginning (*arkhé*) from which it would begin (*árxaito*) . . . ?" (242b).

miâs arxámenos).[513] Aristotle also uses this formula (*Met.* A.2.983a12–3: "they begin by being surprised," *árkhontai apò toû thaumázein;* Z.2.1028b23, "beginning from the one," *apò toû henós arxámenos*), and so did Protagoras,[514] Xenophon,[515] Demosthenes[516] and Simplicius.[517]

A decisive example can be found in Critias, since, as in Parmenides, he is speaking about the starting point of a teaching: "I begin from the origin of man" (*árkhomai apò tê̱s genetê̱s anthrṓpou*) (fr. 32). This would be the sense of *árkhesthai* + *apó* in Parmenides, if he did indeed use this verb in fragment 6, that, as we saw, is to be found in two other passages of the Poem.

The principal consequence of my conjecture is the following: as it does not assume a criticism (either of one or of *two* ways, as was the case with *éirgo̱*), but a new presentation of the two possibilities given in fragment 2, there is no need to imagine a third way, which would be the second way to be criticized (since, obviously, it is not possible to criticize the first). Regarding this hypothesis, F. Fronterotta wrote that "the meaning of the message [of fr. 6] changes completely" if different conjectures from that of Diels are accepted: "it is more reasonable to suppose that the way being spoken of in lines 1–3 of fr. 6 coincides with the first way in fr. 2."[518] This is what I have demonstrated.

(j) Discovering the Foundation of the Two Ways in Fragment 6

I said that in the passage 6.1–2, Parmenides returned to formulating the first way of investigation, and that from 6.4 onward a description of the second way, the way of error, clearly appeared. When the Goddess presented her program of studies, she had already told the future disciple that he had to "be abreast" (*puthésthai*) of everything, both truth and mistaken

513 Cf. also the formula "*apò Hestías árkhesthai*" (*Euthyphro,* 3a) or "*arkhṓmetha*" (*Cratylus,* 401b), which is also found in **Aristophanes** (*Frogs,* 845) and in other fifth-century authors, although its origin is very ancient. The usual meaning is "begin with the essential," since Hestia represents the very center of the *pólis,* the "home" (cf. **Dorion**, L. A., *Euthyphro* [Paris: GF-Flammarion, 1997], 291, note 16). In Sophron and Crates we find the equivalent expression "*ex Hestías árkhesthai.*"

514 **Protagoras**, fragment 3, "you have to begin learning from infancy (*apò neóte̱tos, arxaménous*)."

515 **Xenophon**, *Memories,* 3.5.12: "begin with the parents (*apò tô̱n paterô̱n árkhontai*)."

516 **Demosthenes**, 18.297 (= 325, 7), "beginning with you" (*arxámenos apó sou*).

517 **Simplicius**, *Phys.* 1014.26: "[Zeno's argument known as "The Stadium"] begins with Achilles from the beginning of the stadium . . ." (*arxaménou . . . apò tê̱s arkhê̱s toû stadíou*).

518 **Fronterotta**, F., "Essere, tempo e pensiero: Parmenide et l''origine dell'ontologia'," *Annali della Scuola Normale Superiore di Pisa,* Classe di Lettere e Filosofia, Serie II, Vol. 24 (1994) 841.

opinions. Logically, learning must *begin* with the knowledge of a thesis, and then *begin* with the other. Why must it begin twice? Because Parmenides' reasoning is circular: "it is common [*xunón*] for me that where [*hoppóthen*] I begin [*árxo̱mai*], there I shall return again" (fr. 5). Years later, Plato followed Parmenides' example, since the method proposed in his *Parmenides* as intellectual "gymnastics" for the young Socrates consists in *beginning* (*arxómetha*) with the examination of a certain hypothesis (137a), and once this is exhausted, *beginning* with the opposite hypothesis (*elthóntes pálin epì té̱n arkhé̱n* . . .) (165e). As the starting point is arbitrary, the Parmenides of Plato's *Parmenides* proposes *beginning with* (*ap'emautoû árxo̱mai*) his own hypothesis (137b).

But the situation is more radical in Parmenides, since according to the content of the thesis, it is enough to state it, to realize that its negation is impossible; thus, even if you begin with the negation, you have to recognize that the positive statement is necessary. Therefore, the starting point of the reasoning is *common:* the conclusion of one way is the starting point of the other; you begin with being and come back to being.[519] In fragment 5 it is the Goddess expounding her method, and therefore she says that "for her" (*moi*), the starting point of the double argument is "common" (*xunós*). This term has the same meaning in Parmenides as it does in Heraclitus (fr. 2 and 103) and in the ancient *Etymologica:*[520] *koinós,* "common, that is, coincident."[521] This does not mean an "indifferent" viewpoint, as Tarán[522] maintains, but one that is "shared" (gemeinsamer[523]). It is "from" this common point that you have to "begin": the Goddess begins her explanation and the disciple begins first to receive her teaching and then to test it. He begins by one way and then begins again by another.[524] So when the Goddess ends her exposition of the first way, she indicates: "here I end for

519 This is the meaning of fragment 5, according to Meijer (**Meijer**, P. A., "Das methodologische im 5. Fragment des Parmenides," *Classica at medievalia* 30 [1969] 104–5). Cf. also **Meijer** (1997), 23–24.

520 Cf. **Hesychius**, *Lexicon,* Vol. III (Amsterdam: A. M. Hakkert, 1965), 173; *Etymologicum magnum,* ed. Gaisford, T. (Amsterdam: A. M. Hakkert, 1967), 416; *Etymologicum graecae linguae* (Leipzig: J. A. G. Weigel, 1818), 416.

521 **Kirk**, G. S., *Heraclitus: The Cosmic Fragments* (Cambridge, England: Cambridge University Press, 1954), 115.

522 **Tarán** (1965), 51.

523 **Meijer**, "Das methodologische," 104.

524 It should be noted that the meaning of the correlation "*pró̱te̱s gár . . . autár épeita*" (6.3–4) is not adversative, as it appears in most translations, but simply correlative. In **Homer** this is a habitual formula corresponding to "on the one hand . . . and then" (cf. *Il.* 3.315, 11.420, 12.191, 23.237, 23.683, 24.791). The presence in all these cases of *pró̱ton* instead of *pró̱te̱s* led **Karsten** to modify Parmenides' text (cf. *supra*). Denniston says that the commonest use of *autár* is "weakly adversative, or purely progressive" (**Denniston**, J. D., *The Greek Particles* [Oxford: Clarendon Press, 1934], 55) and that the formula *autár epeí* "often indicates the progressive stages of an account." Cf. *atár* in 8.58.

you (*soi*) reasoning and thinking about the truth" (8.50–51) and she begins *then* (*d'apò toûde . . .*) (8.52) the presentation of the opinions of mortals, about which she can only offer "a deceitful series of words" (8.52).

So the verb *árkesthai* offers a content that could be applicable to the gap in line 6.3. In the first place, since it does not assume a rejection of what has just been expounded, it gives the connective *gár* (which joins 6.2 and 6.3) its normal value, since if Parmenides had wanted to distance himself from what was said in 6.1–2, he would not have then said "since" or "given that." As Mourelatos observed about Tarán's interpretation, Parmenides would surely have written "*allà*"—"but," "however"—but would never have used a particle that implies continuity.[525] Then, if what we have is not a rejection, the Goddess's exhortation to her disciple continues normally in 6.4 (and that is why I believe that the verb might have been in the second person). And as the teaching in question is situated in the future (the first thesis in 8.1–50; the second from 8.51 onward), the verb, I believe, must be conjectured as being in the future tense. So my conjecture is "*you will begin,*" "*árxei*" in the middle voice (as is the case with all the examples we have already seen of *árkhomai* + *apo;* there are no examples of this formula in the active voice). This conjecture leads us to leave out the pronoun "*s'*." Since now the verb is in the second person, "*s'*" would have been an apocopate [shortened form] of "*sú*" ["you"], "you will begin," but the elision of "*u*" is highly unlikely. However, if we take into account the manuscript tradition of line 6.3, we find two codices offering the reading "*t'*" instead of "*s'*": manuscripts B and C. Another codex, G IV, gives us no term between *gár* and *aph'* (this was the model followed by the 1526 Aldine edition), which might mean that the copyist hesitated between "*s'*" and "*t'*" and preferred to suppress the pronoun. *I should say that I accept the pronoun* "**te**" ("**t'**")[526] *and I complete the hexameter with the verb* **árxei**: *"pró̱te̱s gár t'aph'hodoû dizé̱sios árxei."* So my version of the beginning of fragment 6 is as follows: "It is necessary to say and to think that by being, it is, since it is possible to be, and nothing[ness] does not exist. This I order to proclaim since you <will begin> with this first way of investigation, but then with that made by mortals who know nothing . . ." (6.1–4). We already know what is the foundation of the first way, that is, the thesis: "that which is being is, and nothing[ness] does not exist." In the next chapter we shall see what is the foundation of the negation of the thesis.

---

525 **Mourelatos** (1970), 77, note 7.

526 With regard to the construction *gár te,* cf. **Denniston**, *Greek Particles,* 529. Cf. also *Il.* 23.156, *Od.* 7.307, 12.105.

Chapter VII: The Negation of the Thesis, "Opinions," and the Nonexistent Third Way

After expounding his thesis once again in the first two lines of fragment 6, Parmenides presents the negative aspect of it (as he did before in fragment 2) still in fragment 6, from line 3 onward. But this time the negation of the thesis is accompanied by its foundation, that is, its "cause." This wrong way is not autonomous, proved on its own evidence, as the first one is (since, indeed, who can deny that there is being, that that which is being is?). This time we have an artificial way, invented by those who ignore the unbearable weight of the fact of being and therefore relativize it. Nevertheless, faithful to his program of study (in which the Goddess invited the future philosopher *also* to "inquire" about human opinions), Parmenides proposes studying this false way, in order to discover what its foundation is. Once the origin of the error has been grasped, only one way will remain as a real possibility, which will be discussed in the lengthy fragment 8. A hypothetical "third" way has no foundation whatsoever.

If my interpretation is correct, the passage that begins in line 6.4 represents the negation of the thesis that, as we saw, is expounded in the second way. A strong witness comes to my aid: Simplicius. Indeed, when this author cites lines 6.1b–9, he does so to give an example of the position of those who admit nothing besides (or "apart from," *pará*) being. W. Leszl, who has studied this Simplicius passage in minute detail, states the following: in the first place, Parmenides announces "the fundamental alternative [or separation], which constitutes the first way: 'being is, but nothing[ness] is not' (6.1b–2a). This is the alternative that mortals ignore when they set being and not-being side by side."[527] According to this same author, lines 4 ff. of fragment 6 illustrate this ignorance, and if Simplicius "quotes these lines it is to confirm in Parmenides the presence of *two* ways, and certainly not three."[528] F. Fronterotta arrives at the same conclusion, saying "in Simplicius' eyes, fragments 2 and 6 are not in contradiction, since Parmenides

---

527 **Leszl**, W., *Parmenide e l'Eleatismo.* Dispensa per il corso di Storia della Filosofia Antica, Università degli Studi di Pisa, Dipartimento di Filosofia (May 1994) 137–38.

528 **Leszl**, *Parmenide,*123.

indicates only two ways of investigation in each of them,"[529] so that the possibilities "in Simplicius' presentation are therefore certainly two and not three," since Reinhardt's hypothesis on the existence of a "third" way "is based exclusively on the opposition between fragments 2 and 6" and on Diels's conjecture for the gap in 6.3.[530]

So now let us see how Parmenides describes this second way.[531] The first words of line 4 of fragment 6 clearly show that the way that begins to be expounded here is different from the previous one, presented in 6.1–2: "*autàr épeita,*" "but then . . .". Nevertheless, in order to understand the true structure of this way, we must clarify certain things about the original text, which, once again, was subjected to certain abuses by interpreters. I say this because in line 6.5 there is a verb *pláttontai* ("make," "create") whose subject is "mortals." This enables us to state that, for Parmenides, the way is the product of human activity. This verb *pláttontai* occurs in *all* the manuscripts of Simplicius, the only source of fragment 6. Failing to take into account this unanimity, the editor of the 1526 Aldine edition replaced this verb with *plázontai* ("stray," "miss," "wander"). Nothing justifies this change.

Nevertheless, this conjecture was adopted and even created a rule, since in the rigorous Liddell, Scott, and Jones *Lexicon* we read that when Parmenides writes *pláttontai* he is merely using an unprecedented form of the middle voice of *plázo̱*. H. Diels, who supports this change, offers similar examples in the dialect of Tarento.[532] This argument is more than weak. D. Sider states ironically that regarding Parmenides as an Italian poet is like believing that Joyce was also an Italian novelist.[533] A. Capizzi demonstrated that perhaps in the dialect of Tarento one might be able to find *plázo̱* instead of *plásso̱* (which, according to Diels, would have been the verb used by Parmenides), but what needs demonstrating is the reverse: why does Parmenides use *plásso̱* instead of *plázo̱*,[534] if he really wanted to refer to "straying"? Those who support the reading "*plázontai*" recognize that Parmenides could have written "*plássontai*" in his usual Ionian, and that later "a Byzantine copyist, used to the Attic of Simplicius, transformed it into *pláttontai.*"[535] This hypothesis could be accepted, but it is difficult to take the final step,

529 **Fronterotta**, F., "Essere, tempo e pensiero: Parmenide et l''origine dell'ontologia,'" *Annali della Scuola Normale Superiore di Pisa,* Classe di Lettere e Filosofia, Serie II, 24 (1994) 845.

530 **Fronterotta**, "Essere, tempo," 389 and 845, note 27.

531 I repeat once more that as in fragment 2 there were only two ways to think, and as at the beginning of fragment 6 Parmenides expounds the first of these ways, the way that will be described after that has to be the second way.

532 **Diels** (1897), 73.

533 **Sider**, D., "Textual Notes on Parmenides' Poem," *Hermes* 113 (1985) 364.

534 **Capizzi**, A., *La porta di Parmenide* (Rome: Edizioni dell'Ateneo, 1975), 75.

535 Cf. **Diels** (1897), 72.

which is the assimilation of "*plásso̲/plátto̲*" and "*plázo̲.*"[536] When Parmenides uses the notion of *pláttontai,* he uses it with its normal, banal meaning of "make," "create,"[537] and in the slightly subjective sense of "make for yourself," "imagine."[538] If we take into account that the creation of this false way is the work of mortals, that it consists of a series of words "established" by them, we find a very suggestive echo in a passage in the *Laws,* where Plato says that the legislator must begin by "creating with speech" (*plásasthai tô̲i logô̲i,* 800b7). This interpretation of the verb enables us, finally, to find a justification for the relative "*hê̲n*" (6.4), which is generally translated in an arbitrary way as "in (or 'by') which," as if it were a locative.[539] The Goddess simply says that this is a way *that* (*hè̲n*) mortals make, and that they "believe" is right.[540]

This impossible way is referred to by the pronoun "*tê̲s*" ("that") (6.4), but the text does not give a complete formulation of it. This proves that this way is not new: *it has already been presented,* in particular, in line 5 of fragment 2. It is the wrong way, the negation of the thesis. In fragment 6 the Goddess expands on it, explains who made it and who its hypothetical "users" are (hypothetical, since the way is untravelable). The reason is this: this way was made by mortal human beings who know nothing, or, if you prefer, who know "nothing[ness]": *brotoì eidótes oudén* (6.4). This formula, which is a real "stereotype in ancient lyric poetry"[541] is the polar opposite, in Parmenides, to the formula "*eidóta fô̲ta,*" "the man who knows," which characterizes the Goddess's disciple in fragment 1.3. If this is so, whereas mortals who know nothing are condemned to make themselves a way that leads nowhere, the philosopher, who is a "mortal who knows," sets out along the "way of the Goddess, full of signs" ("*hodòs polúphemos daímonos,*" 1.2–3), a way that lies "far distant from the path of men" ("*ap'anthro̲pô̲n ektòs pátou éstin,*" 1.27).[542]

---

536 Ballew notes that no important philologist has related *plázo̲* to *plátto̲/plásso̲* (**Ballew**, L., "Straight and Circular in Parmenides and the *Timaeus,*" *Phronesis* 19 [1974] 193).

537 Cf. **Hesiod**, *Works* 70; **Lysias**, 19.60.

538 **Ballew**, "Straight and Circular," 193.

539 Cf. Conche: "*upon which* mortals stray" (**Conche** [1996], 100); and Wiesner, "auf welchem . . . Sterbliche irren" (**Wiesner** [1996], 252).

540 For the mortals of Parmenides, the world they "believe" is real has the same value as the account given by **Critias** of Atlantis: "it is not a myth created [*plasthénta,* participle of *plátto̲*], but a true report" (*Timaeus,* 26e).

541 **Mansfeld** (1964), 4. This scholar picks up the subtle analysis of **Pfeiffer,** R., "Gottheit und Individuum," in *Ausgewählte Schriften* (Munich: Beck, 1960).

542 Parmenides is thinking of ordinary men who have not decided to set out on a way in search of truth. It remains to be said that in the Poem, the word *brotoí* ("mortals") is synonymos with *anthrópoi* ("men"). Cf. 8.38–39: "*ónoma . . . brotoì katéthento*" ("names . . . that mortals assigned") and 19.3, "*ónom'anthrópoi katéthento*" ("names that men assigned"). *Contra,* cf. **Coxon,** A. H., "The Philosophy of Parmenides," *Classical Quarterly* 28

Here we find a new confirmation of the erroneous character of the way described in passage 6.4–7 that continues in 7.1–5: on this way the *nóos* ("intellect") of mortals is driven, as if traveling in a chariot,[543] but the driver is "incapacity" (*amekhaníe̱*, 6.5). Deprived of their infallible guides—the Daughters of the Sun, the wise horses, and, especially, the Goddess—men are now "carried" (*phoroûntai*)[544] along a way made by an intellect that has lost its object (which is, as we saw in our analysis of 8.34–35, the fact of being, the single possible thinkable "object"), and so this intellect lacks the necessary resources to arrive at its goal. "Incapacity"[545] is the *moîra kaké̱* ("evil fate") which plays the same role on the way of error as Themis and Dike played on the way of truth (cf. 1.26–28). As Vlastos says,[546] this *amekhaníe̱* is the natural state of humanity before divinity (Prometheus, in his example) brought help (skills) to it: men were blind and deaf.[547] These same defects belong to the mortals in fragment 6 (*ko̱phoì homô̱s tuphloí te*, "deaf and blind"), whereas the formula by which Aeschylus sums up this state of affairs ("everything happened to them at random, confusedly," *Prom. vinc.* 450) reappears in Parmenides with the term *tethé̱potes* ("amazed"), a true résumé of the situation. Mortals, lacking the Goddess's teaching, are swept along, deaf and blind, like automata:[548] they do not know where to head for, since, unlike the "mortal who knows," as Coxon[549] observes, these people do not know what road they are on, which is not extraordinary, seeing that this way is *panapeuthéa* ("completely unknown") (2.6) or, as P. Destrée proposes, they shuffle on drunkenly, with faltering steps, "backwards and forwards, forwards and backwards," as the term "*palíntropos*"[550]

(1934) 134; and **Bormann** (1971), 101, which establish a difference between the *brotoí* of fragment 6 and those of the rest of the Poem. Further on I will offer my interpretation of the identity of these "mortal men."

543 "Drive" is *ithúno̱*, the verb used for driving chariots and riding horses: cf. **Homer** *Il.* 11.528, 16.475, and **Hesiod**, *Shield*, 324.

544 The allusion to the images in fragment 1 is clear: this verb echoes a *phérousin* (1.1, 1.25), *phérei* (1.3), *pherómen* and *phéron* (1.3), applied in the passage to the traveler who goes in search of the Goddess and who is "carried."

545 The term *amekhaníe̱* alludes to the impossibility, because of the lack of the necessary *resources*, to carry out any kind of task. Cf. **Empedocles**, fragment 12.1: *amé̱khanos* = *adúnatos* ("incapable = impossible"). For Mansfeld, *amekhaníe̱* = Machtlosigkeit (**Mansfeld** [1964], 11 ff.). Snell relates the term with action (*drân*, "do"), on the basis of **Aeschylus**, *mekhané̱ drastérios* ("way of doing") (**Snell**, B., "Aischylos und das Handeln in Drama," *Philologus,* Supp. 20, I (1928) 14).

546 **Vlastos**, G., "Equality and Justice in Early Greek Cosmologies," *Classical Philology* 42 (1947), 163.

547 Cf. **Aeschylus**, *Prom. vinc.* 447–48: "In the beginning, they had eyes, but their eyes did not show them anything useful; they had ears, but they did not hear."

548 Cf. similar images in **Homer**, *Il.* 4.262, 21.64, and especially *Od.* 23.15.

549 **Coxon**, "The Philosophy of Parmenides," 131, note 1.

550 **Destrée**, P., "La communauté de l'être (Parménide, fr. B 5)," *Revue de philosophie ancienne* 18(1) (2000) 12.

indicates. There can be no doubt that this human way is the negation of the thesis, that is, the wrong way of fragment 2, and for that reason the Goddess exhorts the disciple to withdraw thought from it in 7.2. It is true that men usually move forward blindly, but Parmenides writes his Poem to show them the way to go, so that long habit, their usual guide,[551] does not force them to use eyes that cannot see what they ought to see (and therefore are as if blind), ears that do not hear what they ought to hear (and therefore are as if deaf), and a tongue[552] that only utters deceitful words (7.3–5; 8.52).[553]

(a) The Senses and the Wandering Intellect Do Not Distinguish Between Being and Not-being

This critique of the senses[554] gathers the last six lines of fragment 6 and all of fragment 7 into a homogeneous whole. By means of an argument we have already come across in fragment 2 (and which M. Untersteiner, with respect to fr. 1, calls "composizione ad anello"[555]), the whole of this passage begins and ends with a critique not only of sense experience but also of the "wandering intellect." This coupling should not surprise us: the boundary separating thought and sensation in the Presocratics is vague. Even in Xenophanes, scholars do not agree about the translation of *noeî* in fragment 24, whose subject is divinity; as the verb is accompanied by "see" and by "hear," to translate it as "think," as do the vast majority of interpreters, is perhaps excessive. In *Il.* 15.422, Hector "saw" (*enóe̱sen,* from the verb *noeîn*) "his cousin with his eyes," and in *Il.* 24.294, Hecuba says to Priam that soon "you will see [*noé̱sas*] the portent with your eyes." If we take into account

551 According to Becker, here Parmenides is contrasting a usual way with a way being traveled for the first time (**Becker**, O., "Das Bild des Weges und verwandte Vorstellungen im frühgriechischen Denken," *Hermes* Einzelschriften 4 [1937] 142, note 13).

552 Cf. **Bacchylides**, 10.51.

553 For Aubenque, in this passage there is an allusion to the "bavardage vide, la glossolalie," in strong contrast to the true speech of the Goddess (**Aubenque**, P., "Syntaxe et sémantique de l'être dans le Poème de Parménide," in *Études sur Parménide,* Vol. II, ed. Aubenque, P. [Paris: Vrin, 1987], 119). Cf. also **Mansfeld**, J., "Parménide et Héraclite avaient-ils une théorie de la perception?" *Phronesis* 44 (1999) 331. Hölscher, on the basis of **Empedocles**, fragment 3.11, proposes another interpretation and says that here the tongue represents the sense of taste (Geschmack) (**Hölscher**, U., *Anfängliche Fragen* [Göttingen: Vandenhoeck & Ruprecht, 1968], 52. *Contra,* cf. Patin, for whom "using the tongue" here means *onomázein* ("naming") (**Patin** [1899], 633). Cf. also **Verdenius** (1942), 55, note 7; and **Mansfeld** (1964), 43.

554 Vlastos speaks of "insensible senses" (**Vlastos**, G., "Parmenides' Theory of Knowledge," *Transactions and Proceedings of the American Philological Association* 77 [1946] 69).

555 **Untersteiner** (1958), lxxix.

that in an indirect version of Xenophanes' text, transmitted by Diogenes Laertius, the verb "*noeî*" was replaced by "*anapneî*" ("breathe"), perhaps a translation such as "observe" would fit fragment 24. Aristotle had already said that for the "ancient" philosophers, thinking (*tò noeîn*) was "like sensation, something bodily" (*De anima* 426a26), and J. Mansfeld recently defended the idea according to which "the pre-Platonic philosophers did not make a distinction between sensation and thought,"[556] since both factors are the cause, in Parmenides, of the wrong way habitually followed by mortals, that is, the adoption of a method of investigation that denies the fundamental thesis and therefore leads nowhere. *This wrong way is, without any doubt, the second way expounded in fragment 2, a way considered* ***a priori*** *as a way of investigation* (let us not forget that in line 2.2 the Goddess says that she will present the **only** ways of investigation, and then goes on to present just two) *and which subsequently shows itself to be completely impracticable.* The critique in line 7.2 refers to this way.

The formula in line 7.1, *eînai mḛ eónta* ("there are things that are not"), is a summary of the last two lines of fragment 6 (6.8–9): mortals' way of thinking based on the senses, allowing itself to be guided by a wandering intellect, leads them to suppose that *there are things that are not.* This way of thinking must never prevail ("*ou mḛ́pote toûto damḛ̂i*") (7.1a). But if men think like that it is because they are *díkranoi* ("two-headed") (6.5). The time has come to consider this fundamental characteristic of the "human condition," as Parmenides conceives it. Men have two heads: "with one they look at being and with the other at non-being."[557] This *conjunction* is the key to the error of mortals. They are incapable of accepting the principle of noncontradiction and the excluded middle, which requires a "decision": either the one or the other. As they do not know what being is, and therefore, the extent to which it is impossible not to be, they confuse the one with the other, as if it were possible to say that there are things that are not. Remember that the way of error consisted in a combination of contrary notions. This combination emerges clearly from lines 8 and 9 of fragment 6, which describe the content of the wrong way as seen by its "user." So we should not think that these lines present a precise formula, proposed by the Goddess, as was the case in 2.3 and 2.5. The passage shows how men "conceive" (*nenómistai*) the only possible "objects" of all thought: being and non-

---

556 **Mansfeld**, J., "Aristote et la structure du *De sensibus* de Théophraste," *Phronesis* 41 (1996) 158 ff., and "Parménide et Héraclite," 331.

557 The expression belongs to Loew (**Loew**, E., "Ein Beitrag zum heraklitisch-parmenideischen Enkenntnisproblem," *Archiv für Geschichte der Philosophie* 31 [1917] 45). We should not make the mistake of believing that the expression *díkranoi* refers to "double-thinking." In Parmenides' time you did not think with your head but with your breast. The head is the receptacle for the principal senses: sight, hearing, smell, taste.

being, existence and nonexistence.[558] By mortals, the text says, "*tò pélein te kaì ouk eînai*" ("being and not-being") are *considered* "*tautòn kou tautòn*" ("the same and not the same"). By means of the verb *nomízo* ("consider") related to *nómos* ("custom," "habit," among other things), Parmenides stresses the "habitual" character of this human opinion that is based on a "wandering intellect" (*plagktòs nóos*).[559] It is "long habit" (*éthos polúpeiron*) (7.3) that leads men to create (*pláttontai*) (6.5) a method that mixes up being and not-being, and therefore, to state that they are both the same and different at once.

The expression we find in 6.8–9 simply means that mortals *attribute being to non-being and non-being to being*. To put it another way, they confuse (mix up, combine, advocate) that which is and that which is not. The verb that Simplicius uses to refer to this operation is "*sunphérein*" ("bring together"), and he says that this operation takes place "in thought" (*Phys.* 78.2). It is interesting to note that when Plato refers to the predication or attribution of being to non-being and vice versa, that is, when he quotes line 7.1 of Parmenides in order to refute it, he also uses a series of verbs synonymous with *sunphérein,* which all refer to language: *prosgígnesthai* (*Soph.* 238a4, 6), *prosarmotteîn* (238c), and *prosáptein* (239b). Finally, when he searches for an epithet to describe those who say that "*tò mē̱ ón, eînai po̱s*" ("that which is not, in a certain way is")—namely, the way that for Parmenides is the way of error, but which Plato wishes to defend—he uses the term "*poluképhalos*" ("many-headed") (240c).

For all these reasons, I do not share the opinions of researchers who see in 6.8–9 a simultaneous allusion to the two ways of investigation stated in fragment 2 (a conjunction that would amount to a "third way"). This hypothesis ignores the fact that the formula "*tautòn kou tautòn*" ("the same **and** not the same") must be taken as a whole. The point of this phrase is to stress the confusion between two elements, the failure to differentiate between them by not knowing whether they are the same or not the same. A parallel example can be found in a treatise by Hippocrates: "*pánta tautà kaí ou tautá*" ("it is all the same and not the same"); "*pháos Ze̱ní, skótos Aide̱i*"

---

558 Like most scholars, I consider that "*tò pélein*" (6.8) is synonymous with "*eînai.*" *Contra,* Somigliana considers that *tò pélein* is a verb of movement meaning "to turn," which produces this curious translation of the passage: "That which turns and non-being are the same and not the same" (**Somigliana**, A., "I versi 4 ss. del fr. B 6 di Parmenide e la supposta polemica antieraclitea," *Rivista di filosofia neoscolastica* 67 [1975] 333). However, the author does not tell us how the second part of the statement (sc., "that which turns and non-being [. . .] are not the same") could be false, given that Parmenides expressly says that *tò eón* is immobile (8.26), i.e., "it does not turn." The use of *pélein* in 8.11 and in 8.19 as an obvious synonym of *eînai* refutes Somigliana's hypothesis.

559 Instead of *nóos,* Simplicius codex E proposes *nómos,* and a reviser of codex P also added *nómos* beside *nóos.* This is probably an erroneous reading, but the closeness of *nomízo̱* might be an invitation to reflect on the question.

("light, for Zeus; darkness, for Hades"); "*pháos Aídẹi, skótos Zẹní*" ("light, for Hades; darkness, for Zeus") (*De victu* I.5). This phrase does not contain a statement corresponding to *tautá* ("the same") and another to *ou tautá* ("not the same"), one of which is true and the other false; there is a mixture of four statements, in which the same notions are attributed to two different gods, from which it can be deduced that those who express themselves thus do not know what light or darkness is or to which god they correspond.[560]

From what I have said, the following conclusion can be drawn: lines 6.8–9 do not present a new way of investigation because, among other reasons, to propose a new way after having proclaimed that there are only two possibilities would be equivalent to saying that Parmenides is not keeping to his plan, fundamentally because, given the message the Goddess transmits to her disciple, *everything* can be summed up in one essential alternative. The main fault that this passage seeks to highlight is the admission of a conjunction. Neither of these two requirements are present when there are three possibilities: *either one* **or** *the other,* or *one* **and** *the other.* To maintain that both that which is and that which is not exist is equivalent to maintaining that that which is, both is and is not at once. As I said *supra,* Parmenides' bitterest enemy, Gorgias, grasped the meaning of the way of error with great subtlety. Indeed, when the Sophist claims to "demonstrate"—in order to go on to refute it—that "that which is not, exists," he states: "If that which is not, is [viz., the negation of the thesis, corresponding to the second way, according to my interpretation], then it will be and *at the same time* it will not be; since, to the extent that it is thought of as non-existent, it does not exist; but to the extent that it *is* something that is not, it will be" (fr. 3, § 67).[561] As S. Karsten says, "those who state that non-being is, deny being and, at the same time affirm it."[562] Furthermore, when we examined the content of the second way, we said then that as this consists of the affirmation of a negation and of the negation of an affirmation, we found in it a mixture of being and not-being in which each notion was attributed to its contrary. Here in 6.8–9, we find an attribution (which according to the parameters of Parmenides' thesis must be established in analogous terms) made with regard to contradictory terms. But, fundamentally, we find (1) *the negation of the principle of non-contradiction* and (2) *the postulation of difference.*

We must remember that the principle of non-contradiction was the foundation of the way of truth. To state now that that which is *and* that

560 The same happens with Heraclitus' statement "*eîmén te kaí ouk eîmen*" ("we are and we are not") (fr. 49a). This is not an alternative but a conjunction.

561 Wiesner, who supports finding a "third way," interprets this passage of Gorgias in a radically different way (**Wiesner** [1996], 101).

562 **Karsten** (1835), 152.

which is not are the same *and* not the same assumes that two contradictory judgments are possible at the same time. And this is so because mortals do not respect this principle and believe that being and that which is not are different; that is why they have established (8.39) different names to talk about them. But as they have been unable to choose, they allow contradictory names *simultaneously: eînai* ***te kaí*** *oukhí* ("being **and** not-being") (8.40). Men belong to the *ákrita fûla* (6.7) that is incapable of "separating" (etymologically "deciding" or, as G. Germani didactically translates, "disgiungere")[563] one thing from another, and therefore they construct a theory of reality founded upon the simultaneous presence of contraries. For them, those contraries "necessarily" (*khreó̱n*) (8.54) constitute two forms, instead of one, according to which "everything is full of light and dark night *at the same time*" (9.3). They forget that the only possibility, namely, that which respects the principle of non-contradiction, is an *alternative: pelénai è̱ oukhí* ("being or not [being]") (8.11), a *separation: éstin è̱ ouk éstin* ("being or not being") (8.16). That is why, although they assume that being and not being are different,[564] we may deduce from what they say that they act as if there were no difference between them, and assume that that which is not, is, and that which is, is not.[565]

Finally, we may note that Plato comes to my aid to confirm what I am saying. Indeed, if Parmenides had already admitted a way in which being

563 **Germani**, G., "Per un'interpretazione delle vie parmenidee," *Annali del Dipartimento di Filosofia, Università di Firenze,* Vol. II (1986) 23.

564 According to Jantzen, "mortals do not maintain the existence of being and non-being, but in their statements the categories of being and not being approach one another and, consequently, their statements are false" (**Jantzen**, J., *Parmenides zum Verhältnis von Sprache und Wirklichkeit,* Zetemata 63 [Munich: Beck, 1976], 110).

565 The version of 6.8–9 proposed by Reinhardt, which consists of putting a comma after *eînai* (**Reinhardt** [1916], 87), might give rise to an interesting interpretation of the text, but not in the sense the author imagines. According to this scholar, "*tautón kou tautón*" are not the predicates of the two infinitives, but two terms related to the first group, "*tò pélein te kaí ouk eînai.*" It is difficult to grasp the meaning of this version, since Reinhardt does not offer a translation of it. Nevertheless, given the value he ascribes to "*nomízein*" ("Etwas sich zu seinem Nomos machen"), I believe that Cornford comes fairly close to his thinking when, following the same syntax as Reinhardt, he translates: "Who have determined to believe that it is and that it is not, the same and not the same" (**Cornford** [1939], 32). For his part, Beaufret, who says he is adopting Reinhardt's version, proposes this text: ". . . pour qui l'être et aussi bien le non-être, le même et ce qui n'est pas le même, font loi" (**Beaufret**, J., and **Riniéri**, J. J., *Le Poème de Parménide* [Paris: Presses Universitaires de France, 1955], 81). Later, his translation changes: ". . . dont le lot est de dire aussi bien être que n'être pas, être même et ne l'être pas" (**Beaufret**, J., *Parménide, Le Poème,* 1982 [Paris: M. Chandeigne, 1986] 13). We said that the syntax proposed by Reinhardt could give rise, despite himself, to an interesting reading of the text, since if the formula "*tautón kou tautón*" were independent, it could become an explanation of the previous clause, depending on a possible "*hoîs esti*" (with *esti* understood): "for whom (*hoîs*) [there is] both being and non-being; they conceive (*nenómistai*) both the same and the different (*tautón kou tautón*)."

and not-being combine and, in some way, being is not and non-being is, why did Plato decide to write the *Sophist* to *refute* Parmenides and maintain, polemically, that "a certain union exists between being and non-being" (240b–c), and that "it is necessary to force non-being, in certain conditions, to be and being, in its turn and according to a certain modality, not to be"? (241d). If the mortals of Parmenides had admitted the simultaneous reality of that which is and that which is not, *difference* and *otherness,* whose discovery is the basis of the *Sophist,* would have preceded Plato by almost a century.

(b) Lógos *as the Criterion by Which to Judge the Critique of the Way Made by Men*

Fragment 7 ends in a rather unusual way: the Goddess addresses her disciple and exhorts him to judge by means of *lógos* what she has just said: "*krînai dé lógoi polúderin élegkhon ex eméthen rhethénta.*" This request definitively refutes any interpretation that claims to find a sort of "revelation" in the Poem. For D. Furley, "these lines are the most astonishing in the Poem."[566] There can be no doubt that Parmenides' Goddess is an extraordinary character. Traditional divinities require reverent acceptance of everything they say; they do not ask for their speech to be "judged," much less that this judgment should be carried out by means of a *lógos* (I shall come back to this term). Parmenides' Goddess is a professor of philosophy[567] who asks the student to *analyze* her speech. Why does she want this? The text gives us the answer: what the Goddess has just expounded (*rhethénta*) is really a proof (*élegkhos*) against something that was held to be certain, something habitual, and therefore the speech that contains this proof has a polemical (*polúderin*) aspect. As Verdenius observes, the participle *rhethénta* (perfect aorist) indicates unequivocally that the Goddess is alluding to something *already expounded.*[568] This "already expounded" something is an *élegkhos.*[569]

As we know, this term originally had the meaning "object of shame," even "derision,"[570] but already in Parmenides' time it was beginning to refer

566 **Furley**, D., "Truth as What Survives the *élenchos*" (1987), reprinted in *Cosmic Problems* (Cambridge, England: Cambridge University Press, 1989), 38.

567 Cf. **Cordero**, N. L., "La déesse de Parménide, maîtresse de philosophie," in *La naissance de la raison en Grèce,* ed. Mattéi, J. F. (Paris: P.U.F., 1990).

568 **Verdenius** (1942), 64. Cf. also **Tarán** (1965), 81; **Mourelatos** (1970), 91, note 46.

569 An exhaustive analysis of this notion can be found in **Furley**, "Truth as What Survives."

570 Cf. Homer *Il.* 23.342: "If you destroy your chariot, you will cover yourself with shame," says Nestor to his son.

to a combination of arguments used, generally, to accuse (and, in Plato's time, the meaning of "refutation" will become predominant). In fact, *élegkhos* is a collective term, a singular with plural value, since it combines a series of elements, but these have to be very precise: data, proofs, and arguments. These elements can be used not only to refute, as will happen later on with Socrates, but also to demonstrate, prove, or justify something, especially in the legal sphere, where it is practically synonymous with "proof" (of a crime, for example). An accusation is a series of confirmed facts or data, and this combination adds up to an *élegkhos.* As M. Dixsaut subtly observes, this *élegkhos* is "the proof that [Parmenides] has adduced, if we may so put it, against the 'false witnesses' of custom, the senses and language."[571] This is the meaning of the term in Parmenides.[572]

These proofs must be "judged." The Goddess uses the imperative "*krînai.*" This verb (infinitive: *krínnai*) means "discern," "separate," "decide," and like *élegkhos,* is often found in the legal sphere with the meaning "interpret the proofs," or, directly, "judge."[573] Parmenides uses forms of this verb on three occasions and the related noun *krísis* once. In line 15 of fragment 8, the term *krísis* is used to make a sort of assessment after having presented a long series of *proofs* of the thesis according to which that which is being, is. This is the thesis that constitutes the true way: "the *krísis* ('decision,' 'judgment') on these things lies in this: it is or it is not." And in the following line, Parmenides says that, in fact, the question has already been "decided": "*kékritai* [verb '*krínnai,*' 'it has already been decided'] of necessity that one exists . . ." Finally, the verb *krínnai* is used once more in 8.55, this time in relation to the world of opinions, in which men "decided [*ekkrínanto*] the existence of separate forms." Before I give my view on the meaning of "*krínnai*" here in fragment 7.5, let us look at why the Poem is full of references to the sphere of law.

We saw in the first chapters of this work that Parmenides is a philosopher who tries to "demonstrate" his statements and that, therefore, he holds that thought must follow a "way," that is, "a method." This method leads to knowledge, but even in the first fragment the sphere of knowledge is presented as a "home" (*dṓ,* 1.25) whose gates are guarded by Dike, symbol of justice, "prodigal in punishments" (1.14). The way of the Goddess abounds in "signs," "messages" (it is *polúphēmos,* "rich in news"),[574] and

---

571 **Dixsaut**, M., "Platon et le *lógos* de Parménide," in *Études sur Parménide,* Vol. II, ed. Aubenque, P. (Paris: Vrin, 1987), 243.

572 Cf., *contra,* Furley, for whom the term means "refutation" (**Furley**, "Truth as What Survives").

573 Remember that "judge" in Greek is "*kritḗs*" and that one of the terms for "court" is "*kritḗrion.*"

574 **Leszl**, *Parmenide,* 146.

when the moment comes to "demonstrate" the foundation of the thesis, Parmenides offers a series of "proofs," "*sḗmata,*" in fragment 8. In fragment 8 we find proof or evidence of the absolute, total, and unique character of the fact of being. In the group made up of fragments 6 and 7, this combination of proofs goes to show that the opinions of mortals are based on sensations and a wandering intellect that strays from its objective. Here we have an *élegkhos,* and this must be "judged" by means of "*lógos,*" as if it were on trial. So what is the role of *lógos* at this trial?

(c) The Meaning of **lógos** *in Parmenides*

Given that Parmenides criticizes a way that is based on the senses, the temptation exists to translate "*lógos*" as "reason" and to see the alternative "feeling vs. intellect" in the text. However, we must not fall into this temptation. A detailed study of the term "*lógos*" from Homer onward shows that in all its uses there are allusions to a certain "reasoning" (either in the criterion that must be applied to "combine" separated elements to form a "col*lec*tion," a term that keeps the root "*leg-* [= *lec-*]"; or to speak: *legein,* in a combination of words; or to argue, etc.), but it is practically impossible to know at what moment the meaning of "reason" arose as the dominant meaning of the term "*lógos.*" With regard to Parmenides, although Guthrie exclaims enthusiastically that in 7.1 "for the first time, the senses and reason are contrasted" and that "reason alone is to be trusted,"[575] I am inclined toward Verdenius's interpretation, according to which "*lógos* never meant reason [Vernunft] in the Presocratics."[576] As in the vast majority of Greek authors writing before Stoicism, the term *lógos* in Parmenides fundamentally has the meaning of "speech." However, there are various kinds of speech, and perhaps Parmenides' originality lies in his attempt to establish a hierarchy among them.

The term appears on three occasions in the passages of the Poem that have come down to us, and I do not think I am exaggerating if I say that, as with Hesiod, the notion acquires a different meaning if it is used in the singular or the plural. In the plural, as was already the case with Homer[577] (and Hesiod does the same),[578] *lógos* refers to a speech (that is, a combination of words) that may be superficial or directly false (as is the case in

575 **Guthrie** (1965), 25.

576 **Verdenius**, W. J., "Der Logosbegriff bei Heraklit und Parmenides," *Phronesis* 12 (1967) 100.

577 Cf. Homer, *Il.* 15.393: "consoled him with *words . . .*"; *Od.*1.55: "lulled him with caressing *words.*"

578 Cf. Hesiod, *Theogony* 890 and *Works* 789: "caressing *words*"; *Works* 78: "deceiving *words.*"

Hesiod).[579] For example, in the first fragment of Parmenides, the Daughters of the Sun convince Dike with "gentle words [*lógoi*]" (1.15) to open the heaven gates of the Goddess's realm. On the other hand, when the word is used in the singular, it refers to a speech, but to a very special speech. As we said, Parmenides follows—perhaps without knowing he does—the example of Hesiod, who uses *lógos* to refer to an "account," which is presumed to be true, since it describes the history of humanity.[580] Indeed, in fragment 8, after expounding the "proofs" or "evidence" that confirm the true thesis, Parmenides says: "Here I end for you the trustworthy *lógos* and thought about the truth" (8.50–51). Once again we have a speech, but the speech reproduces a thought (which is, in its turn, a reasoning, i.e., a series of arguments) and it concerns something true: so it is to be presumed that this *lógos* is also true.

What happens in our fragment 7? The term is found in the singular, and in the dative. Once we have set aside the meaning "reason" (there is no need to say "judge *by means of* reason, that is, "rationally"), I do not share the opinion of Verdenius, who gives the dative the value of a modal dative: "judge by arguing" (since, according to him, *lógos* has the meaning "argument," "debate").[581] I believe that as in fragment 2 onward, the Goddess has presented an argumentative speech (and will continue to do so in fragment 8, where the term *lógos* will reappear); the moment has come to tell the disciple to judge—by means of (instrumental dative) [this] speech (*lógos*)—the polemical[582] proof against the foundation of opinions that she has just expounded. The alternative "sensation vs. reason" does not make sense, because Parmenides also criticizes the activity of the intellect when it wanders astray. Of course, the senses must be set aside (since they only apprehend apparent changes and do not grasp the profound reality of the fact of being), but an intellect (*nóos*) must also be rejected that ultimately only depends on the "mixture of limbs" ("*krásis meléo̱n*") (fr. 16) of mortals.[583] And as for the faculty of judging, even though it acts positively in fragment 8 (where it eliminates the second way and only keeps the first) it can also make mistakes and judge (*ekrínanto,* 8.55) that there are opposite forms. The Goddess asks the listener to judge by means of (or "in accordance with") true reasoning the value of the way made by men who know

579 Cf. Hesiod, *Theogony* 226: "lying words."

580 Cf. Hesiod, *Works* 107: "I will end my *account* (*lógon*) by another . . ."; this is an account of the "ages" of humanity, which claims to be relating real facts.

581 **Verdenius**, "Logosbegriff," 99.

582 "Polemical" (*polúde̱rin*) has an active meaning. Cf. **Mourelatos** (1970), 91, note 46.

583 According to von Fritz, the intellect wanders in search of *eón* (**Fritz**, K. von, "*Noûs, noeîn* and Its Derivatives in Presocratic Philosophy [Excluding Anaxagoras], I, From the Beginnings to Parmenides," *Classical Philology* 40 [1945] 239).

nothing. The sentence following the judgment will be proclaimed in fragment 8: "it has already been decided" that the wrong way should be abandoned.

(d) The Hypothetical "Third Way"

According to my interpretation, in the combined passages 6.4–9 and 7.1–5, I find a new presentation of the second way, now completed with the viewpoint of its "makers" and its "users." This way is clearly formulated in 7.1 (*eînai mḕ eónta*), and 7.2 says it is to be rejected. Nevertheless, the vast majority of scholars *today* find in this passage the presentation of a "third way of investigation." I stress the word *today* because for twenty-one centuries nobody ever found three ways, routes, or paths in Parmenides' thought. The strong disjunctions between day (or light) and night in the Proem, between the only two ways proposed in fragment 2, and between Truth and Opinion, which form part of *all* that is to be known, were always elements that excluded any compromise *a priori.* In the philosophy of the inventor of the principle of identity and non-contradiction, there is no third possibility (= *tertium non datur*).

So let us see how people came to speak of a third way of investigation in Parmenides. First of all, we may say that today this third way is *vox populi:* indeed, 99 percent of works on Parmenides speak of a third way. According to my interpretation, for this to be possible, first it is necessary to relativize or distort the text of the Poem. When the text is distorted, this automatically nullifies the interpretation. This is the case with scholars who say that when Parmenides presents ways of investigation, only two of them are thinkable, but there may well be others that are unthinkable. This viewpoint distorts the text of fragment 2.2, in which Parmenides wrote "*noễsai*" ("to think": final infinitive with instrumental value) and not "*noẹtaí*" ("thinkable": passive participle). Moreover, if the latter were right, how could Parmenides have presented ways characterized by "unthinkability"? One of the only two ways, once examined, will be shown to be "unthinkable," but *a posteriori* (fr. 8.17), and rigorously speaking, it could also be called "unthought." And then, if one of the ways turns out to be "unthinkable" (which is authentically Parmenidean), how could it be differentiated from other ways that were also "unthinkable"?

There remains the case of those who have relativized Parmenides' words. For these interpreters it would be possible to admit other ways, but these would not be "ways *of investigation.*" For example, L. Couloubaritsis shows no doubt in saying that in the presentation of the ways there is "a mythical way of speaking" on Parmenides' part, and that it is necessary to distinguish between the way and what is dealt with on it.[584] Nevertheless, we can reply to this that the whole of fragment 8 is the fullest possible exposition of the intrinsic value (dramatized by Parmenides, since his contemporaries do not appear to grasp it) of the single term "*éstin*," which is, at the same time, the single word (*múthos*) that remains of the way ("there remains one single word of the way: 'is,'" fr. 8.1–2). And the *sḗmata* that follow are proofs of the word ("*éstin*") and are *on* the way.

Despite what is usually believed,[585] K. Reinhardt was not the first to find three possibilities in Parmenides. It was H. Stein, although his three possibilities do not agree with the classical "three ways" that were to be systematized definitively by Reinhardt. Stein recognizes that there is a way expounded in 6.1–2, another from 6.4 onward, and finally, another from 8.1 on.[586] This position, difficult enough in itself to maintain (indeed, what difference could there be between the way presented in 6.1–2 and that expounded in fr. 8?), becomes even more obscure because of Stein's very personal restructuring of the original text of Parmenides, leaving it unrecognizable.

On the other hand, K. Reinhardt scientifically systematized three possibilities, which he presents in two different ways, but whose content is the same: (a) being is, (b) being is not, (c) being is and is not; or (A) being is, (B) non-being is, (C) both being and non-being are.[587] It is impossible to know the reasons that led Reinhardt to construct this tripartite scheme (although, as we shall see, there are *material* elements in the Poem that might justify this process). Once the scheme has been proposed, the three ways have to be located. There can be no doubt that the first two, (a) and (b), as well as (A) and (B) are the two "classical" ways, the ones in fragment 2. As for (c) and (C), there only remains a part of fragment 6, from line 4 onward to try to place them. This then would be the way of mortals (or of Heraclitus, as some have interpreted it) who mix being and not being.

The great majority of cases then go on to say that this way reappears from line 51 of fragment 8, since this, they hold, is about the way of *dóxa*, a description of appearances, and presents a "probable" (fr. 8.60)[588] speech about them. In this assimilation, M. Heidegger, a disciple of Reinhardt,

---

584 **Couloubaritsis** (1990), 182.

585 Cf., for example, **Kahn**, C. H., review of Tarán, *Gnomon* 20 (1968) 126; and **Couloubaritsis**, L., "Les multiples chemins de Parménide," in *Études sur Parménide,* Vol. II, ed. Aubenque, P. (Paris: Vrin, 1987), 26.

586 **Stein**, H., "Die Fragmente des Parmenides *Perí Phúseo̱s,*" in *Symbola philologrum Bonnensium in honorem F. Ritschelii* (Leipzig: Teubner, 1864–67), 780.

587 **Reinhardt** (1916) 36.

588 Even if this were so, it would be the *diákosmos,* not the world, that was "probable" (**Finkelberg**, A., "Being, Truth and Opinion in Parmenides," *Archiv für Geschichte der Philosophie* 81 [1999] 237). For this reason, I prefer to translate "*eoikóta*" as "apparent in opinions."

played a salient part: for this scholar, the third way has the same aspect as the first, but it does not lead to being: "it is the way of *dóxa,* in the sense of appearance."[589] On the basis of this interpretation, a great majority of scholars find in the second part of the Poem a plausible speech about appearances, and various Anglo-Saxon scholars call the section of the Poem devoted to opinions the "Way of Seeming."

What relation does all this have to the philosophy of Parmenides? Little or none. Let us begin at the end. In Parmenides, "*dóxa*" never means "appearance." Parmenides is not Plato. In the next chapter we shall analyze this notion, but we can say immediately that Parmenides says nothing about "appearances" because for him there is only one subject of study: that which is being. On this subject, either the truth can be told or opinions can be ventured. Therefore, the student must assimilate the truth; that is what will decide whether everything is full of "opinions" or not. Lastly, we may say that, as we shall see, the term *dokoûnta* (in 1.31) does not introduce a new dimension of study; it is simply synonymous with *dóxa.*

The Goddess's speech on opinions in fragment 8 ("henceforward learn the opinions of mortals . . . ," line 51 ff.) is the deceitful exposition of a probable (*eoikóta*) cosmic order (*diákosmon*) (8.60). For Parmenidean logic, the "probable" is synonymous with the erroneous, the untrue (and, had he used the term, the "false"). The Goddess is clear and precise: when she announces that she is going to present this speech, she says that it will be a deceitful (*apatelón*) combination of words (*kósmon epéon*) (8.52). A "probable" speech is not a speech about appearances; it is the speech that is apparent, not the object of the speech. And moreover, how can it be believed that a speech described *a priori* as "deceitful" could be probable? As De Rijk observes, "by revealing the basic error in human opinions about the world (8.51–59), the Goddess had fulfilled what she promised in lines 30–1 of fragment 1,"[590] where she said that all "true conviction is absent from opinions." As Hesiod's Muses had already said, on the one hand, there is true speech, and on the other, there are "falsehoods" (*pseúdea*) that appear like reality (*Theogony* 27–28).

This is the case with Parmenides' speech about opinions. Its purpose is to tell the listener what to hold on to when listening to a combination of mere words claiming to be true. When we look in detail at this passage about opinions, I shall come back to this point.

---

589 **Heidegger**, M., *Einführung in die Metaphysik* (Frankfurt am Main: Max Niemeyer, 1983), 120.

590 **Rijk**, L. M. de, "Did Parmenides Reject the Sensible World?" in *Graceful Reason,* ed. Gerson, L. P. (Toronto: Pontifical Institute of Mediaeval Studies, 1983), 47.

Let us now return to the nucleus of the so-called third way. It would mix together being and non-being by saying that there is non-being and that being is not. *But why propose a third way, if, as we saw, the second way says exactly the same?* Thus we come to the root of the problem. Those who maintain that there is a third way of investigation in Parmenides believe that the second way is "the way of not being." If this were so, what does this way assert? That there is non-being, or that being is not. *In both cases it is assumed that there is being,* that is, the content of the first way, either because the quality of "being" is ascribed to non-being (and in order to state that non-being is, it is necessary to possess the notion of "being"), or because it is said about "being" that it is not. Being is omnipresent, and it could not be otherwise, since being is a primary, necessary, and absolute certainty, at least for Parmenides.

The so-called formula of the "third way" is none other than the formula of the second way, mixing being and not-being. As there is no way of "non-being," we could state with a certain irony that we accept the existence of a third way provided that it is admitted that there is no second way; then there would be two ways: the first and the third. Those who find the expression of a second way in line 2.5, different from that which is found in passages where being is predicated of not being, which they would call the third way, do not take into account the fact that the statement of each way (that is, the thesis and its negation) in fragment 2 is *double:* the second hemistich of each formula clarifies the first. J. Wiesner wrongly says that the second way maintains "*ouk éstin,*"[591] that is, just the negation of the verb, and that when a subject is added there is a mixture of being and not being, or a third way. This second statement is totally correct, but the second hemistich of line 2.5 shows clearly that "*ouk éstin*" *already* presupposes a subject, whose necessity is stated in 2.5b: "it is necessary not to be." To say that is already a mixture of being and not being, and the concise *ouk éstin* already presented the same idea by stating that "there is not."

From line 4 of fragment 6 onward, Parmenides presents the foundation of the second way, that is, the negation of the thesis. How is it possible to offer a foundation for saying that that which is being is not? It is very simple: "mortals who know nothing" do not know the basic thesis ("there is being because it is not possible not to be"), and so "being and not being are *considered* as the same and not the same" (6.8–9). Parmenides stresses the "habitual" character of this human opinion, which is supported by a "wandering intellect" (*plagktós nóos,* 6.6). It is "long habit" (*éthos polúpeiron,* 7.3) that leads men to "create" (*pláttontai,* 6.5) a method that mixes being

591 **Wiesner** (1996), 84 ff.

and not being and, therefore, to state that these are both identical and different at once. But, as we saw, the text of this fragment 6 came down to us containing a very unfortunate conjecture *that allows the introduction of a new possibility.* Indeed, if the Goddess orders the disciple to withdraw from two different ways ("*prǭtẹs gàr, épeita de*") ("for from this first . . . and then from . . .") it is inconceivable that *one* of these should be the first, true way, since the Goddess would not order the disciple to withdraw from that; *therefore,* there must be three ways: the true one, and the two ways that are rejected.[592] But an essential fact eludes all these interpreters: it is not Parmenides who speaks of *rejecting* two ways, but the editor of the Aldine edition of Simplicius, followed by H. Diels, whose text unfortunately nobody now discusses. F. Fronterotta confirms that Reinhardt's interpretation is based exclusively upon "the completion conjectured by Diels for the end of line 3 of fragment 6."[593] A reading of fragment 6 with the gap as it stands, that is, without any conjecture at all, clearly shows that in this fragment Parmenides presents only *two* possibilities: one in 6.1–3 and another in 6.4–9. If the gap is filled with a verb that is valid for both ways, as I proposed on the above pages, it is not necessary to imagine a possible third way. This possibility only appears if we assume that Parmenides used a verb that required a rejection, and in that case, as there are two ways to be rejected, we have to imagine that there remains a third way to be adopted, making three ways in all.

From line 4 of fragment 6 onward we find what Plato had called a "*élegkhos perì toû mẹ̄ óntos*" ("refutation of that which is not") in the passage already quoted from *Sophist* 239b. Its full scope is grasped with the quotation from the first line of fragment 7, in which the particle *gár* has a strong explanatory-causal value:[594] mortals mix that which is and that which is not and find themselves on a way that is a dead end *because* it is equivalent to stating that there are things that are not. This occurs because they are incapable of grasping the scope of the thesis, that is, the absolute and necessary

---

592 Heitsch is a good example of this way of thinking. According to this scholar, the two ways presented in 6.3 ff. cannot be the same as those in fragment 2, since fragment 6 *clearly* says that both must be avoided. (**Heitsch**, E., *Gegenwart und Evidenz bei Parmenides* [Wiesbaden: Franz Steiner Verlag, 1970], 39). So Heitsch imagines a third way and then sets out on a long march to avoid the "conflict"—as he calls it—between the dichotomous scheme of the whole Poem, and the "trichotomy" of the three ways (**Heitsch**, *Gegenwart und Evidenz,* 40–53).

593 **Fronterotta**, "Essere, tempo," 839.

594 Cf. **Denniston**, *Greek Particles,* 60–67. This line refers to the content of fragment 6. Both Untersteiner and Diels maintained that the text that is called fragment 7 today was a continuation of fragment 6: "it can be considered as a definite fact that B7 and 8 come immediately after B6" (**Untersteiner** [1958], cxxvi); "7.1 immediately follows 6.9" (**Diels** [1897], 73).

character of the fact of being. When the Goddess's teaching has been assimilated, then final "judgment" can be brought (that is, the moment of the decision [*krísis*] arrives) (cf. 8.16), and this is when *one single way is eliminated and one single way is kept.*

(e) Confirmation of the Existence of Only Two Ways of Investigation

A "third way" does not form part of this way of thinking. Indeed, in lines 8.16–18 we read that "it has been decided, of necessity, that one remains unthinkable and unnamable [i.e., "anonymous": it cannot be expressed, since it is not the true way], and that the other exists and is genuine." There is not even the slightest reference to a third way. One of the *two* ways that were presented, *a priori,* as capable of directing thought (2.2), is *now*[595] found to be deprived of the "thought" (from *nóēma:* it is *a-nóētos*) of its possible user, who must withdraw his thought from it (7.2). That confirms the Goddess's prognosis: this way is *panapeuthéa,* "totally unknowable" (2.6), since one cannot know what one cannot think. Moreover, if we take into account what is said in the passage 8.35–36 about the relationships between thinking, being, and saying, it is obvious that following an unthinkable way we do not find any reference to that which is, and for that reason the way is *anṓnumos,* "anonymous," that is, etymologically, nameless.[596] Finally, we may say that in the passage 8.17 one single way is eliminated, the one that is not true (cf. the clause in brackets). This means that if Parmenides had presented three ways, and if one had been rejected in 8.17, that would still leave two; but the beginning of fragment 8 is explicit: "one single word of the way [singular] remains."

My rejection of a possible "third way" is based on the impossibility of finding a middle term between being and not being, according to the foundations of Parmenides' philosophy. And I have stressed that the Parmenidean schemes are essentially dichotomous, since his philosophy assumes—perhaps without being conscious of his discovery—the principles of non-contradiction and the excluded middle. With this way of seeing things, it is not possible to admit a *tertium* between the two contradictory elements that constitute his system:[597] "it is or it is not" (8.15); "it is neces-

595 That is, after having been described as a way based on the senses and wandering intellect. The Goddess speaks in the past: *kékritai;* its impossibility has *already* been decided upon. "Already," that is, before fragment 8.

596 On this term cf. **Aristotle**, *Eth. Eud.*, 1221a.

597 Seligman observed that an intermediate position between being and not-being is not allowable (**Seligman**, P., *Being and Not-being: An introduction to Plato's* Sophist [The Hague: Martinus Nijhoff, 1978], 5).

sary to be absolutely, or not" (8.11). Moreover, both being and not being are absolute[598] in themselves (which will not escape criticism by Plato and Aristotle).

Although the traditional interpretations of Parmenides, apart from very rare exceptions, find three ways of investigation in his philosophy, there are certain, somewhat timid, attempts to consider that in fragment 6 there is only the presentation of a new "possibility," which does not actually become a "way." This is a minor possibility, adopted by some pre-Parmenidean thinkers or by people in general, in an almost intuitive way. A. Pasquinelli was the first to expound this viewpoint. According to this scholar, both fragment 2 and fragment 8 are completely explicit on the existence of only *two* ways of investigation, since there is no *tertium* between being and non-being. But in 6.4 ff. there is a false possibility: the thesis implicit in the world of *dóxa,* which constitutes a new position.[599] When we come to analyze the content of so-called "*dóxa*" we shall see that here we do not have a separate possibility from the original dichotomy; and as for Pasquinelli, although ultimately there are not three "ways," there are three "possibilities," his position belongs to the traditional schemes.

For his part, L. Tarán explicitly states that "there is no third way of investigation in Parmenides,"[600] against scholars who think they can find one, but in his analysis of 6.4–9, he admits that here there is "a doctrine that is incapable of distinguishing being from non-being," a doctrine that might refer to Heraclitus (that is, which did not accept the Parmenidean dichotomy and proposed something different). For this reason, when he refers to the rejection by the Goddess, Tarán states that that rejection relates to the second way of investigation *and* "the impossible path along which mortals wander who know nothing."[601] That is to say, there is a positive way and rejection of a negative way *and* of an impossible path. Finally, A. P. D. Mourelatos makes a distinction between a negative way and that "of mortals," although he recognizes that the latter "lapses" into the former.[602]

To date I have only found a position similar to my own in L. Robin and E. Loew, although neither of these two scholars drew the final conclusions that result from admitting the fundamental dichotomy in Parmenides' thought. These two scholars—who, however, did not criticize Diels's conjecture for line 6.3—vehemently maintain that there are only two ways of

598 "Parmenides does not make any difference at all between relative being and absolute being" (**Verdenius** [1942], 54).

599 **Pasquinelli**, A., *I Presocratici* (Turin: Einaudi, 1958), 397.

600 Tarán, L., (1965), 208.

601 Tarán, L., (1965), 81.

602 **Mourelatos** (1970), 78, note 7; and **Mourelatos** (1970), 91. A similar position can be deduced from the words of **Loenen** (1959), 94.

investigation in Parmenides, but, as we shall see, they find certain specific nuances within the second way and so, we might say, they also offer three possibilities, though these are reducible to a fundamental alternative.

For L. Robin, who in 1923 expounded a most subtle interpretation of Parmenides' thought in barely nine pages, "the principle of contradiction obliging thought to opt for an absolute 'yes' or 'no' is thus stated for the first time and rests on the ontological impossibility of something claiming to be different from being it is not nevertheless non-being."[603] This rigorous dichotomy leads Parmenides to work out his system around two ways of investigation, a true one and a false one; nevertheless, this false way "assumes a double direction (fr. 6), which appears to correspond to different degrees of rationality":[604] on the one hand, a way that was perhaps followed by the Heracliteans, in which being and non-being are considered as identical, and on the other, a way in which they get confused and lost and which contributes to the creation of a physics based on opinion.[605]

For his part, E. Loew expounded a similar viewpoint in a series of works published between 1917 and 1935: he said that in Parmenides, "there are only two ways of investigation, the true and the false,"[606] between which "*tertium non datur.*" And as there is no not-being, neither is there the combination "being and not-being." "For this reason, the Goddess warns first against the way of not-being, and then, even more vigorously, against the way of being and not-being, along which men wander."[607] It is worth noting that, for Loew as well, "the Goddess rejects two wrong ways."[608]

Be that as it may, in the work of these two scholars we find an element essential to our search: the conviction that the two ways correspond to *alḗtheia* and to *dóxa,* that is, to the two parts that have always been recognized in Parmenides' Poem. Thus Robin states that, in Parmenides, "there are two routes or methods: one, that of immutable and perfect truth, to which logical thought belongs; the other, that of opinion and its different

603 **Robin**, L., *La pensée grecque et les origines de l'esprit scientifique,* 3rd ed. (Paris: La Renaissance du Livre, 1963), 104.

604 **Robin**, *La pensée grecque.*

605 Wahl accepts this thesis of Robin's: "Parmenides only ever speaks to us about two ways; one, which is inevitable, which is the way of being; and another, which is inaccessible, which cannot be used, and is the way of non-being" (**Wahl**, J., *Vers la fin de l'ontologie* [Paris: Société de l'Enseignement Supérieur, 1956], 118).

606 **Loew**, E., "Das Verhältnis von Logik und Leben bei Parmenides," *Wiener Studien* 54 (1935) 3.

607 **Loew**, "Verhältnis von Logik," 10.

608 **Loew**, E., "Das Lehrgedicht des Parmenides: Gliederung und Gedankengang," *Rheinisches Museum* 78 (1929) 153. For Guazzoni Foa, there are only two ways in fragment 6, but then he states that *dóxa,* which has a positive aspect, cannot be identified with either of the two ways (**Guazzoni Foa**, V., *Il problema delle "vie di ricerca" in Parmenide* [Bergamo: Arti Grafiche Mariani & Monti, 1979], 23–59, 55–67).

and changing appearances, condemned by custom and the confused experience of the senses."[609] For his part, Loew characterizes the two ways in the following manner: the first is the logical-critical way (that is, the way of truth), whereas the second is the empirical-physical way that corresponds to the opinions of mortals.[610]

I accept this position of Robin and Loew, but at the same time, I hold that the two possibilities offered by Parmenides are radical and do not allow for any intermediate nuance. In other words, the alternatives Parmenides presents throughout his Poem are always different aspects of the same main alternative. It makes no sense to find in one passage of the Poem, for example, an alternative between a first true way and a second wrong way, and in another passage a choice between a first true way and a third way represented by opinions. There is one single alternative, since the second way *corresponds to the opinions of mortals,* and against this stands its *contradictory* pole, the true way. Consequently, and before drawing the conclusions that have to be drawn, we must look further at this equivalence between the way of error and the way of opinions, on which I based my ideas when proposing a solution for the gap in 6.3. Now we need to study a series of passages that show this equivalence, which are diametrically opposed to the content of the way of truth.

Even in the incomplete form in which it has come down to us, the passage 6.4 ff. diametrically opposes a way created by mortals who know nothing, to the one that states that being is possible and nothing[ness] does not exist. The way of men maintains that that which is not being, is (7.1), which was the thesis of the second way of investigation. The first way stands at the antipode of this dead-end way. Already in fragment 1 the Goddess had said that "her" way (that is, the way of truth) was to be found far from the path of men (1.27), who before they become "men who know" are in the realm of night. That is, even the first fragment speaks of two ways of investigation.[611] The alternative is clear: on the one hand, the first way, the true way, that is, the way of the Goddess; on the other, the way of mortals. The first way is related to truth; the second depends on men's way of thinking, that is, opinion.

This same alternative reappears in other passages, in which Parmenides refers again to two ways of investigation, which set truth against non-truth. For example, in fragment 2.4 Parmenides tells us that the first way "accompanies"[612] truth, and for that reason, this way is "genuine" (*etē̱tumos*) (8.18). Its content is "trustworthy" (*pistón*) (8.50), since knowledge of the "heart of

609 **Robin**, *La pensée grecque,* 104.

610 **Robin**, *La pensée grecque,* 104.

611 Cf. **Leszl**, *Parmenide,* 158.

612 According to Ballew, this verb means "to follow after, as a servant" (**Ballew**, "Straight and Circular," 192).

truth" is the essential content of the teaching the Goddess offers her disciple (1.28). In contrast, the second way belongs to the sphere of the not-true.[613] This way is "completely unknowable" (*panapeuthéa*) (2.4), since it is not possible to say or to think that which is not being. Consequently, this way is described as "unthinkable" (*anóe̱tos*), "anonymous" (*anónumos,* i.e., nameless, unnamable), and fundamentally "not true." No faith can be placed in this way, and for this reason, the Goddess had already announced in fragment 1 that no trust can be put in "opinions" (*ouk éni . . . pístis ale̱thé̱s*) (1.30). They amount to a deceitful combination of words (*kósmos . . . epéo̱n apate̱lón*) (8.52). There can be no doubt that the wrong, untrue way is the way of the opinions of mortals. So everything leads to the basic alternative: truth vs. opinions, or, if you prefer, the first way (or first thesis) vs. the second way (or negation of the thesis).

In the Poem's introduction, the Goddess announces to the young man who has decided to set out on a hazardous journey to find her that, first, he must learn the heart of *truth* and then the *opinions* of mortals. Then in fragment 2, the disciple, who has become an attentive and, we may suppose, obedient pupil, must listen to what are the *only* two ways offered to thinking, and these are none other than the way of truth (2.3) and the wrong way (2.5). Finally, in fragment 8 the Goddess says that she has just expounded her "reasoning and thought about the truth" and that from now on it will be the turn of the "opinions of mortals" (8.52). Let us not forget that in 8.17–18 the Goddess returns to the scheme in fragment 2 and expresses value judgments about her teaching: one way is true and the other is false.

Finally, we may say that the whole of classical antiquity found only two possibilities in Parmenides' Poem: *alé̱theia* and *dóxa.* For example, Alexander of Aphrodisias states that Parmenides "marched along *two* ways"[614] (*ep'amphotéras ê̱lthe tàs hodoús*), since his doctrine stated that, according to truth (*kat'alé̱theian*), everything is one, whereas, according to opinion (*katá dóxan*), principles had been made up to explain phenomena (*Met.* A.3.984b = DK 28 A 7). Diogenes Laertius shares this opinion since, according to him, the philosophy of Parmenides can be divided into two parts: one, according to truth; the other, according to opinion (IX.22.4 = DK 28 A 1). As I have already said, this interpretation remained in force until the end of the nineteenth century.[615]

613 In the quotations from Parmenides' Poem that have come down to us, the word "false" (*pseudé̱s*) is absent.

614 Somewhat unusually, Untersteiner states that Alexander made a mistake: "perché le vie sono tre" (**Untersteiner** [1958], 34).

615 In Parmenides, wrote Brucker, "philosophia duplex est, vel secundum opionem, vel secundum veritatem" (**Brucker**, I., *Historia criticae philosophiae,* I [Leipzig: B. C. Breitkopf, 1742], 1158).

I have stated my completely dichotomous interpretation of Parmenides' philosophy (according to which there is no imaginable third possibility between the thesis and antithesis) from my 1971 doctoral thesis onward.[616] An article published in *Phronesis*[617] widened the readership that might encounter and possibly adopt my viewpoint. The most direct result of this publication was the adoption, two years later, of my verb "*árkhesthai,*" albeit in the active voice, *árkho̱,* by the Greek-American scholar A. Nehamas, who kindly admits that I had already preceded him[618] in his choice.[619] Even so, my position is radically different from that of Nehamas, and the fact that this scholar proposed the same verb as myself does not mean we share the same point of view. Indeed, I proposed the verb in the middle voice *árkhomai,* and, for metrical reasons, I decided upon *árxei,* the second person aorist. In contrast, Nehamas's conjecture proposed the verb should be in the active voice and in the first person future: "*árxo̱.*" Given that it is the Goddess who is speaking, this conjecture appears more coherent than mine, but it is not. The reason is very simple: Nehamas explains that "the use of *árkhein* with *apó* occurs in L.S.J. (see *árkho̱,* I.2),"[620] but in *all* the examples given, the verb is found in the middle voice, and so Nehamas cannot adduce a single passage in support of a possible use of "*árkho̱ + apó,*" either in L.S.J. or in any classical source. In order to maintain the coherence of his interpretation, which requires a first person, Nehamas should have proposed *árkhomai,* which is impossible from the metrical point of view; on the other hand, *árxei,* though not an ideal solution, does respect the meter.[621]

G. Germani adopted my hypothesis in his work "Per un'interpretazione delle vie di Parmenide,"[622] and without ostensibly basing himself on my

---

616 **Cordero**, N. L., *L'être et le non être dans la philosophie de Parménide,* Université de Paris IV, directeur: Pierre-Maxime Schuhl, December 1971, passim.

617 **Cordero**, N. L., "Les deux chemins de Parménide dans les fragments 6 et 7," *Phronesis* 24 (1979).

618 This admission by Nehamas has not prevented certain scholars (for example, O'Brien) from becoming a source of disinformation when they frequently speak of "the conjecture of Nehamas and Cordero," a phrase suggesting that I was inspired by a work that was published two years later than my own (cf. **O'Brien**, D., *Études sur Parménide,* Vol. I, ed. Aubenque, P. [Paris: Vrin, 1987], 222–25, who makes eight references to my hypothesis, and inverts the relevant chronology in six of them. Even alphabetical order is in my favor.). Moreover, given that my conjectures only have a verb in common (imagined by us and attested also by Nehamas), whose meaning differs considerably when it is used in the active or middle voice, it does not make sense to speak of "the" conjecture of Cordero and Nehamas.

619 **Nehamas**, A., "On Parmenides' Three Ways of Inquiry," *Deucalion* 33–34 (1981) 110.

620 **Nehamas**, "On Parmenides," 105.

621 Inexplicably, Couloubaritsis does not take this syntactical evidence into account and believes that the difference "operates [only] on the level of the status of the Goddess's speech" (**Couloubaritsis**, "Les multiples chemins," 27).

622 **Germani**, G., *Annali del Dipartimento di Filosofia,* Vol. II (Firenze: Università di Firenze, 1986), 23 ff.

solution to the gap in 6.3, G. Giannantoni concludes that in "B6 not three but two ways are proclaimed, in a form that is coherent with fragments 2 and 8."[623] For her part, D. de Cecco[624] bases herself upon my "new integration" (which she considers "extremely fruitful") to propose a very subtle and original interpretation of the last sentence of fragment 6: "the way of all of them returns to the starting point," in which the Goddess makes a "correction," since "the journey towards truth is circular." Finally, we may say that perhaps with excessive optimism and after mentioning my interpretation, E. Berti states that "whatever the correct addition that should be added to the text (which certainly has a gap, as is proved by the meter), present-day commentators hold that the ways mentioned by the Goddess are only two."[625]

If my interpretation is valid, in the final lines of the combined whole made up of fragments 6 and 7 (since, as Untersteiner stated, it is a "fatto acquisto dalla critica" that fragment 7 follows immediately on from fragment 6),[626] we find an exhortation to judge by reasoning the polemical proof that the Goddess has given (7.5–6) about the way created by mortals. The basic thesis (that is, the first way) does not need to be submitted to any test; as soon as the Goddess states it, at the beginning of fragment 6, she orders it to be proclaimed (6.2) and tells her listener that later on, he will begin to study it. In contrast, the opposite way harbors a pernicious virus beneath the apparent familiarity of long habit. The senses and the wandering, wavering intellect have worked out a tentative but false worldview, whose foundation was set forth by the Goddess. This way of conceiving reality through "proofs" that only someone situated outside this daily life could adduce has been criticized. The totality of these proofs form a polemical, combative *élegkhos.* The hearer of the Goddess could blindly accept the arguments that his teacher dictates to him, but she urges him to "judge" these proofs. There will be no appeal from the result of the judgment, the verdict: one single way remains, and this way can be reduced to the single word "is." The first lines of fragment 8 contain this verdict.

---

623 **Giannantoni**, G., "Le due 'vie' di Parmenide," *La parola del passato* 43 (1988) 226.

624 **De Cecco**, D., "Parmenide 28 B 6,8–9 DK," in *Esercizi Filosofici (1992)* (Trieste: Edizioni Lint, 1993), 14.

625 **Berti**, E., "Parménide," in *Le savoir grec,* ed. Brunschwig, J., and Lloyd, G. (Paris: Flammarion, 1996), 725.

626 **Untersteiner** (1958), xxxvi.

Chapter VIII: The Meaning of the "Opinions of Mortals"

Parmenides' Poem is presented as the development of the two possibilities the Goddess has offered as a program of studies toward the end of fragment 1. Anyone wanting to advance into the realm of knowledge (some time later this desire to know will be called "philosophy") must take into account that there is one basic and irrefutable truth, but human beings may not know it. In that case, they will be condemned to wander aimlessly. Thought must either follow the way of truth (*alḗtheia*), which is founded upon a necessary and irrefutable thesis, or it will be reduced to empty and contradictory opinions (*dóxai,* plural of *dóxa*). This conceptual dichotomy (which culminates in a gnoseological monism, since "only one word of the way remains," 8.1), excludes any middle term, and therefore excludes any third possibility that might result from a combination of both positions. The Parmenidean problem, as Fülleborn maintained, only allows for two possibilities: "either things are, they have reality; or they are not and they have no reality."[627] *This is the alternative corresponding to the two parts that make up the structure of the Poem.* The exposition of the fact that there is that which is, and that it is impossible that it should not be, is called *Alétheia.* The presentation of the hypothetical possibility that argues as if that which is being did not exist is called *Dóxa.* This attempt to propose an explanation of reality in terms of a radical alternative had already had certain antecedents in pre-Parmenidean cosmogonies, especially in Hesiod,[628] for whom the muses usually express plausible lies but, when they wish, they proclaim the truth (*Theogony* 27–28). Parmenides inherits this schema and states it in terms of philosophical canons and then, if speech captures the reality of that which is being, it can only be true. From Parmenides on, the notions of *lógos* (reasoning, argued speech) and of *alḗtheia* begin to fuse, to the point where later philosophy, especially in Plato's time, will become involved in titanic efforts to justify a *lógos* that can be erroneous, mistaken, or directly false (i.e., *pseudḗs*).[629] We saw earlier that the trustworthy *lógos* was the ex-

627 **Fülleborn** (1795), 95.

628 Cf. **Schwabl**, H., "Hesiod und Parmenides," *Rheinisches Museum* 106 (1963) 139.

629 Probably Antisthenes is claiming to be the faithful heir of Parmenides when he states that "every *lógos* says the truth (*alētheúei*), because anyone who speaks says something (*ti*),

pression of a thought (*nóēma*) "about the truth" (8.50) and that this speech constitutes the positive aspect of Parmenides' thesis.

But we also saw that, as any genuine teacher must, Parmenides, through the intermediary of the Goddess, warns his disciple about the danger of being seduced by a "deceitful (or deceptive) order of words" (8.52). Knowing the error of error is part of the truth, and for that reason it is necessary for the disciple *also* "to inform himself" about the opinions of mortals, as the last lines of the first fragment say. The exposition of this negative part of the thesis is fundamental, since Parmenides shows the hidden aspect of the virus that is apt to contaminate philosophical thought. I say "hidden" because, obviously, no one (except perhaps Gorgias) openly admits that there is nothing, that that which is being, is not. Nevertheless, long habit leads us to relativize the fact of being, to believe that it exhausts itself in "things" ("beings," in Greek). If this is so, how can we justify the absolute and necessary character of the fact of being? Relativizing the fact of being is equivalent to contaminating it with its negation and ignoring the fundamental alternative: it is or it is not (8.15). Those who are incapable of making this choice are "*á-kritoi*" ("people with no capacity for discernment"), and they can only create opinions.

We have seen already in our commentary on fragments 6 and 7 that opinions (the patrimony of "mortals") constitute the way made by men who know nothing (or know "nothing[ness]"). Opinions are mere fantasies, combinations of empty words claiming to replace the truth. There is no "true conviction" in them (1.30); they form part of a deceitful *speech*, certainly persuasive, against which one has to take precautions, as Odysseus had to tie himself to the mast of his ship so as not to allow himself to be seduced by the song of the sirens. All interpreters who have decided to defend the positive value of "opinions" have had to relativize, or even distort, Parmenides' words.[630]

(a) Dóxa *Is Not Appearance*

Despite Parmenides' insistence on always relating the notion of *dóxa* to the sphere of speech, that is, of knowledge, a large number of interpreters of

---

and anyone who says something says something that is being (*tò ón*), and anyone who says something that is being, says the truth (*alētheúei*)" (text transmitted by **Proclus** in his commentary on *Cratylus,* 37).

630 Curd, for example, asks why, if Doxa is false, it constitutes the "best" possible explanation, but she admits that she has taken the word "best" from the classic work of Long (**Long**, A. A., "The Principles of Parmenides' Cosmogony," *Phronesis* 8 [1963] 90–107) (**Kenig Curd**, P., "Deception and Belief in Parmenides' *Doxa,*" *Apeiron* 25 [1992] 112). Then she goes on to ask whether *all* human opinions must be rejected, since the *koûros*

the Eleatean's thought tend to give the term an ontological value, as a synonym of "appearance." This error is most common among Anglo-Saxon scholars, who are apt to describe the second way (and hence the second part of the Poem) as the "way of *seeming*."[631] Here we have a grave sin of anachronism. As I said in the previous chapter, Parmenides is not Plato. The term *dóxa* appears three times in the Poem, and twice it is accompanied by the subjective genitive "*of* mortals" (1.30, 8.51). Mortals (subject) have "opinions," that is, viewpoints, assessments, conjectures. There is never a question of the "look," that is, the appearance, *of* mortals. The third case is even clearer, since men "established" opinions in order to name things (19.1). Parmenides says nothing about "appearances," since he knows that on that subject it would be possible to say something and also say the opposite. In Parmenides there is no theory, not even a plausible theory, of appearances. If they exist (and given Parmenides' concept of being, the way of being that might correspond to them would have to be justified, something that Parmenides does not do), nothing true can be said about them.

Some interpreters base their ideas on the term "*dokoûnta*" in fragment 1.31 in order to state that Parmenides took "appearances" into account. I said earlier that *dokoûnta* is synonymous with *dóxa* (whose root it shares). It is a question of what "seems" to mortals, not what "appears" to them. Parmenides (who, I repeat, is not Plato) does not make any distinction between "being" and "appearing," simply because this would be contradictory in relation to his philosophy. For Parmenides, things—"*tà ónta,*" in Greek—are beings, are "particularizations," "presentations" of the fact of being, not *appearances* of it. The difference is enormous. The philosopher grasps it; mortals believe that there are only these "presentations," which they call "things" (which for one who has had access to the truth are "apparent forms" *morphás:* cf. fr. 8.5) and to which they give a name in order to recognize them (8.38–41), but this has nothing to do with "appearances." The "*dokoûnta*" in fragment 1.31 "might have existed" (*khrḗn:* unreal imperfect) *if* truth had not made itself present. *Dokoûnta,* like *truth,* belongs to the realm of knowledge.

The fact of always associating the term *dóxai*[632] with the subjective genitive "of mortals" shows clearly and distinctly that when Parmenides de-

---

who listens to the Goddess is also a mortal. There should be no need to point out that in Parmenides, "mortal" does not have a biological meaning; it is synonymous with the masses, who believe what is said. The *koûros* is a mortal who has become a "man who knows" (1.3), and therefore does not belong to the bewildered masses.

631 Cf., for example, Gallop, who speaks of the "so-called 'Way of Seeming"' (**Gallop** [1984], 5), but who makes this formula the title of his Chapter V (**Gallop** [1984], 21).

632 An exception would appear to be 19.1, where the term *dóxa,* in the singular, forms part of the modal expression "according to opinion"; however, it is not an exception, since line 8.39 states that it was "mortals" who established these names to designate "things."

scribes "the human condition," he is suggesting that it can only create opinions. If we take into account that the most complete description of this situation is found in the passage that runs from 6.4 to 7.5, we see that the way from which it is necessary to withdraw in 7.1 is, without any doubt whatsoever, the way of *dóxa,* whose formulation matches word for word the impossible way in fragment 2: "that which is not being, is." Let us remember that already in antiquity the opinions of mortals were considered as an exemplification of the second way of investigation, that is, the negation of the thesis. When Plato quotes lines 7.1–2 in the *Sophist,* he does so, as we have seen, in order to try to refute the proposition that there is no not-being (i.e., the thesis, *lógos,* of Parmenides, 237a). Sextus Empiricus is even more explicit, since he quotes the same lines as a demonstration of the statement contained in line 1.30, according to which there is no true conviction in the *opinions* of mortals (*Adv. Math.* VII.111). That is, the way condemned in 7.2 is without any doubt the one containing the opinions of mortals mentioned in 1.30.

(b) The Object of Opinions

If, as my interpretation states, opinions are mere empty words created by mortals who know nothing, what do these words claim to reflect? To put it another way: as I do not agree that we find in Parmenides a speech about "appearances," what is the object of these opinions? What are these opinions about?

To answer this question, we must be aware of the abyss that separates Parmenides from Plato. Indeed, for Plato, anyone who opines (*doxázei*) has an opinion on something, but this object is neither that which is nor that which is not (*Rep.* 478c), but a combination of both (479d) (and for that reason opinion is halfway between ignorance and knowledge, and in certain dialogues this fact allows him to speak of true opinion or false opinion). Parmenides stands at the antipode of this view. *For Parmenides, the "object" of opinions is* ***that which is.*** But on this object opinions present an empty, illusory speech, that is, they have to be wrong. As W. Leszl observes, "without any doubt Parmenides attributes to *dóxa* a character not only of absence of truth, but also of deceit, error or falsehood."[633] Although Parmenides never uses the term "false" (*pseudés*) (at least, it is not found in any of the quotations of the Poem that have come down to us to this day), for him, opinion is always false, untrue. A *dóxa ale̱thés* would be inconceivable.

633 **Leszl**, *Parmenide,* 223.

That is, the genuine philosopher (the one who advances methodically from the basic, indisputable thesis) and mortals who know nothing (among whom previous philosophers are certainly to be found—as I shall try to show) share the same object of study. And it could not be otherwise. Since philosophical thought began (and as I have said above, in the passage on "Parmenides' *theoría*") *everything* became amazing, and *everything* means all that is being, which, as we know, is expressed in Greek as "*tà ónta.*" But the same object can be looked at in a deeper or shallower way. When we speak of water, for example, only the scientist grasps its inner structure, its *lógos,* as we might say, and expresses it in a formula: H_2O. The two molecules of hydrogen, added to one of oxygen, are not visible or audible, and a wandering intellect would not even know that they existed. A lay, nonscientific viewpoint believes that water is "just" a liquid, colorless, tasteless, and odorless element. But this "opinion" is a description of the way in which a manifestation of water presents itself to the witness attempting to define it.

Exactly the same happens with reality as a whole, with the totality of everything that is being. The philosopher who has set out on the right way grasps its "truth," that without which there would be no reality: the fact of being, because by being, reality is. Traditional philosophers (we may say) or mortals guided by habit "opine," for example, that the being of things is exhausted in themselves, that they are what they are, and as Plato would say later in the *Sophist,* the central problem for them will then come down to *poîa kaì pósa* are *tà ónta* (242c), that is, "what" and "how many" "beings" there are. The essential question, "What is the fact of being that allows there to be beings?" remained unmentioned.

Both precedent philosophers and those "amazed" mortals who want to know consider (*nenómistai,* 6.8) that the principle or principles that they have found "exist." But if this is so, the fact of being and the reality of the principles coincide, even though such principles may, as tends to happen, be contrary. On the other hand, for a philosopher who "knows" that point of view will be only a combination of words, since anyone reasoning thus does not know what being is and what not-being is, or to put it another way, believes that being and not-being are the same and not the same. As we know, this combination is the nucleus of the negation of the thesis. The opinions of mortals set out upon the second way of investigation, and for that reason, they are condemned to fail. Instead of recognizing the alternative "it is **or** it is not," they maintain the combination "it is **and** it is not." The things that "are" being are born, die, change—that is, "cease to be." The principles that "are" being transform themselves, unite, or separate—that is, they become "that which they were not," they deny themselves. This relativism only leads to viewing reality as if it were composed of "names."

(c) Dóxa *and Names*

As soon as Parmenides begins his exposition of the reality based on opinions, he states their arbitrary character: "they [mortals] established two viewpoints to name external forms" (8.53). This phrase, which has been much discussed, deserves detailed analysis. We must not forget that it is not mortals who are speaking, but the Goddess, and therefore she expounds in "her" terms: that which is "real" for mortals is a simple verbal form, and consequently external. For this reason I have translated "*morphā́s*" as "external forms," and if I have related this term with speech it is because that is its meaning in Homer. Indeed, on the two single occasions when the term *morphḗ* appears in the *Odyssey*, 8.170 and 11.367, it is accompanied by the genitive "*épos*" ("word"). In our passage, the verb "name," ("*onomázein*") picks up this meaning.

I said that this passage is susceptible to various interpretations because the numeral adjective "*dúo*" ("two") may refer to "forms" or to "viewpoints" ("*gnṓmas*"). So does it mean establishing (*katéthento,* a verb already used in 8.39 when the Goddess confirms that everything mortals *establish* is just "name") *two* viewpoints in order to name external forms, or establishing viewpoints in order to name *two* external forms? Most interpreters have followed H. Diels's[634] line, for whom "*gnṓmē katatíthestai*" constitutes a habitual formula, and consequently, the two terms should not be separated; therefore, the number must refer to "forms." I support associating the number with viewpoints ("*gnomas*") for two reasons: (1) because the meaning of the term is associated with a sort of criterion (it reappears with this meaning in the last line of fr. 8: "so that no viewpoint [*gnṓmē*] of mortals will prevail over you," 8.61), and a criterion is precisely what Parmenides' philosophy establishes (cf. *supra* the analysis of the verb *krînai* and the noun *krísis*) for judging arguments. But, of course, he only proposes one single criterion, one single viewpoint: that of the disjunction: "either . . . or . . ." The failure of mortals or previous philosophers consists in holding to a double viewpoint, to the conjunction ". . . and . . . ," that is, two viewpoints. This is one of the reasons leading us to link "viewpoint" with "two." The other reason (2) is that Parmenides probably wanted to contrast his "two viewpoints" with the proverbial expression "*one* viewpoint (*mía gnṓmē*)" "in unanimous form."[635]

Mortals' error consists precisely in not having thought it necessary to propose one single viewpoint: "which they did not necessarily bring together (and in that they are mistaken)" (8.54). This phrase inherits the diffi-

634 **Diels** (1897), 92.

635 On this cliché, cf. **Thucydides**, 1.122 and 6.17; **Demosthenes**, 10.59; **Isocrates**, 4.139.

culties of the preceding one, since once more it is a case of relating a numeral adjective, in this case "one" (*mían*) (since a literal translation of the passage would read "with which it is not necessary [for them to make] *one*"). "One" (that is in the feminine) may refer either to "viewpoint" (which is feminine in Greek) or to "external form." According to my interpretation, this number confirms what I have been saying: instead of adopting a single viewpoint (*mía gnṓmē*), mortals established "two viewpoints." That is, there can be no doubt that the number "one" in 8.54 refers to "*gnṓmē*" and not to "external forms."[636] And for this reason the Goddess is able to comment that "in that they are mistaken" (8.54b). The subject of the sentence is definitely mortals, the relative (*en hṓi*) refers to the mistake they have made, and the participle (*peplanēménoi,* corresponding to the verb "*planáō*") describes their attitude: *planáō* means both "stray" and "make a mistake" and even "lose the occasion" (*kairós:* the opportune moment).[637] Mortals have made a mistake, because as the Goddess had already said in fragment 6, "lack of resources drives the *wandering* intellect in their breasts" (6.5–6).[638] As G. Germani says, "mortals do not know where to go, they are disorientated, they proceed at random in a movement full of waverings."[639] And we have already seen that P. Destrée had compared this erratic gait to that of drunks.[640]

The following lines show that not only have mortals established two viewpoints, but that, consequently, this choice has led them to "distinguish [*ekrínanto*][641] a form [the term here is *démas,* which alludes to form in the sense of external aspect, a sort of "configuration"] contrary to itself [*antía*]." Fortunately, Parmenides expresses this idea in a phrase coordinated with the preceding phrase by means of the conjunction "*kaí*" ("and"), in which he says that mortals *also* "set [*éthento*] proofs [*sḗmata*] [of it] separated [*khōrís*] from each other" (8.55b–56a). This passage is very important because Parmenides begins to "identify" "mortals." They are people who have offered "proofs" of something, but instead of these proofs being based on the conjunction that, as we have seen, is the nucleus of Parmenides' thesis, they are victims of double-thinking that *separates* two universes. As we shall see, Parmenides will also offer "proofs" ("*sḗmata*") of his thesis, but these "proofs" are coherent: they are not separated from one another, but derive from one another. As mortals decided to express themselves by means

636 Cf., *contra,* Coxon: "to name only one Form is not right" (**Coxon** [1986], 220).

637 Cf. **Pindar**, *Nem.* 8.4.

638 "Straying" (*plaktón*) is a form of the verb *plázō,* which is synonymous with *planáō.*

639 **Germani**, G., "*Alḗtheie* in Parmenide," *La parola del passato* 43 (1988) 202.

640 **Destrée**, P., "La communauté de l'être (Parménide, fr. B 5)," *Revue de philosophie ancienne* 1 (2000) 12.

641 Coxon translates as "choose" (**Coxon** [1986], 221).

of a form that is contrary to itself, logically they must offer contrary "proofs" that are separate, even contradictory. So what kind of proofs could these be?

In the final lines of our current fragment 8, Parmenides gives various examples. The fragments that follow, up to the so-called "fragment 19," in which he says that "thus these things arose, according to opinion, and thus they exist now," propose a sort of apparent (therefore, deceptive, because it is "like" truth) description of reality. This is an explanation based on opinions that, as we saw, depend on two opposing viewpoints and even offer "proofs" of these.

(d) The Opinion-Makers

Who held the worldview that Parmenides unfolds from 8.56 onward? The candidates are so numerous that the most sensible position is not to take them into account. Faithful to his discovery, Parmenides could have said, as another important person would say centuries later, that "he who is not with me is against me."[642] Every philosophical system, ideology, or way of thinking that ignores that "by being, it is" will be a victim of opinions, because it will be condemned to relativize the fact of being and make it cohabit with its opposite, that which is not-being. To illustrate this position, in the part of his Poem called "*Dóxa,*" Parmenides works out a fictitious philosophical system, a true summing up both of "what is said" and of the previous philosophical schools. The question: who is Parmenides arguing against here?[643] It makes no sense. Parmenides is opposing any philosopher, layperson, or other who has been incapable of recognizing the necessary and absolute character of the fact of being, and who, consequently, has left a space open to admitting that that which is not (and even that a certain way of not-being) can enter into a way of conceiving things.

Most scholars of Parmenides' thought have seen in the philosopher a criticism of Pythagorism. It is possible, but the Pythagoreans are not the only target of Parmenides' criticisms. It is normal that when one is criticizing ideas that one does not share, one should begin by settling accounts with the predominant ideology of the time. Plato did this with the Sophists, the Stoics did it with Aristotelianism and Platonism, and perhaps so did Parmenides with Pythagorism. Let us not forget that at the end of the sixth

642 Words attributed to Jesus Christ by Luke (11.23).

643 There are even some scholars who have maintained that Doxa expounds a theory held by Parmenides in his youth (cf. **Rüstow**, A., "Über Parmenides," *Verhandl. d. 52 Vers. deutsch. Philol. u. Schulm. zu Marburg* [1913] 164).

and beginning of the fifth century B.C., southern Italy was a region under strong Pythagorean influence, and the first philosopher Parmenides heard was the Pythagorean Ameinias. Perhaps for this reason, we can detect a certain abundance of Pythagorean[644] notions in Parmenides' criticism, but it is also clear that in the "apparent" explanation of reality that he expounds (and whose "deceptive" character he does not fail to point out) there are elements that could be found in other philosophical movements.

The didactic example chosen by Parmenides, light (that is, the light of a flame) and darkness, which reappears in fragment 9 as light and night,[645] does not have any special significance. Fundamentally they are opposites, irreconcilable opposites. As is explained in lines 8.57–58, each is what it is and, consequently, is different from the other, but the previous lines have said that there is a difference in the sense of an opposition. However, it is interesting to point out that a century (or perhaps less) before Plato, Parmenides is aware of the notions of "sameness" (*toutón*) and "otherness" (*hetéroi*) (8.57–58) and of the fact that the one assumes the other. The use of such notions is clearly different (although the philosophers coincide on one point: both notions define the identity of every thing), since for Plato, as everything shares in both these notions, each thing can cohabit with its opposite; whereas for Parmenides, this would be valid for everything except for the principle that, for him, is the existence of that which is being.[646]

It is obvious that, apart from "certainties" that belong to common sense (and are usually expressed in all kinds of proverbs) some previous philosophical systems, which Parmenides was sure to know of, could be included among the "opinions" criticized in the Poem.

The indefinite (*tò ápeiron*) of Anaximander, which is considered to be eternal (if the opinion transmitted by Hippolytus, *Adv. haer.* I.6.1 [= A 11 DK], is authentic) and that then originates everything that is from contrary germs, might belong to the "two-headed" (6.5), as well as Anaximenes' evolutionary cosmogony.[647] And regarding the falsehood of opinions, it is

---

644 We shall see below that light and darkness are presented as examples of "external forms," and we know that, according to Aristotle, *phôs* and *skótos* figured among the ten opposing principles admitted by the Pythagoreans (*Met.* A.5.986a22). Cf. **Parmenides** 8.56–59 (*pûr . . . nuktós*), 14.3 (*pháos kaì nuktós*). In 8.41 Parmenides speaks of *khrôs,* which, according to **Aristotle** (*De sens.*, 439a31), was a specifically Pythagorean term, which was confirmed by **Aëtius**: "the Pythagoreans called the surface of the body *khrôs*" (I.15.2).

645 Earth as a "principle" is, as we know, only mentioned in doxographical texts (cf. **Aristotle**, *Gen. and corr.*, II.3.330b13). Aristotle also speaks of two "causes" (*aitías*), "the hot and the cold, as for example fire and earth" (*Met.*, A.5986b33–34).

646 Even so, when Plato finds at least five forms that are more important than the others (cf. *Sophist,* 254c), he does not propose a form that is opposite of, contrary to, or simply different from that of being, which is why these "important" forms are only five (being, rest, movement, identity, and difference) and not six.

647 Reinhardt accepted this hypothesis (**Reinhardt** [1916], 50).

probable that Parmenides was thinking of Xenophanes, for whom sometimes "that which is held as an opinion is close to the real" (fr. 35).[648] For Parmenides, there is nothing more dangerous than the plausible, because it is similar to the true, although it is not true.

(e) The Content of Opinions

Even at the risk of disappointing possible readers of this book, I shall not go further with the analysis of Parmenidean "*dóxa*." My decision rests on two assumptions. The first is that Parmenides himself says that the combination of words (*epéo̱n*) that he allows himself to present is deceptive (*apate̱lón,* 8.52). This term "more than any other in the Parmenidean Poem leads us to think of an antithesis between *alé̱theia* and falsehood."[649] As I have repeated in the above pages, Parmenides would have found it difficult to call a speech deceptive that proposes his own thesis. Therefore, contrary to certain scholars,[650] I think it makes no sense to speak of a Parmenidean "cosmology." My second assumption is this: even if the deceptive character of this part of the Goddess's speech is admitted, as in my case, if we want to understand what type of "cosmology" is contained in the Parmenidean *dóxa,* we have to resort, almost exclusively, to doxographical witnesses. Hardly anything can be drawn from the quotations of passages of the Poem that have come down to us to this day. A clear example of this dependence on the doxographies is the work of J. Bollack mentioned in note 650, which is nearly 90 percent made up of texts by Aëtius and Cicero, grouped together by Diels and Kranz in testimony A37. Nevertheless, if there is a Presocratic author about whom the interpreter *must completely disregard* the opinion of ancient commentators, that author is Parmenides. The "doxographer" nearest in time to the real Parmenides, Plato, admits with sincerity and courage: "I am afraid that we may not understand [*suniô̱men*] his words [*tà legómena*] and I am even more [*polù pléon*] [afraid] that what he was thinking of when he said them goes quite beyond us" (*Thaeat.* 184a). So what can be expected of more recent witnesses, especially when they do not provide textual quotations to accompany their commentaries? Little or nothing.[651] Parmenides (and perhaps the same applies to Heraclitus) is a

---

648 According to Tarán, in this text Xenophanes is saying that, on certain subjects, the only guide for men is opinion (**Tarán** [1965], 207, note 15).

649 **Germani**, "*Alé̱theie,*" 199.

650 Especially Bollack, author of an extensive work (**Bollack**, J., "La cosmologie parménidienne de Parménide," in *Herméneutique et Ontologie.* Hommage à Pierre Aubenque, ed. Brague, R., and Courtine, J. F. [Paris: P.U.F., 1990] 17–53).

651 In the chapter dedicated to the study of fragment 2, I already displayed my surprise at the fact that a decisive text like this had not drawn the attention of ancient commentators,

philosopher who must be interpreted from what remains of his writings, and ancient testimonies should only be listened to if they are commenting on texts that we possess and know what they are saying.

There are two types of content among the texts making up the Parmenidean *dóxa.* Some describe a cosmology that perhaps some philosophers followed, but, given the principles established by the Poem, they come within the sphere of ignorance of the thesis that by being, it is, and therefore lack any kind of truth. We will concern ourselves with these texts very briefly. Other texts offer a sort of reflection on such a cosmology, and we shall also look at those. Finally, there is a text which is difficult to place, because although it deals with a "physical" problem (the material foundations of thought), its consequences are felt in the sphere of thought: fragment 16. We shall also look at that text.

Let us begin with the group of texts describing a "cosmology" that Parmenides, as I have said, not only does not share, but considers "deceptive." The group includes fragments 10, 11, 12, 13, 14 and 15.[652] Fragments 17 and 18[653] have a content we could describe as "biological," but that nevertheless falls within a "cosmogonic" sphere. A brief reading of the context of the passages in which various commentators (Plato, Clement, Simplicius, Stobaeus, Plutarch, Sextus Empiricus) have quoted fragments 10–15 shows us that in every case the authors appear to know of a Parmenides text that we do not, and that they have extracted certain lines from a precise context to illustrate topics that interested them. Needless to say, we shall never know what the *original* Parmenidean context was in which each quotation was to be found.

Fragments 17 and 18 simply confirm that Parmenides was interested in biological, gynecological, or directly medical problems. However, these texts pose a very serious problem. Indeed, do they expound the same Parmenidean ideas? If they do, we would have to reconsider the value of Parmenides' *dóxa.* I believe that, once again, Parmenides is expounding "what is said" about topic A or B; in this case, conception and birth.

The text preserved today as fragment 16 gathers, I believe, genuinely Parmenidean ideas about mortals' way of thinking. We could say it presents the material foundation of erroneous thinking, since it says that what thinks (*hóper phronéei*) is the nature (*phúsis*) of bodily limbs. Like everything belonging to the sphere of *dóxa,* we suppose that these limbs are made up of opposing principles and that they determine the way of thinking since,

---

and that for more than a thousand years (until Proclus and Simplicius decided to quote it) they appear to have ignored it (unless possible quotations from it in works dating before the sixth century A.D. have been lost).

652 Cf. a translation of these fragments at the end of this book.

653 See previous note.

ultimately, feeling (*aisthánesthai*) is thinking (*phroneîn*).[654] B. Cassin and M. Narcy lucidly state that, in the absence of the authentic Parmenidean context, it is practically impossible to pronounce upon the real problems that the text presents.[655] Even so, I venture the following hypothesis. In Parmenides, that which is is always the basis of thinking, since it is thanks to that which is that thinking occurs (cf. *supra* the analysis of lines 8.33–36). This principle is also valid for others, but in that case it is the conception of being that others (mortals, philosophers) have that will be the foundation of their thinking, and as we know, from a double, "conjunctive" base nothing can come except double, "conjunctive" thinking.

There remain the texts that propose a sort of reflection on this cosmology. In this set we can include lines 38–41[656] of fragment 8 and fragments 9 and 19. The beginning of the speech on the *dóxa* has already confirmed that mortals established viewpoints to "name" (*onomázein*) external forms. For Parmenides, *opinions are a question of words.* But these words are just "names" (*onómata*) (8.38, 19.3), mere sound signals (*epéo̱n*) (8.52), and talking about "reality" consists merely in "naming" (8.53, 9.1). But as mortals are victims of long habit, they believe that *something* corresponds to these names, and that that something is real. It is here that Parmenides stands at the opposite pole to mortals, because only that which is can be said, and only that which is is real. Birth and dying, changing appearance, changing position (changing places), even being and not-being (8.38–41) are mere names; the real, the true cannot be reduced to these labels stuck onto "things" that are, but are not real.

The listing of "names" by Parmenides is not random. We saw that among them are "being and not-being" (*einaî te kaì oukhí*) (8.40). This example luminously shows that, as I said above, the object of study of opinions and of the thesis is *the same.* The difference consists in the way of confronting these objects. The positive way, which is the development of the thesis, grasps the truth of both and judges (*krísis*) that a disjunction is required: "either it is completely, or it is not at all" (8.11). Opinions of mortals, who do not know what being is (and therefore do not know why that which is not should be rejected) accept both "being **and** not-being" at once. They do not know that the decision is to choose between "it is **or** it is not" (8.15).

Fragment 9, which belongs to the texts offering reasons in favor of the choice by mortals of a dualist cosmology, confirms that "everything [*pánta*] has been given the names [*onómastai*] of light and night" and that in virtue

654 Cf. the sources of this text: **Aristotle** (*Met.*, 1009b21) and **Theophrastus** (*De sens.*, 3).

655 **Cassin**, B., and **Narcy**, M., "Parménide sophiste," *Études sur Parménide,* Vol. II (Paris: Vrin, 1987), 291.

656 For Ebert as well, this passage forms part of the content of the Doxa (**Ebert**, T., "Wo beginnt der Weg der Doxa?" *Phronesis* 34 [1989] 123).

of both possibilities,[657] that name is applied[658] to this or that. But as the only *dunámeis* are light and night, it can be said that everything is full of both *at the same time* (*homoû*). And as only they exist, between them there is nothing (*mēdén*). If the whole is made up of two principles, and besides them nothing exists, these principles represent that which is; but in that case, they could not be opposites. Plato, who doubtless takes his inspiration from Parmenides, says that when a philosopher states the existence of two contrary principles, he assumes, without daring to confess it, that being is a third thing that "provides" its existence to the two principles (cf. *Sophist* 243d).

Finally, fragment 19 appears to conclude the presentation of *dóxa,* since it refers to a current (*nûn*) state of affairs, which has already been (*éphu*) produced. As it is talking about the explanation of reality proposed by mortals, this current state of affairs is a consequence of opinion: things are like this "according to opinion" (*katà dóxan*) (19.1). Each thing is represented by its own *ónoma,* established by men. In accordance with his circular method, Parmenides repeats his starting point of 8.38: men have established names and things are like that now.

---

657 The term that I translate as "possibilities" is "*dúnamis.*" This notion will be present in Plato with a meaning it surely already has in Parmenides' time: the power to do or suffer an action. My translation "possibility" tries to recover this double value of *dúnamis,* which is not only active, as is usually believed, but also passive.

658 On the idea according to which a name "rests" on (*epí*) the thing, cf. *supra,* my analysis of line 8.35.

Chapter IX: The Foundation of the Thesis: The Way of Truth

After showing in fragments 6 and 7 that the negation of the thesis leads to a dead end (and that, therefore, thought must withdraw from it; 7.2), it only remains to bring proofs in favor of the only way that remains. Fragment 8 begins with precisely these words: "So there remains one single word[659] of the way." Through the use of the term *múthos,* this formula returns to the beginning of the Goddess's speech, where she had announced (in fr. 2) that her *múthos* would consist in presenting the "only ways of investigation there are to think" (2.2). We know that both possibilities were critically examined, and in lines 17 and 18 of fragment 8 the Goddess confirms that one of the ways has been abandoned. Therefore, we suppose, there remains one single way, and that is represented by a single word, the same that characterized it in fragment 2: "*éstin.*"

(a) The Only Way That Remains

Only two authors have quoted these first lines of fragment 8, Sextus and Simplicius. On the other hand, from line 3 onward, the citations are superabundant. This shows that, for a good part of the classical tradition, it is in this fragment 8 that the nucleus of Parmenides' thought is to be found. Let us return for a moment to the first two lines. I said that only Sextus and Simplicius had quoted them, but it is important to point out that both authors saw clearly that the way presented in them is opposed to the possibility of the existence of that which is not, criticized in fragments 6 and 7, that is, the negation of the basic thesis. The way that exposition begins in fragment 8 is, without any doubt, the opposite way to that of opinions which ignored the principal and only thesis. The text I have proposed for the beginning of fragment 8 corresponds to the version transcribed by Simplicius on page 142 of his Commentary on Aristotle's *Physics* (in other passages, on pages 78 and 145, there is a slightly different text), which makes clear that these lines follow immediately after the text preserved as fragment 7: "after rejecting the way that investigates non-being, 'withdraw your

659 On the translation of *mûthos* as "word," cf. Chapter III (a).

thought from this way of investigation [fr. 7.2]', [Parmenides] continues: 'so there remains one single . . .'" *Phys.* 78). Further on, Simplicius confirms this assessment: "here there is what he says after the exclusion [*anaíresis*] of non-being: so there remains one single word of the way . . ." (*Phys.* 146).[660] There can be no doubt that for Simplicius the way that now begins is the *negation* of the possibility that "that which is not-being, is" (7.1), which was the second way. Here, as in the rest of the Poem, there is no vestige whatever of a third way.

The same happens with the quotation of these first two lines by Sextus. Here we find a curious fact, since Sextus quotes in continuous form the last line of fragment 7 (which consists of a hemistich) and the first line of fragment 8 (which also consists of just one hemistich).[661] The anomaly is the following: Sextus only quotes the last five lines of fragment 7, and this quotation comes immediately after line 30 of fragment 1. This means that Sextus lacks the sentence "for this shall never prevail: that things that are not being, are [*eînai mē̱ eónta*]" (7.1). That is to say, for him, the way from which it is necessary to withdraw mentioned in 7.2 is the way stated immediately beforehand, which, in his version, is not our text 7.1, but "the opinions of mortals in which there is no true conviction" (1.30). In the most natural way possible, for Sextus, opinions are the way that states that "things that are not being, are." Nevertheless, it is odd that the last two lines of fragment 1 should be missing from Sextus' quotation, and that his text runs on immediately into fragment 7.2. This is not the moment to venture a hypothesis about this anomaly, but we might imagine that Sextus had an abbreviated version of the Poem in which, now as plainly as possible, the way presented in 8.1 follows immediately upon the suppression of the way that affirms the existence of not-being presented in 7.2.[662] It is worth pointing out that both Sextus and Simplicius give us to understand that a way has been eliminated in fragment 6 and that another has been retained, and this is what the text they quote from the beginning of fragment 8 is concerned with. D. Furley sums up these stages of Parmenides' reasoning thus: "Either *p*, or *q*, or both *p* and *q*; but not *q*; and if not *q*, then not both *p* and *q*; therefore only *p* remains."[663]

---

660 On the context of Simplicius' quotations, cf. **Stevens**, A., *Postérité de l'Être: Simplicius interprète de Parménide* (Brussels: Ousia, 1990).

661 Furley finds in 8.1 the reply to the "judgment" carried out by the *lógos* in 7.5–6 (**Furley**, "Truth as What Survives," 44).

662 Sextus' text is different from that of Simplicius. In it we read *dé ti* (a reading that is also found in **Simplicius**, *Phys.*, 78) *thumós*. Vitali follows this version, but unexpectedly translates "*thumós*" as "conoscenza" (**Vitali** [1977], 35).

663 **Furley**, "Truth as What Survives," 39. Despite the clarity of this scheme, the weight of prejudice leads Furley to say that Parmenides "rejects all the ways, except one" (**Furley**,

So the only way that remains is the fundamental thesis. The other possibility presented in fragment 2 was abandoned because a precise analysis of its content showed that, in reality, it does not exist. Those who claim to follow this nonexistent way are merely playing with words: they believe they are finding the meaning of reality, and only find what they themselves have created: words, names. This way is a vicious circle, and therefore has already been abandoned. This the Goddess proclaims when, in the middle of the arguments she presents in fragment 8, she engages in a sort of recapitulation. Her use of the perfect tense shows that the exclusion of one way (just one; so just one remains, since at first there were only two) has already taken place and has been necessary: "it has already been decided [*kékritai*], of necessity [*anágkē*], that one remains unthinkable [*anóēton*] and unnamable [*anṓnumon*] [since it is not the true way] and the other exists [*pélein*] and is genuine [*etḗtumon*" (8.16–18). The exclusion occurred when, faced with a "judgment" in fragments 6 and 7, the wrong way could not defend itself against the "polemical proof" (7.5) to which it was subjected.

These three lines (8.16–18) give us complementary information of great importance. Although Parmenides does not use the term "false" (*pseudés*) (at least in the passages of the Poem that have come down to us), we now know that one of the ways "is not true." It is worth pointing out that fragment 8 completes the polar opposition between the two ways already established in fragment 2: one way was accompanied by *the truth* and the other was completely unknowable. Now we know that, in addition, this second way *is not true.* Let us remember that as the negation of the thesis, this way was self-contradictory, since it claimed to state a term with respect to its negation: of that which is being, it said that it did not exist, and that it was necessary that it should not exist (2.5), and already in fragment 2 Parmenides had said that it was not possible to know or to utter "that which is not." Fragment 8 confirms both impossibilities: the way was abandoned because it is unthinkable and unnamable. If we take into account that, as fragment 3 states, "thinking and being are the same" we understand that that which is not is unthinkable. Although the epithet "*anṓnumon*" is also negative, it is more difficult to interpret. I prefer to translate it as "unnamable," with the meaning "impossible to utter," basing my ideas on the trilogy be-think-say that was discussed in Chapter V. Nevertheless, the term could also mean "without name," as in a passage of Aristotle's *Nicomachean Ethics,*[664] an allusion, perhaps, to the human habit of naming "everything."

"Truth as What Survives," 38). If this scholar believed in his own interpretation, he would have to recognize that only two ways are possible, *p* and *q*, and that *one* is rejected and *one* is retained.

664 Passage 1107b2, which says that various states of mind do not have a name of their own.

(b) The s̱ēmata *of* éstin

At the beginning of fragment 8, the Goddess says that one single word remains as the content of the way: "is." Thanks to this single term, an assimilation is produced between "is" and the way, to the point where the explanation of the meaning of "is" is found in a series of *s̱ēmata* which are "upon" (*epí*) the way. These *s̱ēmata* are multiple (*pollá*), which means that the single word "is" possesses unsuspected riches. This was brought out by Parmenides by means of the opposition between "one single word" and "multiple *s̱ēmata*." As I said, these *s̱ēmata* are "upon" (or "on") the way. Up to this point, Parmenides has presented his ideas directly, and it was only regarding the wrong way that he gave a sort of justification that was both theoretical and practical: theoretical when in fragment 2 he said that that which is not cannot be the object either of thought or of utterance; practical when he showed, in fragments 6 and 7, that this wrong way is untravelable, since it is a fiction created by mortals. So now "proofs" have to be brought in favor of the thesis, that is, the way accompanied by truth. This way maintained that there is being because it is not possible not to be, and given the necessary character of this thesis, the fact of being (whose impossibility has proved unimaginable) acquires a necessary and absolute character.

The *s̱ēmata* of fragment 8 are indications, even proofs (not to say "demonstrations"), of the necessary and unique character of the fact of being. They are *on* the way because the way is a route to travel, on which there are stages, milestones, and signposts that indicate that thought is going the right way. This "argumentative" moment in Parmenides' thought is found between lines 2 and 49 of fragment 8, which constitute a "trustworthy reasoning [*lógos*] and thought [*nóe̱ma*] about the truth" (8.50). But what does "*s̱ēmata*" mean in this context? The singular term is *s̱ê̱ma,* and its meaning is very broad, but in every case there is a reference to a certain type of sign, signal, or pointer. This must be the meaning of the word in 8.55 in relation to the external forms (which we have already discussed above). At the beginning of fragment 8, as Parmenides is speaking of a way, we may consider that the *s̱ēmata* are signposts to be found along the way. But what is the purpose of these signposts? They are witnesses to the necessary and absolute character of the presence signified by *éstin,* and all that that presence implies. A *s̱ê̱ma* is a *s̱emeîon:* a sign or proof.[665] Melissus of Samos, who without any doubt knew Parmenides' Poem, says that the principal *s̱emeîon*

665 Cf. L. S. J.: "*s̱emeîon* . . . = *s̱ê̱ma,* in all senses; . . . in reasoning, a sign or proof." This position was to be found before that in Albertelli (**Albertelli** [1939], 240, note 2), and **Simplicius** had already stated that "*tò gàr òn . . . àlla ékhei s̱emeîa*" (*Phys.*, 77.30).

of his philosophy is the argument according to which only one being exists, but that, apart from that, there are also other *sēmeîa* (fr. 8.1). These are signs pointing to proofs in favor of a doctrine.

Let us return to the beginning of fragment 8. The single word that remains as a subject of study, reflection, and investigation is, finally, "*éstin,*" standing alone. Now we understand why Parmenidean truth is circular (*eukukléos*) (1.29) and why the succinct and enigmatic text preserved as fragment 5 says that "it is common for me that where I begin, there I shall return again." The starting point coincides with the arrival point. After a long journey, the beginning of fragment 8 says exactly the same as line 3 of fragment 2, "*éstin.*" And just as in the second hemistich of this line 2.3 it was "demonstrated" that is "is," because "it is not possible not to be," in the *sḗmata* of fragment 8 it will be "demonstrated" with *proofs* that is "is" because the fact of being is necessary, absolute, and unique.

Parmenides says that there are many proofs (*pollá*) of (or "upon," *epí*) the single term that remains as a valid way. This statement confirms that the way and its content have fused: the proofs of the existence of the way will be the proofs of the existence of "*éstin.*" Then an unusual fact confirms that "*éstin*" is inseparable from the "subject" that it itself has produced (since, as I have said on a number of occasions, "is" can only be said of "that which is being," since the proofs of the absolute, necessary, and unique character of "is" refer to "being" [*eón*]: "that which is being" represents "is," since only "that which is being, is"). Hence all the *sḗmata* of fragment 8 are sorts of predicates, attributes, or properties of *eón,* with which Parmenides very rarely uses the article "*tò*" to turn it into a noun, since the participle, without an article, which I have translated as "being," captures more precisely the dynamic character of the presence denoted by *éstin,* because "by being, it is."

Fragment 8 will present the foundations ("proofs") of the thesis stated rather dogmatically in line 2.3: "[that which is being] is, and [or "because"] it is not possible not to be." I said at the time that this thesis assumes (or postulates) the necessary and absolute (and therefore unique) character of the fact of being. This thesis is set against its negation as a contradiction, and this opposition occurs between absolute possibilities, excluding an intermediate term. In the middle of the presentation of the proofs in support of the necessary character of the thesis, in fragment 8, Parmenides reminds us that the fundamental decision (*krísis*) (8.15) is between "*éstin ḕ ouk éstin*" ("is or is not"), but this alternative is between absolute terms: "It is necessary to be absolutely [*pámpan pelénai*] or not [be absolutely]" (8.11). But why does the fact of being that characterizes that which is being have this absolute character? Lines 3–6a of fragment 8 list a series of "proofs" that lead to this conclusion.

(c) The Field in Which the **s̲ēmata** *Operate*

It is not my intention to go more deeply into the study of the *s̲ēmata* in fragment 8.[666] I will only refer to a few points and, in particular, we shall constantly remind ourselves that, as these *s̲ēmata* concern the fact of being, that is, a sort of activity, potency, even energy, *any analysis of them in terms of spatial coordinates makes no sense.* It is Melissus, Parmenides' illegitimate heir, who will study this fact of being in terms of time and space and, hence, will deduce that as the void does not exist, being has nowhere (*hók̲ei*) to go (!) and therefore is one; and as it was neither born nor will die, it is, always (*aeí*) was (!) and always will be (!) (fr. 2). Both space and the three temporal tenses are inapplicable to the fact of being, which, at most, can be recognized as a permanent presence.[667] Parmenides does not forget that already in fragment 1 he used allegorical images to present his ideas, and he does the same in this fragment 8, in which Dike and Moira will reappear and Ananke will enter on the scene. References to limits, chains, and even a sphere clearly have an allegorical value, as was the case with light and darkness in fragment 1, since who can imagine that being can be "chained," unless it is metaphorically?

(d) The First **s̲ēma**: *That which Is Being Is Everlasting*

Parmenides begins the presentation of the *s̲ēmata* of "is" with a sort of summing up of the characteristics that will be developed from line 6b onward: "that which is being is unbegotten and incorruptible, whole [*oûlon*], unique [*mounogenés*], unshakable [*atremés*], and finished [*telestón*]." The way of presenting these first *s̲ēmata* by Parmenides is valid for those that will come later. The Greek text says: "*agene̲ton éòn, kaì anṓlethron estin,*" literally, "being unbegotten, it is also incorruptible." The subject, which once more is assumed, is none other than the fact of being, and will only reappear in line 19 as "that which is being," *tò eón.* Lines 3–19 develop an authentic demonstration, in which argument from the absurd plays an essential part, without what is said therefore referring to a concrete subject, which shows brilliance in arguing.

---

666 On this subject I recommend the excellent analyses of Tarán (**Tarán** [1965], 82–160); Bormann (**Bormann** [1971], 150–79); and, with respect to lines 5–21, Wiesner (**Wiesner**, J., "Die Negation der Entstehung des Seienden: Studien zu Parmenides B 8.5–21," *Archiv für Geschichte der Philosophie* 52 [1970] 1–34).

667 Ruggiu speaks of a "timeless presence" (**Ruggiu** [1975], 251).

The Parmenidean machine sets out to prove that that which is being is everlasting (without temporal origin or ending), and the pseudo-questioning to which the Goddess subjects her disciple ("What origin will you seek for it? How and when might it have increased?" [8.6–7]) is purely formal: if there is only that which is being, this cannot beget itself or cease to be. The secondary consequence of this everlastingness of the fact of being is its permanent presence. The present of "*estin*" is not the verbal present tense. We would need to imagine a sort of temporal presence that endures, whose intensity is constant and which cannot be controlled through temporal parameters. L. Tarán speaks of the timeless present, aloof from time and its structures.[668] Although F. Fronterotta does not share this viewpoint, he asks a basic question, which I answered in my own way when I looked at the context in which the *sē̱mata* occur: why, in a word, must being "belong" to time?[669] According to my interpretation, that which is being has nothing to do with time that is structured in temporal "moments." Parmenides characterizes *éstin* with a present-tense verb because, in Greek grammar, it is the tense that allows him to show the presence proper to the "now" (*nûn*), but that does not mean that this present comes after a past or before a future. If we keep the category "present," as I have already said, here it means a permanent present.

The everlasting character of that which is, is assured because Dike, who does not loosen or untie the links, does not permit it either to be born or to die (8.13–14). In line 30, another divinity, Ananke, and in line 37, Moira, will also exercise similar coercive force over it: the former will keep it in the bonds or chains that hold it, and the latter will force it to remain unalterable. These three divinities replace the Daughters of the Sun at this higher stage of the philosophy "course." Indeed, the Heliades led the traveler to the heavy gates kept by Dike. Once it had been confirmed, allegorically, that the future philosopher had the "right" to continue on his journey, the way led inexorably toward the truth. And as we saw in the previous chapters, the way of truth is rigorous: it starts from axioms, covers stages, overcomes problems.[670] Randomness and digression belong to opinions. The true way follows a *necessary* course. Thought is chained to it and no straying is allowed. This is the meaning of the links, ties, even chains that

---

668 **Tarán** (1965), 180, note 2. Fronterotta criticizes this position of Tarán's (**Fronterotta**, "Essere, tempo," 856–58). For this scholar, even if being is located in an instantaneous present, it belongs to time, and this condition is necessary to explain the process of knowledge, which implies contemporaneity between subject and object (**Fronterotta**, "Essere, tempo," 867).

669 **Fronterotta**, "Essere, tempo," 866.

670 Remember that *próble̱ma* in Greek means "obstacle," "barrier."

hold that which is being. "The beautiful image of the 'chains of Necessity' means without any possible doubt the impossibility that being should not be."[671]

When he expounds the first *sḗmata* (according to which that which is being is unbegotten and incorruptible), Parmenides says clearly that the power of Dike is none other than the force of conviction (*pístios iskhús*) (8.12). Conviction, which was absent from opinions (1.30), reappears in line 8.28 to exile (that is, "send far away") generation and corruption once again, and if Parmenides stresses this aspect it is because all philosophical systems have followed a sort of genetic scheme in which a certain principle, defined *a priori* as eternal, then "becomes" this or that (i.e., elements, things) and thus beings come to take the place of being. This leads to confusion, and then it is not known what is that which is. For there to be things (beings) that are, there has to be a force that is not subject to the vicissitudes of generation, destruction, and change. That genuine principle (the others are illusory) is the fact of being.

The stability and solidity of this necessary and absolute force of being is the object of two more *sḗmata,* also given at the beginning of fragment 8: "unshakable" (*atremés*) and "finished" (*telestón*). It is impossible not to relate the term "unshakable" with the same epithet applied to the "heart" of truth in line 1.29. When we analyzed that passage, I suggested that truth possesses a content, a nucleus: metaphorically, a "heart." This nucleus is the total presence of that which is being. And as that which is being is *already* that which is (it was not born, will not be born, was not corrupted, and will not be corrupted), it is "finished"; it is complete, perfect (etymologically, *per-* [wholly]; *-factum* [made]).

For the Greek mentality, the finished is the symbol of perfection, since it lacks nothing; Parmenides himself says so in line 32: "it is not permitted [*ouk . . . thémis*] that that which is being should be imperfect [*ateleúteton*]." Parmenides resorts once more to legal terminology: just as Dike did not allow it to be born or to die, now it is not allowed to remain unfinished, and this prohibition, which in line 32 has an impersonal origin, is in fact an imposition of powerful necessity (1.30). As I have already said, this coercion derives from the necessary linking of the argument, which advances by stages and follows a rigorous method. The links that it establishes "tie" that which is being to itself; they are "ob-ligatory."[672] This is how "remaining identical *in* the same, it abides in itself" (8.29). Unshakable, it resists and

---

671 **Reale**, G., in **Zeller**, E., and **Mondolfo**, R., *La filosofia dei Greci,* Part I, Vol. 3, (Florence: La Nuova Italia, 1967), 217.

672 An echo of the relation there is between perfection and the coherent unity between the parts of the whole will be found in **Plato**, when he states that it is the good (*tò agathón*), i.e., that which unites (*deón*), that "maintains" (*sunékhein*) (*Fedón,* 99c).

remains constant (*émpedon*) (8.30). As it does not have to face polemical proofs, as was the case with the wrong way, it remains wholly intact (*ásulon*) (8.48).[673] B. Cassin finds a parallel between these lines and a passage in the *Odyssey,* in which Odysseus resists the sirens' song and says that "by its self-limitation being escapes the coercion of events, birth and death [. . .] Being, which is, but which 'never was and never will be' is only immobilized in an identity present to itself if it leaves time and becoming beyond its limits."[674]

(e) Immobility

Line 37 says that Moira[675] forces it to remain whole (*oûlon*) and immobile (*akíne̱ton*). This immobility has already appeared in line 26: "immobile within the bonds of mighty chains . . ." We have already seen that these chains, links, and ties are the requirements imposed by the argument that "ties" the reasonings; if you like, it is a question of "logical necessity." There can be no doubt that, for inexplicable reasons, "immobility," together with "oneness," is the *sê̱ma* that even in antiquity achieved most popularity and marked Parmenides forever as the philosopher who denied the reality of movement. Zeno's demonstration of the impossibility of a *rational explanation* for movement (from which its nonexistence was erroneously deduced) has nothing to do with Parmenides. Neither does Melissus' demonstration of the impossibility that "being" should move, as a consequence of the nonexistence of the void (fr. 7 [7]). Probably, Plato's[676] invention of the Eleatic school contaminated Parmenides with these ideas of his fellow citizen Zeno and his reader Melissus (a distant reader, since he lived on Samos). Given what we have said up until now, the interpretation of this "immobility" does not present any difficulty whatsoever. As Parmenides says nothing about the "beings" who constitute the field that Plato calls the "sensitive field," any negation (or affirmation) of the movement of "things"

673 "Inviolable" is the translation of Couloubaritsis (**Couloubaritsis** [1990], 372).

674 **Cassin**, B., "Le chant des syrènes dans le Poème de Parménide (Quelques rermarques sur le fr. VIII, 26–33)," in *Études sur Parménide,* Vol. II, ed. Aubenque, P. (Paris: Vrin, 1987), 168–69.

675 Parmenides had already introduced Dike, and also Ananke, if we consider that "necessity" is also a divinity. According to Reale, they are three names for the same divinity (**Reale**, *La filosofia dei Greci,* I.3, 217).

676 On Plato's invention of the Eleatic school, cf. **Cordero**, N. L., "Simplicius et l' 'école' éléate," in *Simplicius, sa vie, son oeuvre, sa survie,* ed. Hadot, I. (Berlin/New York: Walther de Gruyter, 1987), 166–82; and **Cordero**, N. L., "L'invention de l'école éléatique (Platon, *Sophiste,* 242d)," in *Études sur le "Sophiste" de Platon,* ed. Aubenque, P. (Naples: Bibliopolis, 1991) 91–124.

is excluded. Given the analysis of the fact of being in fragment 8, the relevant question is not, "why does being not move?" but, "why should being move?" Indeed, what sense does it make to apply the category of movement to a necessary and absolute notion? Like most of the *sḗmata* in fragment 8, "movement" has an allegorical value, like the limits, chains, sphere (which we will look at below), and so forth. History has been stricter with Parmenides than with Plato, whom it has forgiven for saying the opposite: that "existing reality" (*ousía*), that is, Form, "*moves*" (*kineîsthai*) (*Sophist* 248e); nobody took the expression literally,[677] although there can be no doubt that Plato and Parmenides were trying to say the same thing: *kineîsthai* means "shake," "alter." By being known, Form in Plato becomes an object of knowledge, a *nóēma;* now it is not what it was, although the change it has undergone only consists of acquiring a new property, that of being known. In Parmenides, that which is being does not alter or change, since any change would mean becoming what it is not, or acquiring that which it lacks, and in that case it would have to be admitted that something exists "as well as" that which is, which was denied *a priori* by the other *sḗmata.* As it is "perfect," "finished" (*tetelesménon*) (8.42), it lacks nothing. With a touch of irony, Parmenides says that, as it is "whole," if it lacked anything, it would lack *everything* (8.33).

(f) Homogeneity

Indeed, that which is being is homogeneous (*homón*) (8.47), everywhere equal to itself (*îson*) (8.49). There are no degrees of being: it is (absolutely) or it is not (absolutely).

Who could hold that it is possible to half-exist? The fact of being exists now (*nûn*) in a wholly homogeneous way (*homoû pân*) (8.5); it is itself wholly homogeneous (*pân estin homoîon*) (8.22) and wholly continuous (*xunekhès pân estin*) (8.25), so that it presents no "gap" whatsoever: "that which is being touches [*pelázei*] that which is being" (8.25).

To illustrate this homogeneity, Parmenides resorts to the image of the perfect solid, the sphere, whose "sphericity" depends on the homogeneity of its mass. Indeed, if the mass of a sphere has different densities at some points, then its surface will be bound to reflect this anomaly. A perfect (that is, well-made) sphere cannot present a rough surface. Everything depends on the homogeneity of its mass. For this reason, Parmenides states that

---

677 Cf. the classic article of De Vogel (**De Vogel**, C., "Platon a-t-il ou n'a-t-il pas introduit le mouvement dans son monde intelligible?" *Actes du XIe Congrès International de Philosophie* XII, Brussels [1953] 61–67).

"that which is being is not as if it had a greater quantity of that which is, either here or there" (8.48). That which is cannot be quantified: either it is or it is not; it is "like [*enalígkios*] the mass of a well-rounded sphere,[678] completely equidistant from the center, since it is not possible that it should be a bit stronger or a bit weaker, here or there" (8.43–45). Likeness does not mean identity. To encourage Diomedes, Athena made to spring from her helmet "an indefatigable fire, like [*enalígkios*] the autumn star [Sirius]" (*Il.* 5.5); that does not mean that the star itself sprang from her helmet. Menelaus rises from his bed "like [*enalígkios*] a god," but that does not mean he is a god. In Parmenides, the fact of being is *like* the mass of a well-rounded sphere, because just like the mass that makes this kind of sphere possible, it is homogeneous, everywhere equally "dense." The image is didactic: "the perfection of the curve of the sphere is clarified by 'not a bit stronger or a bit weaker': it is the negation of all difference in the power or intensity of being, since any difference of this kind in the *manifestation* of being would reinforce the illusions of mortals."[679]

(g) Oneness

As there are no degrees of intensity in being, it is homogeneous, continuous, one (8.5). Together with "immobility," the *sē̱ma* of "one" (*hén*) made Parmenides become the greatest representative of "Eleatic oneness." As in the case of the first "immobility," this does not apply to the object of Parmenides' reflection either. As we know, only two sources of this line 8.5 have come down to us: Simplicius and Asclepius, and the term "*hén*" appears only in Simplicius (*Phys.* 78, 145). Instead of "*hén, sunekhés,*" Asclepius gives us "*oulophués*" (*Met.* 42), which M. Untersteiner, who adopts this version, translates as "is a whole in its nature."[680] As we shall see, Plato's criticisms of Parmenides are largely based on the notion of "wholeness" that appears to abound in the Poem and that would be contradictory to the oneness, and in the text offered by Asclepius there is a new reference to the "whole," so it is very probable that Plato knew Parmenides' text through this version of Asclepius.[681] Even so, we do not believe there are reasons to distrust Simplicius' text; it is simply a question of interpreting it.

---

678 Dixsaut translates "of a ball (boule)" (**Dixsaut**, M., "Platon et le *lógos* de Parmenide," in *Études sur Parmenide,* Vol. II, ed. Aubenque, P. [Paris: Vrin, 1987], 233.

679 **Dixsaut**, "Platon et le *lógos,*" 234–35.

680 **Untersteiner** (1958), 145. On the basis of this reading, this scholar maintains that "l'essere di Parmenide è *oûlon,* non *hén*" (**Untersteiner** [1958], xxvii–1).

681 Reale thinks it possible that both versions are authentic and correspond to different periods in Parmenides' life (**Reale**, G., *Melissus: Testimonianze e frammenti* [Florence: La Nuova

What does the statement that that which is being is "one" mean? Let us see (1) what *can* be said about this characteristic; and (2) what *must not* be said about it.

(1) As we have already said with respect to movement and other notions assuming spatial-temporal parameters, any reference to a physical—*ergo* quantifiable —universe must be excluded. If a philosopher asks a question about the quantity of beings, it is reasonable to expect he will reply with numeral adjectives: one or more than one. But, as J. Barnes points out: "as far as we know, the question of how many items the universe contains did not concern him [Parmenides]."[682] K. Reinhardt had already said that the predicate of oneness was almost marginal (nebensächlicher) in Parmenides.[683] "*Hén*" means that that which is being is a total presence that, tautologically, monopolizes the fact of being: "Being is the only thing there is."[684] In this sense, "being" is a unique, singular "fact." And for this reason, for the first time in the terminology of Greek philosophy (unless he was preceded by texts now lost to us), Parmenides, who like all philosophers reflects upon "*tà ónta*" ("things"), discovers that if these exist it is because they have "something" in common, which is unique, and for that reason they are considered to be "*tò ón,*" "that which is being." The only oneness detectable in Parmenides is linguistic; the singular replaces the plural; reflection upon *ón* replaces reflection upon *ónta.* Just as the life studied by a biologist is "one," although it manifests itself differently in every kind of living thing, the fact of being that Parmenides discovered is also "one," since there cannot be various kinds of "being": it is or it is not (8.15).

(2) In my commentary on "opinions" (cf. Chapter VIII), I said with reference to a possible Parmenidean cosmology that the commentaries of doxographers should not be trusted. The same thing happens—I may add now—with the opinions of some philosophers about others. In the case of Parmenides, I cited the confession of Plato (who was both a doxographer and a philosopher): "I am afraid I do not understand his words" nor what he was thinking of when he said them (*Theaetetus* 184a). This does not prevent him from commenting on and criticizing the Eleatean, as Parmenides himself had also criticized previous philosophers. The same thing happened with Aristotle with respect to Plato, with the Stoics with respect to Aristotle, and so on. Philosophy is a perpetual, salutary, ongoing dialogue, and thanks to this dynamic it will never end. When we have the good fortune to possess authentic texts, these must be analyzed themselves, and

---

Italia, 1970], 111). For Barnes, this position is "romantic" (**Barnes**, J., "Parmenides and the Eleatic One," *Archiv für Geschichte der Philosophie* 61 [1979] 11, note 35).

682 **Barnes**, "Parmenides," 21.

683 **Reinhardt** (1916), 108.

684 **Tarán** (1965), 190.

commentators can be listened to when they are based on these texts. Nothing in what remains of Parmenides' Poem supports the sentence with which Plato sums up the credo of the "Eleatic group": "all things [*tô̱n pánto̱n*] are considered to be one single thing [*henòs óntos*]" (*Sophist* 242d). The sentence makes sense only if it is interpreted in the way I have suggested: Parmenides is referring to everything *as if it were* one single thing, because it, the fact of being, is a common denominator of all things. But we do not know whether Plato would have agreed with our interpretation. In short, Parmenides says that the fact of being is unique, not that everything is one, and certainly not that being is The One. It is true that in the above-mentioned passage of the *Sophist,* Parmenides is not mentioned, but it is from this text that the Eleatic group, whose most distinguished representative was Parmenides, was established. From this to attributing the aforementioned creed to Parmenides is a mere step, which commentators did not hesitate to take.

In the *Sophist,* Plato is interested in overcoming a conception of being that, according to him, led philosophy down a blind alley. An absolute conception of being does not enable crucial problems to be resolved, such as the justification of predication, false speech, images. Philosophers contemporary with Plato who were considered to be Parmenides' heirs are the causes of this situation, especially Melissus and Antisthenes. Parmenides is innocent, but Plato, who is not a historian of philosophy but a philosopher, battles against a system of ideas as this system had come down to him. And the "one-being," which prevents any justification of multiplicity, the sensitive universe, or change, is the main enemy.

However, Plato is not tilting at windmills. A philosophical current defends this one-being, and its origins are to be found in Melissus. Perhaps Plato wanted to suggest to readers of the *Sophist* that Elea itself was not the cradle of this conception when he says that these pernicious ideas arose later "starting from Elea."[685] But it is certain that Melissus does clearly proclaim the unity of being. "Melissus is the only Eleatic who promoted the theme of the *hén* to the level of critical knowledge, and who offers a rigorous demonstration of this attribute of the *eón.*"[686] To carry out this demonstration, as we know, Melissus distorts Parmenides' philosophy because he makes the fact of being a spatial-temporal Being, which—unlike the dynamic force of that which is being, which is "perfect," that is, "finished"—is

---

685 The Greek text of the passage does not say "*par'he̱min*" ("among us"), as is read by those who follow a reviser of the manuscript *Parisinus* 1808, but "*par'he̱mô̱n*" ("starting from us"), as the whole of the manuscript tradition attests. Cf. my translations: Platón, *Diálogos,* "El sofista," Vol. V (Madrid: Gredos, 1988), 403, note 165; and Platon, *Le Sophiste* (Paris: GF-Flammarion, 1993), 242, note 193.

686 **Reale**, *Melissus,* 121.

characterized by being infinite (*ápeiron,* i.e., without limits) in "size" (*mégethos*)! The oneness of being is the consequence of this unlimitedness: "if being was not one, it would be limited by something else" (Melissus, fr. 5). There can be no doubt that "Melissus could go down in posterity, in the history books, as the inventor of real monism."[687]

If Plato combats this conception of the one-being, why does he not criticize Melissus directly? For two reasons: (1) Plato tends to trust the philosophical culture of the reader (especially if the reader has been his pupil in the Academy) and he knows his reader cannot fail to be aware that in a passage of his book Melissus had stated that "only one thing exists" (*hén mónon ésti*) (fr. 8.1). So when in the *Sophist* the criticism of the monists begins, the protagonist of the dialogue asks the anonymous monist: "Do you say that 'only one thing exists' [*hén . . . mónon eînai* (in direct speech, '*ésti*')]?" (244b). No one can doubt that this is Melissus. (2) It is usual for Plato to blame the originators of a system for the developments to be found in those who claim to be heirs of the system, as if the germs of the danger were already to be found in its origin. This is the case with Heraclitus, who never wrote the phrase "everything is in flux" (which, moreover, would be contradictory to the eternal law of the *lógos*), even though the phrase is attributed to the "Heracliteans" (*Cratylus* 438–39) and also exaggeratedly ascribed to their founder. Doubtless Plato believes that Parmenides' absolute conception of the fact of being was responsible for the developments of philosophers such as Antisthenes, who stated that all speech (*lógos*) is true (cf. Proclus' testimony *In Crat.* 37), which produced unacceptable secondary consequences for Plato's system, since if lying, falsehood, and illusion do not exist, what difference is there between the sophist and the philosopher? Plato wrote the *Sophist* in order to answer this question, and the figure to be eliminated was not Melissus or Antisthenes, but Parmenides.

(h) Truth

After repeating that that which is being "persists in homogeneous form to its limits" (i.e., it remains protected in its identity), Parmenides indicates that those words mark the ending of the "trustworthy reasoning" (*pistón lógon*) and the thought (*nóe̱ma*) about (or around: *amphís*) the truth (*ale̱theíe̱s*) (8.50–51). The pair thought-reasoning deserves an explanation. The *nóe̱ma* has a content, and that content is expressed in speech. As the speech took the form of an argument, I have preferred to translate "*lógos*" as "reasoning," but "speech" would also have been a correct translation, since speech

---

687 **Barnes**, "Parmenides," 21.

and reasoning fuse. The reasoning was made up of the presentation of a series of "proofs," and as these revolve around the truth, the reasoning was "trustworthy." Here we find the same schema as in fragment 2, when Parmenides stated that the way of persuasion accompanied the truth. "Persuasion" and "trustworthiness" go together. Sophistry has not yet been born, and the persuasive *lógos* is not deceptive (as it will be in the case of Gorgias, cf. *Encomium of Helen* [fr. 11], § 8, "*lógos ho peísas . . . apatḗsas,*" "the speech that persuades . . . deceives"). If persuasion accompanies the truth, it is because only the truth is trustworthy, and already in fragment 2, truth accompanies the way that expounds the thesis. Moreover, in fragment 8 it will be said that the negation of this way is not a true way, from which it can be deduced that the other way "is" true. So can it be deduced that the way is true because its content is the truth? Yes, but with reservations. If the content of the way is the truth, it is because the way says something true. That means that truth will be a prerogative of a *lógos* (speech) that is presented by a way, and in presenting a true speech, through a sort of perhaps illegitimate generalization, Parmenides says that the way itself is true. It is for this reason that I have said that I hesitate to apply the epithet "true" directly to the way (that is to say, I do so with reservations).

The problem of truth in Parmenides is very complex. Scholars who blindly accept the Heideggerian thesis, according to which, at the start, truth is an ontological category (which is still far from being proved), show no doubt in stating that as "being" is true, then a speech that speaks about being must also be true. *Alēthḗs* is absent from the *sḗmata* of that which is being, which is wholly coherent with the reasoning of fragment 8, in which Parmenides confirms that the thought expressed up to line 49 was a trustworthy *lógos* that revolved "around" (*amphís*) the truth. As always, from Homer on, truth lies in a speech that, if valid, has the privilege of being accompanied by the truth, and in that case it can be said that the speech revolves around the truth, as in 8.49. But in Parmenides, truth is still the truth of speech. As this speech is a speech about "being," Antisthenes (perhaps without thinking of Parmenides) will have no doubt in stating that "that which is, is true." We do not know whether Parmenides reached this level. Remember that even at the end of fragment 1, Parmenides admits that truth has a "heart," and, according to my interpretation, that heart is a content: there is being. But to state that "there is being" is a speech. So what is true is the speech.

Epilogue

Any respectable work ends with an "epilogue." I would be ashamed to break this rule, although I feel sad at the idea of writing an *epilogue* to the philosophy of Parmenides, since that would mean that his ideas might be exhausted at any particular time. But an epilogue can also bear witness to the permanence of certain ideas, and can analyze why an innovative and revolutionary author could have been marginalized and misunderstood even by his immediate successors. Several times in this work I have quoted Plato's confession in the *Theaetetus:* "I am afraid I do not understand his words" or what he was thinking when he said them (184a). Nevertheless, Plato goes on to comment upon (and criticize) Parmenides, and there can be no doubt that Plato's interpretation of the Eleatean is indebted to the philosophers who presented themselves as the master's heirs. So are there any philosophers before Plato who explicitly refer to Parmenides? The answer is negative, but this fact is normal. If we leave aside Heraclitus, who alludes to some of his predecessors,[688] treatises by Presocratic philosophers present themselves as oracular texts without references to the past. Nevertheless, there are two philosophers who, even from antiquity, although they are not named, are usually associated with Parmenides. They are Zeno of Elea and Melissus of Samos. Let us begin with Zeno. Can a Parmenidean legacy be detected in this philosopher? My reply is negative. It is not enough to be a citizen of Elea, and to possibly have heard Parmenides speak, in order to share his ideas. If we carefully read Plato's testimony on the relationship between the two philosophers, we can state that Plato himself invites us to distrust Zeno's "Eleaticism."[689] Indeed, if we leave out the reference to be found at the beginning of *Parmenides* (128a–b) and the *Sophist* (216a),[690] all Plato's allusions to Zeno present him as a debater (i.e., an eristic) and even as a sophist.

688 Cf. fragment 40, which refers to Pythagoras (who appears again in fr. 129), Xenophanes, and Hecateus, and fragment 39, in which there is a eulogy of Bias de Priene.

689 Regarding the Eleatic "school," in various passages of this work I have referred the reader to my articles (**Cordero**, N. L., "Simplicius et l''école' éléate," in *Simplicius, sa vie, son oeuvre, sa survie,* ed. Hadot, I. [Berlin/New York: Walther de Gruyter, 1987], 166–82; and **Cordero**, N. L., "L'invention de l'école éléatique (Platon, *Sophiste* 242d)," in *Études sur le "Sophiste" de Platon,* ed. Aubenque, P. [Naples: Bibliopolis, 1991], 91–124).

690 Cf. my translations of the *Sophist,* in which I show that even at the beginning of the dialogue, Plato says that the protagonist, the Stranger of Elea, is "different" from the followers of Parmenides and Zeno (Platón, *Diálogos,* Vol. V, "El sofista" [Madrid: Gredos, 1988], 332, note 5; and Platon, *Le Sophiste* [Paris: GF-Flammarion, 1993], 212, note 5).

In his *Parmenides,* Plato makes Zeno say that he wrote his "defense" of Parmenides "for the pleasure of discussion" (*philonikía*) (128d), and the fictitious[691] Parmenides of the dialogue calls Zeno's arguments a "gymnastic exercise" (an exercise that he recommends to Socrates, an inexperienced and somewhat dogmatic youth). These speeches by Zeno refer both to a hypothesis and to its negation (136a), which coincides with the image of the philosopher presented in the *Phaedrus* (if it is Zeno who hides beneath "Palamedes of Elea," as most researchers agree). This character "spoke in such a way that he was able to make it appear to his listeners that the same things were equal and different, single and multiple, at rest and in movement" (261d). And finally, in *Alcibiades I,* the panorama is completed, since Plato says that Pythodorus and Callias "through having paid a hundred mines to this Zeno, acquired talent and enlightenment" (119a). That is, for Plato, Zeno is a mere sophist.

Various post-Platonic commentators share this viewpoint. Aristotle makes an enigmatic reference from which it can be deduced that Zeno was capable of making two different things[692] coincide at the same time, and this skill is also attested to by Isocrates (on what is both at once possible and impossible, *Hel.* 3) and for Proclus (on the equal and unequal, *In Parm.* 620.1 Cousin). We should not be surprised that Pseudo-Galen (*Hist. phil.* 3 Diels = *Dox. gr.* 601.8–9) and Epiphanius (*Adv. haer.* III.11 Diels = *Dox. gr.* 590.20) considered that Zeno was an eristic philosopher and that for the *Souda* (s.v.) and Diogenes Laertius (VIII.57), Zeno was the inventor of dialectic.

The conclusion is obvious: Zeno did not have his own philosophical system.[693] The testimonies that present him as a disciple of Parmenides depend exclusively upon Plato,[694] but only in the *Parmenides.* In 1971, in a revolutionary article, F. Solmsen demonstrated conclusively that Plato arbitrarily combined the ideas of Parmenides and Zeno. Although I do not fully share the viewpoint of this scholar, for whom Zeno represents "a modified version of Eleatism,"[695] a rigorous reading of the *Parmenides* (128a) shows that Plato appears to "discover" the link between Zeno and Parmenides in certain ideas that, for Plato, are similar. That means that the similarity between the two philosophers was not something obvious. For example, Aris-

---

691 "Parmenides" in the *Parmenides* is an archetype: the philosopher as such. No Parmenidean idea is expressed by the Parmenides of the *Parmenides.*

692 "As if it were possible, as in Zeno, to have revenge on both father and mother at once" (*Rhetoric,* A.12.1372b).

693 Cf. **Cordero,** N.L. "Zénon d'Elée, moniste ou nihiliste?" *La parola del passato* 43 (1988) 100–126.

694 Cf. **Cordero**, "Simplicius et l''école'" and **Cordero**, "L'invention de l'école."

695 **Solmsen**, F., "The Tradition About Zeno of Elea Re-examined," *Phronesis* 16 (1971) 140.

totle, who devotes a few pages of his *Physics* to Zeno, never links his name with that of Parmenides, that is to say Zeno, a citizen of Elea, may have "listened" to Parmenides without becoming his disciple. Furthermore—and fortunately—texts of Zeno have come down to us, and these show that he and Parmenides were not talking about the same thing. Parmenides' *éstin* is not an "object"; it is an inexhaustible, complete, perfect force, which cannot be regarded as either one or multiple, as either "divisible to the infinite or indivisible in one part."

From Plato on, posterity has associated the name of Melissus with Parmenides, although this philosopher does not make a single concrete reference to the Eleatean. In the *Theaetetus* (180e, 183e), Plato mentions both philosophers as representatives of the tendency that maintains that there is an immobile One-Being, and from then on anything found in Melissus was attributed to Parmenides. In the chapter on the *sḗmata* of the fact of being (the passage on "oneness"), we already saw that Melissus is the creator of the One-Being, thanks to his refutation of the void, and I gave my own viewpoint there: Parmenides has nothing to do with these ideas.

With or without heirs, it is clear that Parmenides' Poem has immediate repercussions. In Empedocles, practically contemporary with Melissus, and perhaps even a little earlier, there are echoes not only of the problem but also of the terminology—including grammatical expressions[696]—that are found in Parmenides. These details show that Empedocles "read" Parmenides' text, and so did Plato, Aristotle, Theophrastus, Plutarch, and Clement, since all these authors quoted passages from it. The last direct witness to the Poem seems to be Simplicius (sixth century A.D.), who allows himself—those are his words—to quote an extensive passage of it, "given the rarity of the work."[697] From then on, no *new* quotation from Parmenides appears.[698] Already-known texts are quoted again, and there is nothing to show that these sources directly used Parmenides' book; they may be indirect quotations. From this series of textual references going from Plato to Simplicius, the attempt was made to "reestablish" the lost text of the Poem, and in Chapter I we looked at the stages of this long process, thanks to which we can know about Parmenides' thought today.

There is no need to say that we shall never know if our knowledge of the text is precise. And of course that means we shall never know if we have succeeded in interpreting its content. By way of consolation, I have

696 Cf. the clear parallelism between line 8.52 of Parmenides ("learn the opinions of mortals, listening to the deceitful order of my words") and passage 17.26–27 of Empedocles ("Listen to the undeceiving order of the speech . . .").

697 **Simplicius**, *Phys.*, 144.

698 For a detailed analysis of the question, cf. **Cordero**, N. L., "L'histoire du texte de Parménide," in *Études sur Parménide*, ed. Aubenque, P. (Paris: Vrin, 1987), 3–24.

several times quoted the text from the *Theaetetus,* in which Plato, barely a century after Parmenides, said exactly the same thing. Be that as it may, whether faithful to its author or to an approximate image of him, today we possess something of his thought, which both makes us think and forces us to converse with him and, if the verb were not too solemn, we might add, invites us to "philosophize." The rest is silence . . .

Appendix 1
Parmenides' Poem

(a) Text

The text of the Poem I present here is based on a direct revision of the manuscript tradition. It differs in certain places from the last "orthodox" version by Hermann Diels, as given by him in *Die Fragmente der Vorsokratiker.* In the footnotes I tell the reader about any changes I have made. A complete critical apparatus can be found in my work *Les deux chemins de Parménide.*

Fragment 1 ουκ

ἵπποι ταί με φέρουσιν ὅσον τ' ἐπὶ θυμὸς ἱκάνοι,
πέμπον, ἐπεὶ μ' ἐς ὁδὸν βῆσαν πολύφημον ἄγουσαι
δαίμονος, ἣ κατὰ πάν[699] τα<ύ>τῃ[700] φέρει εἰδότα φῶτα.
τῇ φερόμην, τῇ γάρ με πολύφραστοι φέρον ἵπποι
ἅρμα τιταίνουσαι, κοῦραι δ' ὁδὸν ἡγεμόνευον.
ἄξων δ' ἐν χνοίῃσιν <ἵει> σύριγγος ἀϋτήν
αἰθόμενος (δοιοῖς γὰρ ἐπείγετο δινωτοῖσιν
κύκλοις ἀμφοτέρωθεν), ὅτε σπερχοίατο πέμπειν
ἡλιάδες κοῦραι, προλιποῦσαι δώματα νυκτός,
εἰς φάος, ὠσάμεναι κράτων ἄπο χερσὶ καλύπτρας
ἔνθα πύλαι νυκτός τε καὶ ἤματός εἰσι κελεύθων,
καί σφας ὑπέρθυρον ἀμφὶς ἔχει καὶ λάϊνος οὐδός.
αὐταὶ δ' αἰθέριαι πλῆνται μεγάλοισι θυρέτροις
τῶν δὲ δίκη πολύποινος ἔχει κληῖδας ἀμοιβούς.
τὴν δὴ παρφάμεναι κοῦραι μαλακοῖσι λόγοισιν
πεῖσαν ἐπιφραδέως, ὥς σφιν βαλανωτὸν ὀχῆα
ἀπτερέως ὤσειε πυλέων ἄπο. ταὶ δὲ θυρέτρων
χάσμ' ἀχανὲς ποίησαν ἀναπτάμεναι πολυχάλκους
ἄξονας ἐν σύριγξιν ἀμοιβαδὸν εἰλίξασαι

---

699 Conjecture. All Sextus Empiricus manuscripts, the only source for this passage, present a corrupt text: ΚΑΤΑΙΙΑΝΤΑΤΗ. On this conjecture, cf. **Cordero**, "Le vers 1.3 de Parménide (La Déesse conduit à l'égard de tout)," *La Revue Philosophique* 107(2) (1982) 158–179.

700 < > *Idem* previous note.

γόμφοις καὶ περόνῃσιν ἀρηρότε· τῇ ῥα δι' αὐτῶν
ἰθὺς ἔχον κοῦραι κατ' ἀμαξιτὸν ἅρμα καὶ ἵππους.
καί με θεὰ πρόφρων ὑπεδέξατο, χεῖρα δὲ χειρί
δεξιτερὴν ἕλεν, ὧδε δ' ἔπος φάτο καί με προσηύδα·
ὦ κοῦρ' ἀθανάτοισι συνάορος ἡνιόχοισιν,
ἵπποις ταί σε φέρουσιν ἱκάνων ἡμέτερον δῶ,
χαῖρ', ἐπεὶ οὔτι σε μοῖρα κακὴ προὔπεμπε νέεσθαι
τήνδ' ὁδόν (ἦ γάρ ἀπ' ἀνθρώπων ἐκτὸς πάτου ἐστίν),
ἀλλὰ θέμις τε δίκη τε. Χρεὼ δέ σε πάντα πυθέσθαι
ἠμέν ἀληθίης εὐκυκλέος ἀτρεμὲς ἦτορ
ἠδὲ βροτῶν δόξας, ταῖς οὐκ ἔνι πίστις ἀληθής.
ἀλλ' ἔμπης καὶ ταῦτα μαθήσεαι· ὡς τὰ δοκοῦντα
χρῆν δοκίμως εἶναι διὰ παντὸς πάντα περῶντα.

Fragment 2

εἰ δ' ἄγ' ἐγὼν ἐρέω, κόμισαι δὲ σὺ μῦθον ἀκούσας
αἵπερ ὁδοὶ μοῦναι διζήσιος εἰσι νοῆσαι·
ἡ μὲν ὅπως ἔστιν τε καὶ ὡς οὐκ ἐστι μὴ εἶναι,
πειθοῦς ἐστι κέλευθος (ἀληθείῃ γὰρ ὀπηδεῖ)
ἡ δ' ὡς οὐκ ἐστιν τε καὶ ὡς χρεών ἐστι μὴ εἶναι,
τὴν δή τοι φράζω παναπευθέα ἔμμεν ἀταρπόν·
οὔτε γὰρ ἂν γνοίης τό γε μὴ ἐὸν (οὐ γὰρ ἀνυστόν)
οὔτε φράσαις.

Fragment 3

τὸ γὰρ αὐτὸ νοεῖν ἐστιν τε καὶ εἶναι.

Fragment 4

λεῦσσε δ' ὅμως ἀπεόντα νὅ παρεόντα βεβαίως·
οὐ γὰρ ἀποτμήξει τὸ ἐὸν τοῦ ἐόντος ἔχεσθαι
οὔτε σκιδνάμενον πάντῃ πάντως κατὰ κόσμον
οὔτε συνιστάμενον.

Fragment 5

ξυνόν δέ μοί ἐστιν
ὁππόθεν ἄρξομαι· τόθι γάρ πάλιν ἵξομαι α ὖτις.

Fragment 6

Χρὴ τὸ λέγειν τὸ[701] νοεῖν τ' ἐὸν ἔμμεναι· ἐστι γὰρ εἶναι,
μηδὲν δ' οὐκ ἔστιν· τά γ'[702] ἐγὼ φράζεσθαι ἄνωγα·
πρώτης γάρ τ'[703] ἀφ' ὁδοῦ ταύτης διζήσιος <ἄρξει>[704],
αὐτὰρ ἔπειτ' ἀπὸ τῆς, ἣν δὴ βροτοὶ εἰδότες οὐδέν
πλάττονται, δίκρανοι· ἀμηχανίη γὰρ ἐν αὐτῶν
στήθεσιν ἰθύνει πλακτὸν νόον· οἱ δὲ φοροῦνται.
κωφοὶ ὁμῶς τυφλοί τε, τεθηπότες, ἄκριτα φῦλα,
οἷς τὸ πέλειν τε καὶ οὐκ εἶναι ταὐτὸν νενόμισται
κοὐ ταὐόν· πάντων δὲ παλίντροπός ἐστι κέλευθος.

Fragment 7

οὐ γὰρ μήποτε τοῦτο δαμῇ· εἶναι μὴ ἐόντα.
ἀλλὰ σὺ τῆσδ' ἀφ' ὁδοῦ διζήσιος εἶργε νόημα·
μηδέ σ' ἔθος πολύπειρον ὁδὸν κατὰ τήνδε βιάσθω,
νωμᾶν ἄσκοπον ὄμμα καὶ ἠχήεσσαν ἀκουήν
καὶ γλῶσσαν· κρῖναι δὲ λόγ̈ πολύδηριν ἔλεγχον
ἐξ ἐμέθεν ῥηθέντα.

Fragment 8

μόνος δ' ἔτι μῦθος ὁδοῖο
λείπεται ὡς ἔστιν· ταύτῃ δ' ἐπὶ σήματ' ἔασι
πολλὰ μάλ', ὡς ἀγένητον ἐὸν καὶ ἀνώλεθρόν ἐστιν
οὖλον μουνογενές τε καὶ ἀτρεμὲς ἠδὲ τελεστόν·
οὐδέ ποτ' ἦν οὐδ' ἔσται, ἐπεὶ νῦν ἔστιν ὁμοῦ πᾶν,
ἕν, συνεχές· τίνα γὰρ γένναν διζήσεαι αὐτοῦ;
πῇ πόθεν αὐξηθέν ; οὔτ' ἐκ μὴ ἐόντος ἐάσσω
φάσθαι σ' οὐδὲ νοεῖν· οὐ γὰρ φατὸν οὐδὲ νοητόν
ἔστιν ὅπως οὐκ ἔστι. τί δ' ἄν μιν καὶ χρέος ὦρσεν
ὕστερον ἢ πρόσθεν, τοῦ μηδενὸς ἀρξάμενον, φῦν ;
οὕτως ἢ πάμπαν πελέναι χρών ἐστιν ἢ οὐχί.
οὐδὲ ποτ' ἐκ μὴ ἐόντος ἐφήσει πίστιος ἰσχύς
γίγνεσθαί τι παρ' αὐτό· τοῦ εἵνεκεν οὔτε γενέσθαι
οὔτε ὄλλυσθαι ἀνῆκε δίκη χαλάσασα πέδῃσιν,

---

701 τὸ is found throughout the manuscript tradition. Cf. Chapter V (a).

702 γ' (ε) Manuscript D. Cf. Chapter VI (b).

703 τ' (ε) Manuscripts B, C. Cf. Chapter VI (j).

704 < > Conjecture. All Simplicius manuscripts, the only source for this passage, have a gap. On this conjecture, cf. Chapter VI (g).

ἀλλ' ἔχει· ἡ δὲ κϱίσις πεϱὶ τούτων ἐν τ̃δ' ἔστιν·
ἔστιν ἢ οὐκ ἔστιν· κέκϱιται δ' οὖν, ὥσπεϱ ἀνάγκη,
τὴν μὲν ἐᾶν ἀνόητον ἀνώνυμον (οὐ γὰϱ ἀληθής
ἔστιν ὁδός), τὴν δ' ὥστε πέλειν καὶ ἐτήτυμον εἶναι.
πῶς δ' ἂν ἔπειτα πέλοι τὸ ἐόν ; πῶς δ' ἄν κε γένοιτο ;
εἰ γὰϱ ἔγεντ', οὐκ ἔστ(ι), οὐδ' εἴ ποτε μέλλει ἔσεσθαι.
τὼς γένεσις μὲν ἀπέσβεσθαι καὶ ἄπυστος ὄλεθϱος·
οὐδὲ διαιϱετόν ἐστιν, ἐπτὶ πᾶν ἐστιν ὁμοῖον·
οὐδὲ τι τῇ μᾶλλον, τό κεν εἴϱγοι μιν συνέχεσθαι,
οὐδέ τι χειϱότεϱον, πᾶν δ' ἔμπλεόν ἐστιν ἐόντος.
τ̃ ξυνεχὲς πᾶν ἐστιν· ἐὸν γὰϱ ἐόντι πελάζει·
αὐτὰϱ ἀκίνητον μεγάλων ἐν πείϱασι δεσμῶν
ἔστιν ἄναϱχον ἄπαυστον, επεὶ γένεσις καὶ ὄλεθϱος
τῆλε μάλ' ἐπλάχθησαν, ἀπῶσε δὲ πίστις ἀληθής.
ταὐτόν τ' ἐν ταὐτ̃ τε μένον καθ' ἑαυτό τε κεῖται
χοὔτως ἔμπεδον αὖθι μένει· κϱατεϱὴ γὰϱ ἀνάγκη
πείϱατος ἐν δεσμοῖσιν ἔχει, τό μιν ἀμφὶς ἐέϱγει.
οὕνεκεν οὐκ ἀτελεύτητον τὸ ἐὸν θέμις εἶναι.
ἔστι γὰϱ οὐκ ἐπιδευές· [μὴ] ἐὸν δ' ἂν παντὸς ἐδεῖτο.
ταὐτὸν δ' ἐστὶ νοεῖν τε καὶ οὕνεκεν ἔστι νόημα.
οὐ γὰϱ ἄνευ τοῦ ἐόντος, ἐφ'[705] πεφατισμένον ἐστίν,
εὑϱήσεις τὸ νοεῖν· οὐδ' ἦν γὰϱ <ἢ> ἔστιν ἔσται
ἄλλο πάϱεξ τοῦ ἐόντος, ἐπεὶ τό γε μοῖϱ' ἐπέδησεν
ὖλον ἀκίνητόν τ' ἔμμεναι· τ̃ ῇντ' ὄνομ' ἔσται
ὅσσα βϱοτοὶ κατέθεντο πεποιθότες εἶναι ἀληθῆ,
γίγνεσθαί τε καὶ ὄλλυσθαι, εἶναί τε καὶ ουχί,
καὶ τόπον ἀλλάσσειν διά τε χϱόα φανὸν ἀμείβειν.
αὐτὰϱ ἐπεὶ πεῖϱας πύματον, τετελεσμένον ἐστί
πάντοθεν, εὐκύκλου σφαίϱης ἐναλίγκιον ὄγκ̆,
μεσσόθεν ἰσοπαλὲς πάντῃ· τὸ γάϱ οὔτε τι μεῖζον
οὔτε τι βαιότεϱον πελέναι χϱεόν ἐστι τῇ ἢ τῇ.
οὔτε γὰϱ οὐκ ἐὸν ἔστι, τό κεν παύοι μιν ἱκνεῖσθαι
εἰς ὁμόν, οὔτ' ἐὸν ἔστιν ὅπως εἴη κεν ἐόντος
τῇ μᾶλλον τῇ δ' ἧσσον, ἐπεὶ πᾶν ἐστιν ἄσυλον·
οἷ γὰϱ πάντοθεν ἶσον, ὁμῶς ἐν πείϱασι κύϱει.
ἐν τ̃ σοι παύω πιστὸν λόγον ἠδὲ νόημα
ἀμφὶς ἀληθείης· δόξας δ' ἀπὸ τοῦδε βϱοτείας
μάνθανε κόσμον ἐμῶν ἐπέων ἀπατηλὸν ἀκούων.
μοϱφὰς γὰϱ κατέθεντο δύο γνώμας ὀνομάζειν·
τῶν μίαν οὐ χϱών ἐστιν -ἐν̃ πεπλανημένοι εἰσίν-

705 ἐφ' (= ἐπί) Proclus; ἐν Simplicius. On my preference, cf. Chapter V (a).

ἀντία δ᾽ ἐκϱίναντο δέμας καὶ σήματ᾽ ἔθεντο
χωϱὶς ἀπ᾽ ἀλλήλον, τῇ μὲν φλογὸς αἰθέϱιον πῦϱ,
ἤπιον ὄν, μέγ᾽ [ἀϱαιον] ἐλαφϱόν, ἑωυτ͂ πάντοσε τωὐτόν,
τ͂ δ᾽ ἑτέϱ̆ μὴ τωὐτόν· ἀτὰϱ κἀκεῖνο κατ᾽ αὐτό
τἀντία νύκτ᾽ ἀδαῆ, πυκινὸν δέμας ἐμβϱιθές τε.
τόν σοι ἐγὼ διάκοσμον ἐοικότα πάντα φατίζω,
ὡς οὐ μή ποτέ τίς σε βϱοτῶν γνώμη παϱελάσσῃ.

Fragment 9

αὐτὰϱ ἐπειδὴ πάντα φάος καὶ νὺξ ὀνόμασθαι
καὶ τὰ κατὰ σφετέϱας δυνάμεις ἐπὶ τοῖσι τε καὶ τοῖς,
πᾶν πλέον ἐστὶν ὁμοῦ φάεος καὶ νυκτὸς ἀφάντου
ἴσων ἀμφοτέϱων, ἐπεὶ οὐδετέϱ̆ μέτα μηδέν.

Fragment 10

εἴσῃ δ᾽ αἰθεϱίαν τε φύσιν τά τ᾽ ἐν αἰθέϱι πάντα
σήματα καὶ καθαϱᾶς εὐαγέος ἠελίοιο
λαμπάδος ἔϱγ᾽ ἀίδηλα καὶ ὁππόθεν ἐξεγένοντο,
ἔϱγα τε κύκλωπος πεύσῃ πεϱίφοιτα σελήνης
καὶ φύσιν, εἰδήσεις δὲ καὶ οὐϱανὸν ἀμφὶς ἔχοντα
ἔνθεν [μὲν γὰϱ] ἔφυ τε καὶ ὥς μιν ἄγους(α) ἐπέδησεν ἀνάγκη
πείϱατ᾽ ἔχειν ἄστϱων.

Fragment 11

πῶς γαῖα καὶ ἥλιος ἠδὲ σελήνη
αἰθήϱ τε ξυνὸς γάλα τ᾽ οὐϱάνιον καὶ ὄλυμπος
ἔσχατος ἠδ᾽ ἄστϱων θεϱμὸν μένος ὡϱμήθησαν
γίγνεσθαι.

Fragment 12

αἱ γὰϱ στεινότεϱαι πῆντο πυϱὸς ἀκϱήτοιο,
αἱ δ᾽ ἐπὶ ταῖς νυκτός, μετὰ δὲ φλογὸς ἵεται αἶσα·
ἐν δὲ μέσ̆ τούτων δαίμων ἣ πάντα κυβεϱγ͂·
πάντα γὰϱ <ἣ> στυγεϱοῖο τόκου καὶ μίξιος ἄϱχει
πέμπουσ᾽ ἄϱσενι θῆλυ μιγῆν τόντ᾽ ἐναντίον αὖτις
ἄϱσεν θηλυτέϱ̆.

Fragment 13

πϱώτιστον μὲν Ἔϱωτα θεῶν μητίσατο πάντων.

Fragment 14

νυκτιφαὲς περὶ γαῖαν ἀλώμενον ἀλλότριον φῶς.

Fragment 15

αἰεὶ παπταίνουσα πρὸς αὐγὰς ἠελίοιο.

Fragment 16

ὡς γὰρ ἕκαστος ἔχει κρᾶσιν μελέων πολυπλάγκτων,
τὼς νόος ἀνθρώποισι παρίσταται· τὸ γὰρ αὐτό
ἔστιν ὅπερ φρονέει μελέων φύσις ἀνθρώποισιν
καὶ πᾶσιν καὶ παντί· τὸ γὰρ πλέον ἐστὶ νόημα.

Fragment 17

δεξιτεροῖσιν μὲν κούρους, λαιοῖσι δὲ κούρας.

Fragment 18

Femina virque simul Veneris cum germina miscent,
venis informans diverso ex sanguine virtus
temperiem servans bene condita corpora fingit.
Nam si virtutes permixto semine pugnent
nec faciant unam permixto in corpore, dirae
nascentem gemino vexabunt semine sexum.

Fragment 19

οὕτω τοι κατὰ δόξαν ἔφυ τάδε καὶ νῦν ἔασι
καὶ μετέπειτ᾽ ἀπὸ τοῦδε τελευτήσουσι τραφέντα·
τοῖς δ᾽ ὄνομ᾽ ἄνθρωποι κατέμεντ᾽ ἐπίσημον ἑκάστῳ.

(b) Translation

Fragment 1

1 The mares that lead me carry me as far as my will wishes to go, for, guiding me, they brought me toward the way, full of signs, of the Goddess, who leads <there>, about <everything>, the man who knows.
4 There I was carried, since the wise mares brought me, drawing my chariot, while the maidens showed the way.
6 The axle, which struck sparks in the hubs, whistled like a pipe (as it was pressed on at both ends by round wheels) when the Daughters of the Sun, who abandoned the home of night, hastened to drive me toward the light, with their hands pushing back the veils from their heads.
11 There stand the gates of the ways of night and day, framed by a lintel and a threshold of stone. High in the air, both have great double-doors, whose keys, that alternate, belong to Dike, prodigal in punishments.
15 Coaxing her, the maidens skillfully persuaded her with caressing words at once to draw back from the gates the bolts that barred them. When the doors were opened, they made a wide gap, causing the bronze axles to spin one after another in the hubs, fastened with pins and rivets. There through the middle of them, the maidens guided the chariot and the mares, straight along the great way.
22 The Goddess greeted me kindly, took my right hand in hers, and addressing me, spoke these words:
24 Oh youth, accompanied by immortal guides and the mares that bring you to reach my home, welcome! For it is no sad fate that has impelled you to take this way (which, indeed, lies far distant from the path of men), but Themis and Dike. So it is necessary for you to be abreast of everything; on the one hand, the unshakable heart of well-rounded truth, and, on the other, the opinions of mortals, in which there is no true conviction.
31 But, nevertheless, you will also learn this: how it might have been necessary that things that appear in opinions really existed, ranging over everything incessantly.

Fragment 2

1 Well then, I will tell you—and you who listen, receive my word—what are the only ways of investigation there are to think:
3 one, on the one hand, [to think] that "is," and that it is not possible not to be; this is the way of persuasion, since it accompanies the truth;
5 another, on the other hand, [to think] that "is not," and that it is necessary not to be; I tell you that this path is completely unknowable, since you will not know that which is not (as it is not possible) or utter it.

Fragment 3

since it is the same to think and to be

Fragment 4

Observe how the absent is firmly present to the intellect; since it is impossible to force that which is not to be connected with that which is, neither scattering it completely in regular order, nor gathering it.

Fragment 5

. . . it is common for me that where I begin, there I shall return again.

Fragment 6

1 It is necessary to say and to think that by being, it is, since it is possible to be, and nothing[ness] does not exist. This I order to proclaim since you <will begin> with this first way of investigation, but then with that made by mortals who know nothing, two-headed, since their lack of resources drives the wandering intellect in their breasts. They are carried along, blind and deaf, amazed, people with no capacity for discernment, who consider that being and not being are the same and not the same; the way of all of them returns to the starting point.

Fragment 7

1 For this shall never prevail: that there are things that are not.
2 But you, withdraw thought from this way of investigation and let not long habit force you along this way, to use the eye that does not see, the echoing ear, and the tongue. Judge by reasoning the polemical proof I have stated to you.

Fragment 8

1 So there remains one single word of the way: "is." About it, there are many proofs that that which is being is unbegotten and incorruptible, whole, unique, unshakable and finished.
5 It neither was nor will be, but is now, wholly homogenous, one, continuous. What origin will you seek for it? How and when might it have increased? I do not allow you to say or to think that it [came] from that which is not being, since it is not sayable or thinkable that it is not. What necessity could have made it grow before or afterwards, beginning from nothing[ness]?

11 Therefore, it is necessary to be absolutely, or not. The force of conviction will not permit, from that which is not being, something else to be born beside it, since Dike does not allow it to be born or to die, loosening the ties, for she holds it. The decision on these things lies in this: it is or it is not. It has already been decided, of necessity, that one remains unthinkable and unnamable (since it is not the true way) and that the other exists and is genuine.
19 How could that which is being perish? From what could it have been born? For if it was born, it is not, just as if it will be some day, it is not. Origin is extinguished and destruction is unknown. Neither is it divisible, since it is wholly homogenous.
23 There is not anything to a greater degree, which would prevent its cohesion, neither is there anything to a lesser degree: it is wholly filled with that which is being. It is wholly continuous: that which is being touches that which is being.
26 Immobile within the bonds of mighty chains, it is without beginning and without end, since origin and destruction remain far away: true conviction rejected them.
29 Remaining identical in the same, it abides in itself, and, in this way, it remains constant, since powerful necessity keeps it within the chains of the limit that holds it, for it is not permitted that that which is being should be imperfect. Indeed, it lacks nothing at all; if it did, it would lack everything.
34 Thinking and that because of which there is thinking are the same, since without that which is being, thanks to which it is expressed, you will not find thinking, for there is not and there will not be anything else apart from that which is being, given that Moira forces it to remain whole and immobile. Therefore they are mere names that men have established, believing that they were true things: birth and dying, being and not-being, changing place and altering the outer color.
42 But as there is a supreme limit, it is everywhere finished, like the mass of a well-rounded sphere, completely equidistant from the center, since it is not possible that it should be a bit stronger or a bit weaker, here or there.
46 Since that which is not-being, which would prevent it attaining homogeneity, does not exist; and that which is being is not as if it had a greater quantity of that which is, either here or there, for it is wholly intact. Everywhere equal to itself, it remains in homogenous form to its limits.
50 Here I end for you my trustworthy reasoning and thought about the truth. Henceforward learn the opinions of mortals, listening to the deceitful order of my words.
53 They established two viewpoints to name external forms, which they did not necessarily bring together—and in that they are mistaken. They distinguish a form contrary to itself and offer separate proofs for the one and the other; on the one hand, the ethereal fire of the delicate, nimble

flame, wholly identical with itself, but not the same as the other; and on the other hand, that which is in itself its opposite, dark night, which is thick and heavy.

60 I tell you of this probable cosmic order so that no viewpoint of mortals will prevail over you.

Fragment 9

But as everything has been given the names of light and night, and that which has its own powers was named thanks to these or those, everything is full at the same time of light and dark night, the one the same as the other, since, apart from them, there is nothing.

Fragment 10

You will know ethereal nature and all the signs that are in the ether, and the works destructive of the bright sun's pure flame, and whence all this comes; and you will learn the works of the turning moon's rotation, and its nature and you will also know the surrounding sky, whence it was born, and how the necessity that governs it anchors it to hold the limits of the stars.

Fragment 11

. . . how the earth, the sun, the moon, the common ether, the Milky Way, high Olympus and the burning power of the stars came to be.

Fragment 12

1 The tightest [rings?] are full of pure fire; the next, of night; but between them a lick of flame escapes. In the middle of these [rings?] is the Goddess who governs everything. She rules over fearful childbirth and coupling, driving the female to go with the male, and, likewise, the male with the female.

Fragment 13

. . . She conceived Eros, the very first of the gods.

Fragment 14

Shining by night, wandering round the earth, with borrowed light . . .

Fragment 15

. . . always turned toward the beams of the sun . . .

Fragment 16

Just as on every occasion there is a mixture of prodigious limbs in movement, so the intellect is present in men. Since, for men, both in general and in particular, the nature of the limbs is the same that thinks; since thought is the full.

Fragment 17

On the right the boys, on the left the girls.

Fragment 18

1 When the woman and the man mix together the seeds of Venus, the power that, in the veins, should form bodies with different blood, creates them well-shaped if it keeps proportion;
4 but if the seed-powers conflict and do not unite in the body that results from them, by their double seed they disturb the sex that is to be born.

Fragment 19

Thus these things arose according to opinion, and thus they exist now. And then, once they have developed, they will die. To each thing men have given a particular name.

Appendix 2

Note on the Transliteration of the Greek Alphabet

To transliterate the Greek alphabet I have adopted the following model:

α	a
β	b
γ	g
δ	d
ε	e
ζ	z
η	e̲
θ	th
ι	i
κ	k
λ	l
μ	m
ν	n
ξ	x
ο	o
π	p
ρ	r
σ ς	s
τ	t
υ	u
φ	ph
χ	kh
ψ	ps
ω	o̲

Smooth breathing: not reproduced
Rough breathing: h (e.g., ὕλη = húle̲)
Accents: the same (e.g., é, è, ê)

The type of transliteration adopted will allow the reader to reconstruct the original Greek term exactly. Underlining the letters *eta* (η = e̲) and *omega* (ω = o̲) makes it possible easily to reproduce the cases in which the letter in question has an accent (e.g., σῆμα = sê̲ma).

Bibliography

The bibliography given here includes all books and papers cited in this work. For additional titles, I refer the reader to the new edition of my book *Les deux chemins de Parménide,* 2nd edition (Paris: Vrin, 1997), in which I have listed 817 items dealing *exclusively* with Parmenides. I am currently compiling a comprehensive and up-to-date list of all the material on Parmenides I have collected during my years of teaching and research on the subject. I look forward to making this available online by the end of 2004 at www.parmenides.com.

Aalto, P. *Studien zur Geschichte des Infinitivs im Griechischen* (Helsinki: P. Katara, 1953).

Albertelli, P. *Gli Eleati* (Bari: Laterza, 1939).

Allen, R. E., trans. Plato, *Parmenides* (Oxford: Blackwell, 1983).

Arrighetti, G. "L'eredità dell'epica in Parmenide," *Festschrift für Robert Muth zum 65. Geburtstag,* ed. Haendel, P., and Meid, W. (Innsbruck: Institut für Sprachwissenschaft der Universität Innsbruck, 1983).

Aubenque, P. "Syntaxe et sémantique de l'être dans le Poème de Parménide," *Études sur Parménide,* Vol. II, ed. Aubenque, P. (Paris: Vrin, 1987).

———, ed. *Études Études sur Parménide,* Vol. II (Paris: Vrin, 1987).

Austin, S. *Parmenides: Being, Bounds and Logic* (Yale, CT: Yale University Press, 1986).

Baldwin, B. "Parmenides in Byzantium," *Liverpool Classical Monthly* (1990) 115–116.

Ballew, L. "Straight and Circular in Parmenides and the *Timaeus,*" *Phronesis* 19 (1974) 189–209.

Barnes, J. "Parmenides and the Eleatic One," *Archiv für Geschichte der Philosophie* 61 (1979) 1–21.

Basson, A. H. "The Way of Truth," *Proceedings of the Aristotelian Society* 61 (1960–61) 73–86.

Baumann, A. *Formen der Argumentation bei den vorsokratischen Philosophen,* dissertation (Würzburg, 1906).

Beaufret, J. and **Riniéri**, J. J. *Le Poème de Parménide* (Paris: P.U.F., 1955).

———. *Parménide, Le Poème,* 1982 (Paris: M. Chandeigne, 1986).

Becker, O. "Das Bild des Weges und verwandte Vorstellungen im frühgriechischen Denken," *Hermes* Einzelschriften 4 (1937) 1–223.

———. "Drei Abhandlungen [but "Bemerkungen" in the contents] zum Lehrgedicht des Parmenides," *Kant-Studien* 55 (1964) 255–259.

Benveniste, E. *Problèmes de linguistique générale* (Paris: Gallimard, reprinted 1966).

Béraud, J. *La colonisation grecque de l'Italie méridionale et de la Sicile dans l'Antiquité* (Paris: P.U.F., 1957).

Bergk, T. "Commentatio de Empedoclis Proemio," *Kleine philologische Schriften* II (Halle: Buchhandlung des Waisenhauses, 1886).

Bergson, H. *L'évolution créatrice,* 3rd ed. (Paris: Alcan, 1907).

Bernabé, A. *De Tales a Demócrito* (Madrid: Alianza, 1988).

Berti, E. "Parménide," *Le savoir grec,* ed. Brunschwig, J., and Lloyd, G. (Paris: Frammarion, 1996).

Bicknell, P. J. "Dating the Eleatics," *For Service of Classical Studies, Essays in Honor of F. Letters,* ed. Kelly, M. (Melbourne: Cheshire, 1966), 1–14.

———. "A New Arrangement of Some Parmenidean Verses," *Symbolae Osloensis* 42 (1968) 44–50.

Boardman, J. *The Greeks Overseas* (Baltimore: Penguin Books, 1964).

Böhme, R. *Die verkannte Muse. Dichtersprache und geistige Tradition des Parmenides* (Berne: Francke, 1986).

Bollack, J. "La cosmologie parménidienne de Parménide," *Herméneutique et ontologie, Hommage à Pierre Aubenque,* ed. Brague, R., and Courtine, J. F. (Paris: P.U.F., 1990), 17–53.

Bormann, K. *Parmenides: Untersuchungen zu den Fragmenten* (Hamburg: Felix Meiner, 1971).

Bowra, C. M. "The Poem of Parmenides," *Classical Quarterly* 32 (1937) 97–112.

Brague, R. "La vraisemblance du faux," *Études sur Parménide,* Vol. II, ed. Aubenque, P. (Paris: Vrin, 1987) 44–68.

Brandis, C. A. *Commentationum Eleaticarum.* Pars prima: Xenophanis, Parmenidis et Melisi doctrina a propriis philosophorum reliquiis exposita (Altona: J. F. Hammerich, 1813).

———. *Handbuch der griechisch-römischen Philosophie* (Berlin: G. Reiner, 1835).

Bröcker, W. *Die Geschichte der griechischen Philosophie vor Sokrates* (Frankfurt: Klostermann, 1965).

Brucker, I. *Historia criticae philosophiae,* I (Leipzig: B. C. Breitkopf, 1742).

Brugmann, K. *Griechische Grammatik* (Munich: C. H. Beck, 1913).

Brumbaugh, R. S. "Review of Tarán," *International Philosophical Quarterly* 4 (1966).

Burkert, W. "Das Proömion des Parmenides und die Katabasis des Pythagoras," *Phronesis* 14 (1961) 1–30.

Burnet, J. *Early Greek Philosophy,* 4th ed. (London: A. & C. Black, 1930).

Buroni, B. "Dell'essere e del cognoscere: Studii su Parmenide, Platone e Rosmini," *Memorie della Reale Accademia delle Scienze di Torino,* Serie II (Scienze morali, storiche e filologiche) 29 (1878), 287–528.

Buxton, R. G. A. *Persuasion in Greek Tragedy. A Study of Peitho* (Cambridge, England: Cambridge University Press, 1982).

Calogero, G. *Studi sull'Eleatismo,* 2nd ed. (1932; Firenze: La Nuova Italia, 1977).

———. "Parmenide e la genèsi della logica classica," *Annali della Reale Scuola Normale Superiore di Pisa,* Classe di Lettere, Storia e Filosofia, ser. II, 5 (1936), 143–185.

Capizzi, A. *Introduzzione a Parmenide* (Bari: Laterza, 1975).

———. *La porta di Parmenide* (Rome: Edizioni dell'Ateneo, 1975).

Casertano, G. *Parmenide: Il metodo, la scienza, l'esperienza* (Naples: Guida, 1978).

Cassin, B. *Si Parménide* (Lille: Presses Universitaires de Lille, 1980).

———. "Le chant des syrènes dans le Poème de Parménide (Quelques rermarques sur le fr. VIII, 26–33)," *Études sur Parménide,* Vol. II, ed. Aubenque, P. (Paris: Vrin, 1987).

———. *L'effet Sophistique* (Paris: Gallimard, 1995).

———. *Parménide: Sur la nature ou sur l'étant* (Paris: Ed. du Seuil, 1998).

Cassin, B., and **Narcy**, M. "Parménide sophiste," *Études sur Parménide,* Vol. II (Paris: Vrin, 1987).

de Cecco, D. "Parmenide 28 B 6,8–9 DK," *Esercizi Filosofici (1992)* (Trieste: Edizioni Lint, 1993).

Cerri, G. "Elea, Senofane e Leucothea," *Forme di religiosità e tradizioni sapienziali in Magna Grecia,* ed. Casio, A. C., and Poccetti, P. (Pisa/Rome: Istituti Editoriali e Poligrafici Internazionali, 1993).

———. "Il v. 1.3 di Parmenide: la ricognizione dell'esperienza," *Mousa, Scritti in onore di Giuseppe Morelli* (Bologna: Patron, 1997).

———. *Parmenide di Elea: Poema sulla natura* (Milan: Rizzoli, 1999).

Chalmers, W. R. "Parmenides and the Belief of Mortals," *Phronesis* 5 (1960) 5–22.

Chantraine, P. *Grammaire homérique, II: Syntaxe* (Paris: Kliencksieck, 1953).

———. *Dictionnaire étymologique de la langue grecque* (Paris: Klincksieck, 1968).

Chiereghin, F. *Implicazioni etiche della storiografia filosofica di Platone* (Padua: Liviana, 1976).

Ciaceri, E. *Storia della Magna Grecia* (Milan: Albrighi, Segati & Co., 1927).

Collobert, C. *L'être de Parménide ou le refus du temps* (Paris: Kimé, 1993).

Colombo, A. *Il primato del nulla e le origini della metafisica* (Milan: Publicazioni della Universita Cattolica Sacro Cuore, 1972).

Conche, M. *Parménide: Le Poème: Fragments* (Paris: P.U.F., 1996).

Constantineau, P. "La question de la vérité chez Parménide," *Phoenix* 41 [1987] 217–240.

Corbato, C. "Studi Senofanei," *Annali Triestini* XXII (1952).

Cordero, N. L. *L'être et le non être dans la philosophie de Parménide,* Université de Paris IV, directeur: Pierre-Maxime Schuhl, December 1971.

———. "Acerca de tres pasajes del Poema de Parmenides," *Revista latinoamericana de filosofía* 1 (1975), 237–243.

———. "Analyse de l'édition Aldine du Commentaire de Simplicius à la Physique d'Aristote," *Hermes* 105 (1977).

———. "Les deux chemins de Parménide dans les fragments 6 et 7," *Phronesis* 24 (1979) 1–32.

———. "Le vers 1.3 de Parménide," *La revue philosophique* 107(2) (1982) 159–179.

———. "La version de Joseph Scaliger du Poème de Parménide," *Hermes* 110 (1982) 391–398.

———. *Les deux chemins de Parménide* (Paris/Brussels: Vrin/Ousia, 1984; second edition, augmented and corrected, 1997).

———. "Les sources vénitiennes de l'édition Aldine du Livre I du Commentaire de Simplicius de la Physique d'Aristote," *Scriptorium* 38(2) (1984), 70–88.

———. "L'histoire du texte de Parménide," *Études sur Parménide,* Vol. II, ed. Aubenque, P. (Paris: Vrin, 1987), 3–24.

———. "Simplicius et l' 'école' éléate," in *Simplicius, sa vie, son oeuvre, sa survie,* ed. Hadot, I. (Berlin/New York: Walther de Gruyter, 1987), 166–182.

———. "Zénon d'Elée, moniste ou nihiliste?" *La parola del passato* 43 (1988) 100–126.

———. "La déesse de Parménide, maîtresse de philosophie," *La naissance de la raison en Grèce,* ed. Mattéi, J. F. (Paris: P.U.F., 1990).

———. "L'invention de l'école éléatique (Platon, *Sophiste,* 242d)," *Études sur le "Sophiste" de Platon,* ed. Aubenque, P. (Naples: Bibliopolis, 1991) 91–124.

———. *Les deux chemins de Parménide,* 2nd ed. (Paris/Brussels: Vrin/Ousia, 1997).
———. "Parménide platonisé," *Revue de philosophie ancienne* 18(1) (2000) 15–24.
Cornford, F. M. "Parmenides' Two Ways," *Classical Quarterly* 27 (1933), 97–111.
———. *Plato's Theory of Knowledge* (London-New York: K. Paul-Harcourt, 1935).
———. "Parmenides' Way of Truth." *Plato and Parmenides* (London: Routledge & Kegan Paul, 1939), 38–57.
Cosgrove, M. R. "The *koûros* Motif in Parmenides," *Phronesis* 19 [1974] 81–94.
Couloubaritsis, L. "Les multiples chemins de Parménide," *Études sur Parménide,* Vol. II, ed. Aubenque, P. (Paris: Vrin, 1987).
———. *Mythe et philosophie chez Parménide,* 2nd ed. (Brussels: Ousia, 1990).
Coxon, A. H. "The Philosophy of Parmenides," *Classical Quarterly* 28 (1934) 134–144.
———. "The Text of Parmenides Fr. 1.3," *Classical Quarterly* 18 (1968) 69.
———. *The Fragments of Parmenides* (Assen: Van Gorcum, 1986).
———. "Deception and Belief in Parmenides' *Doxa,*" Apeiron 25 (1992) 109–133.
Curtius, G. *Grundzüge der griechischen Etymologie* (Leipzig: B. G. Teubner, 1858–1862).
Das, A. C. *Negative Fact, Negation and Truth* (Calcutta: University of Calcutta, 1942).
Dehon, P. J. "Les recommendations de la déesse. Parménide, fr. 1.28–32," *Revue de philosophie ancienne* 6(2) (1988).
Deichgräber, K. *Parmenides' Auffahrt zur Göttin des Rechts* (Wiesbaden: Akademie der Wissenschaften und der Literatur in Mainz, 1959).
Denniston, J. D. *The Greek Particles* (Oxford: Clarendon Press, 1934).
Destrée, P. "La communauté de l'être (Parménide, fr. B 5)," *Revue de philosophie ancienne* 18(1) (2000).
Detienne, M. *Les maîtres de vérité dans la Grèce archaïque* (Paris: Maspéro, 1967).
———. "Par la bouche et par l'oreille," *L'invention de la mythologie* (Paris: Gallimard, 1981).
Diels, H. "Chronologische Untersuchungen über Apollodors Chronik," *Rheinisches Museum* 31 (1876) 1–54.
———. "Preface," in *Simplicii In Aristotelis Physicorum [. . .] Commentaria* (Berlin: G. Reimer, 1895).
———. *Parmenides Lehrgedicht* (Berlin: G. Reimer, 1897).
Diels, H., and **Kranz**, W. *Die Fragmente der Vorsokratiker,* Vol. I (Zürich-Berlin: Weidmannsche Verlagsbuchhandlung, 1956).
Dixsaut, M. "Platon et le *lógos* de Parmenide," *Études sur Parmenide,* Vol. II, ed. Aubenque, P. (Paris: Vrin, 1987).
Dorion, L. A. *Euthyphro* (Paris: GF-Flammarion, 1997).
Dumont, J. P., et al. *Les Présocratiques* (Paris: Gallimard, 1988).
Ebeling, H. *Lexicon Homericum* (Leipzig: B. G. Teubner, 1885).
Ebert, T. "Wo beginnt der Weg der Doxa?" *Phronesis* 34 (1989) 121–138.
Eggers Lan, C. *Los filósofos Presocráticos,* I (Madrid: Gredos, 1978).
Estienne, H. *Poiesis philosophica* (Geneva: 1573).
Falcón Martínez, C., **Fernández-Galiano**, E., and **López Melero**, R. *Diccionario de mitología clásica,* Vol. I (Madrid: Alianza, 1980).
Falus, R. "Parmenides-interpretationen," *Acta Antiqua Academiae Scientiarum Hungaricae* 8 (1960), 267–294.
Finkelberg, A. "Parmenides' Foundation of the Way of Truth," *Oxford Studies in Ancient Philosophy* 6 (1988) 39–67.
———. "Being, Truth and Opinion in Parmenides," *Archiv für Geschichte der Philosophie* 81 [1999], 233–248.

Finley, M. I. *The Ancient Greeks* (London: Viking Press, 1963).
Floyd, E. D. "Why Parmenides wrote in verse" *Ancient Philosophy* 12 [1992] 251–265.
Fränkel, H. "Parmenidesstudien" [1930]. Reprinted in *Wege und Formen des frühgriechischen Denkens* (Munich: Beck, 1955).
———. *Dichtung und Philosophie des frühen Griechentums* (New York: American Philological Association, 1951).
von Fritz, K. "*Noûs, noeîn* and Its Derivatives in Presocratic Philosophy (Excluding Anaxagoras), I, From the Beginnings to Parmenides," *Classical Philology* 40 (1945) 223–242.
Fronterotta, F. "Essere, tempo e pensiero: Parmenide et l''origine dell'ontologia'," *Annali della Scuola Normale Superiore di Pisa,* Classe di Lettere e Filosofia, Serie II, Vol. 24 (1994), 835–871.
Fülleborn, G. G. *Parmenídou toû Eleátou leípsana: Fragmente des Parmenides* (Zullichau, 1795).
Furley, D. "Truth as What Survives the *élenchos*" (1987), reprinted in *Cosmic Problems* (Cambridge, England: Cambridge University Press, 1989).
Furth, M. "Elements of Eleatic Ontology," *Journal of the History of Philosophy* 6 (1968) 111–132.
Gallop, D. A. *Parmenides: Fragments* (Toronto: Phoenix, 1984).
García Calvo, A. *Lecturas Presocráticas* (Madrid: Lucina, 1981).
Germani, G. "Per un'interpretazione delle vie parmenidee," *Annali del Dipartimento di Filosofia, Università di Firenze,* Vol. II (1986).
———. *Annali del Dipartimento di Filosofia,* Vol. II (Firenze: Università di Firenze, 1986).
———. "*Alḗtheie* in Parmenide," *La parola del passato* 43 (1988).
Giannantoni, G. "Le due 'vie' di Parmenide," *La parola del passato* 43 (1988).
Gigante, M. "Velina gens," *La parola del passato* 19 (1964).
Gigon, O. *Der Ursprung der Griechischen Philosophie von Hesiod bis Parmenides* (Basel: Schwabe & Co., 1945).
Gómez-Lobo, A. "Parménides. Las puertas de la noche y del día," *Revista latinoamericana de filosofía* 3 (1977) 185–188.
———. *Parménides* (Buenos Aires: Editorial Charcas, 1985).
Gomperz, H. "Psychologische Beobachtungen an griechischen Philosophen," *Imago* 10 (1924), 2–34.
Guazzoni Foà, V. *Attualità dell'ontologia eleatica* (Turin: Società Editrice Internazionale, 1961).
———. *Il problema delle "vie di ricerca" in Parmenide* (Bergamo: Arti Grafiche Mariani & Monti, 1979).
Günther, H. C. "Der Satz des Parmenides von der Identität von Denken und Sein," *Studi Italiani di filologia classica* 15(2) (1997), 125–175.
———. *Aletheia und Doxa, Das Proömium des Gedichtes des Parmenides* (Berlin: Dunker & Humblot, 1998).
Guthrie, W. K. C. *A History of Greek Philosophy,* Vol. I (Cambridge, England: Cambridge University Press, 1965).
———. *A History of Greek Philosophy,* Vol. II (Cambridge, England: Cambridge University Press, 1965).
Hadot, I. ed. *Simplicius, sa vie, son oeuvre, sa survie* (Berlin/New York: Walter de Gruyter, 1987).
———. *Qu'est-ce que la philosophie antique?* (Paris: Gallimard, 1995).

Hegel, G. F. *Wissenschaft der Logik,* 3rd ed. (Leipzig: Felix Meiner, 1929).
Heidegger, M. *Was ist Metaphysik?* (Bonn: Cohen, 1929).
———. *Sein und Zeit,* 9th ed. (Tübingen: Max Niemeyer, 1960).
———. *Parmenides Gesamtausgabe II. Abteilung, Vorlesungen 1923–1944,* Vol. 54 (Frankfurt am Main: Klostermann, 1982).
———. *Einführung in die Metaphysik* (Frankfurt am Main: Max Niemeyer, 1983).
Heitsch, E. *Gegenwart und Evidenz bei Parmenides* (Wiesbaden: Franz Steiner Verlag, 1970).
———. "Sein und Gegenwart im frühgriechischen Denken," *Gymnasium* 18 (1971) 221–237.
———. *Parmenides: Die Anfänge der Ontologie, Logik und Naturwissenschaft* (Munich: Tusculum, 1974).
———. *Parmenides und die Anfänge der Erkenntniskritik und Logik* (Donauworth: L. Auer, 1979).
Hobbes, T. *Elementorum philosophiae,* Vol. II (London: A. Crook, 1655).
Höffding, H. "La base psychologique des jugements logiques," *La revue philosophique* 26 (1901) 374).
Hoffmann, E. *Die Sprache und die archaische Logik* (Tübingen: 1925).
Hölscher, U. "Grammatisches zu Parmenides," *Hermes* 84 (1956) 385–397.
———. *Anfängliche Fragen* (Göttingen: Vandenhoeck & Ruprecht, 1968).
———. *Parmenides: Vom Wesen des Seienden* (Frankfurt am Main: Suhrkamp Verlag, 1969).
Huxley, G. L. *The Early Ionians* (New York: Faber, 1966).
Imbraguglia, C. *Teoria e mito in Parmenide* (Genoa: Studio Editoriale di Cultura, 1979).
Jacoby, F. *Apollodoros Chronik, Eine Sammlung der Fragmente* (Berlin: Weidmann, 1902).
Jaeger, W. *The Theology of Early Greek Philosophers,* English translation (1936; Oxford: Clarendon Press, 1947).
Jantzen, J. *Parmenides zum Verhältnis von Sprache und Wirklichkeit* (Munich: C. H. Beck, 1976).
Kahl-Furthmann, G. *Das Problem des Nicht,* 2nd ed. (Meisenheim/Glan: A. Haim, 1968).
Kahn, C. H. review of Tarán, *Gnomon* 40 (1968), 123–133.
———. "The Thesis of Parmenides," *Review of Metaphysics* 22 (1968/69), 700–724.
———. "The Verb 'Be' in Ancient Greek." Part 6 of *The Verb "Be" and Its Synonyms: Philosophical and Grammatical Studies.* Ed. John W. M. Verhaar. Foundations of Language: Suppl. Series. Vol. 16. (Boston: D. Reidel, 1973).
———. *The Art and Thought of Heraclitus* (Cambridge, England: Cambridge University Press, 1978).
———. "Being in Parmenides and Plato," *La parola del passato* 43 (1988) 237–261.
Karsten, S. *Philosophorum graecorum veterum praesertim qui ante Platonem floruerunt operum reliquiae,* Vol. I, Parte 2: Parmenidis (Amsterdam: J. Müller & Soc., 1835).
Kent Sprague, R. "Parmenides: A Suggested Rearrangement of Fragments in the Way of Truth," *Classical Philology* 50 (1955) 124–126.
Kern, O. "Zu Parmenides," *Archiv für Geschichte der Philosophie* 3 (1890) 13–176.
Ketchum, R. J. "Parmenides on What There Is," *Canadian Journal of Philosophy* 20 (1990) 177–190.
Kirk, G. S. *Heraclitus: The Cosmic Fragments* (Cambridge, England: Cambridge University Press, 1954).

Kirk, G. S., **Raven**, J. E., and **Schofield**, M. *The Presocratic Philosophers,* 2nd ed. (Cambridge, England: Cambridge University Press, 1983).

Klibansky, R., and **Labowsky**, L., eds., *Plato Latinus,* Vol. III: "Parmenides nec non Procli Commentarium in Parmenides" (London-Leide: In Aedibus Instituti Warburgiane-Brill, 1953).

Klowski, J. "Die Konstitution der Begriffe Sein und Nichts durch Parmenides," *Kant-Studien* 60 (1969) 404–416.

———. review of Lloyd, *Archiv für Geschichte der Philosophie* 51 (1969).

———. "Parmenides: Grundlegung seiner Seinslehre (B–27)," *Rheinisches Museum* 120 (1977), 97–137.

Kranz, W. "Über Aufbau und Bedeutung des Parmenideischen Gedichtes," *Sitzungsberichte der Königl.-Preussischen Akademie der Wissenschaften* 47 (1916).

———. "Vorsokratisches," *Hermes* 69 (1934) 114–119, 226–228.

———. *Vorsokratische Denker,* 3rd ed. (Berlin: Weidmann, 1959).

Krug, W. T. *System der theoretischen Philosophie,* Vol. I: "Denklehre oder Logik" (Königsberg: Goebbels und Unzer, 1806).

Kühner, R. *Ausfürliche Grammatik der griechischen Sprache,* 2nd ed., Vol. II(1) (Hannover: Hansche Buchhandlung, 1870).

Lafrance, Y. *La théorie platonicienne de la Doxa* (Paris/Montreal: Bellarmin—Les Belles Lettres, 1981).

———. "Le sujet du Poème de Parménide: L'être ou l'univers?" *Elenchos* 20(2) (1999), 265–308.

Lami, A. *I Presocratici* (Milan: Rizzoli, 1991).

Lepore, E. "Strutture della colonizzazione focea in Occident," *La parola del passato* 25 (1970) 19–54.

Lesher, J. H. "The Significance of *katà pántá<s>te̱* in Parmenides Fr. 1.3," *Ancient Philosophy* 14 [1994] 1–20.

Leszl, W. "Approccio epistemologico all'ontologia parmenidea," *La parola del passato* 43 (1988), 281–311.

———. *Parmenide e l'Eleatismo.* Dispensa per il corso di Storia della Filosofia Antica, Università degli Studi di Pisa, Dipartimento di Filosofia (May 1994).

Levi, A. "Sulla dottrina di Parmenide e sulla teoria della *doxa,*" *Athenaeum* 5 (1927), 269–287.

Lloyd, G. E. R. *Polarity and Analogy* (Cambridge, England: Cambridge University Press, 1966).

Loenen, J. H. M. M. *Parmenides, Melissus, Gorgias: A Reinterpretation of Eleatic Philosophy* (Assen: Van Gorcum, 1959).

Loew, E. "Ein Beitrag zum heraklitisch-parmenideischen Enkenntnisproblem," *Archiv fûr Geschichte der Philosophie* 31 [1917] 63–90, 125–152.

———. "Das Lehrgedicht des Parmenides: Gliederung und Gedankengang," *Rheinisches Museum* 78 (1929), 148–165.

———. "Das Verhältnis von Logik und Leben bei Parmenides," *Wiener Studien* 53 (1935) 1–37.

Long, A. A. "The Principles of Parmenides' Cosmogony," *Phronesis* 8 [1963] 90–107.

———. "Review of Tarán," *Journal of the Hellenic Studies* 86 (1966).

Mabbott, J. D. in *Knowledge, Experience and Realism,* ed. G. Ryle, The Aristotelian Society, Vol. Supp. 9 (1929).

Manchester, P. B. "Parmenides and the Need of Eternity," *The Monist* 62 (1979) 81–106.

Mansfeld, J. *Die Offenbarung des Parmenides und die menschliche Welt* (Assen: Van Gorcum, 1964).

———. review of Tarán, *Mnemosyne* 20 (1967).

———. "Aristote et la structure du *De sensibus* de Théophraste," *Phronesis* 41 (1996), 158–188.

———. "Parménide et Héraclite avaient-ils une théorie de la perception?" *Phronesis* 44 (1999).

Manuzio, A. *Theocritus* (Venice: In Aedibus Aldi, 1496).

Marcovich, M. *Eraclito. Frammenti* (Florence: La Nuova Italia, 1978).

Marsoner, A. "La struttura del Proemio di Parmenide," *Annali dell'Istituto Italiano per gli Studi Storici* 5 (1976–1978).

Martineau, M. "Le 'coeur' de l'Alétheia," *Revue de philosophie ancienne* 4 (1986) 33–86.

Martinelli, F. "Fra Omero e Pindaro: Parmenide poeta," *Forme del sapere nei Presocratici*, ed. Capizzi, A., and Casertano, G. (Athens/Rome: Edizione dell'Ateneo, 1987) 169–186.

Meijer, P. A. "Das methodologische im 5. Fragment des Parmenides," *Classica at medievalia* 30 [1969] 102–108.

———. *Parmenides Beyond the Gates: The Divine Revelation on Being, Thinking and the* Doxa (Amsterdam: J. C. Gieben, 1997).

Merlan, P. "Neues Licht auf Parmenides," *Archiv für Geschichte der Philosophie* 48 (1966) 267–276.

Misch, G. *Der Weg in die Philosophie* (Berlin/Leipzig: 1926).

de Moerbeke, G. trans. Proclus, *Commentaire sur le "Parménide" de Platon*, critical edition of Steel, C., Vol. II (Louvain: Presses Universitaires de Louvain, 1985).

Mondolfo, R. "Discusioni su un testo parmenideo (fr. 8.5–6)," *Rivista critica di storia della filosofia* 19 (1964), 310–315.

Montaner, A. "La struttura del Proemio di Parmenide," *Annali dell'Istituto Italiano per gli Studi Filosofici* V (1976–1978).

Montero Moliner, F. *Parménides* (Madrid: Gredos, 1960).

Mookerjee, S. *The Buddhist Philosophy of Universal Flux* (Calcutta: University of Calcutta, 1935).

Moravcsik, J. M. E. "Being and Meaning in the *Sophist*," *Acta philosophica fennica* 14 (1962).

Morel, J. P. "Les Phocéens en Occident: certitudes et hypothèses," *La parola del passato* 21 (1966) 379–420.

———. "Sondages sur l'acropole de Vélia (Contribution aux premiers temps de la cité)," *La parola del passato* 25 (1970) 131–145.

Morot-Sir, E. *La pensée négative* (Paris: Aubier, 1947).

Morrow, G. R., and **Dillon**, J. M., eds. *Proclus' Commentary on Plato's Parmenides* (Princeton, NJ: Princeton University Press, 1987).

Mossé, C. *La Grèce archaïque d'Homère à Eschyle* (Paris: Seuil, 1997).

Mourelatos, A. P. D. "*Phrázo̲* and Its Derivatives in Parmenides," *Classical Philology* 60 (1965), 261–262.

———. *The Route of Parmenides* (Yale, CT: Yale University Press, 1970).

———. "Heraclitus, Parmenides, and the Naive Metaphysics of Things," *Phronesis*, Supp. I, *Exegesis and Argument*, Studies in Greek Philosophy presented to G. Vlastos, ed. Lee, E. N., Mourelatos, A. P. D., and Rorty, R. M. (Assen: 1973) 16–48.

———. "Some Alternatives in Interpreting Parmenides," *The Monist* 62 (1979) 3–17.

Mullach, F. G. A. *Aristotelis, De Melisso, Xenophane et Gorgia disputationes, cum Eleaticorum Philosophorum fragmentis* (Berlin: 1845).

———. *Fragmenta philosophorum graecorum* (Paris: Didot, 1860).

Müller, M. *Nouvelles leçons sur la science du langage* (Paris: 1868).

Mutschmann, H. "Die Überlieferung der Schriften des Sextus Empiricus," *Rheinisches Museum* 69 (1909).

Napoli, M. "La ricerca archeologica di Velia," *La parola del passato* 21 (1966) 191–226.

———. *Civilità della Magna Grecia* (Rome: Eurodes, 1978).

Nehamas, A. "On Parmenides' Three Ways of Inquiry," *Deucalion* 33–34 (1981) 197–211.

Nutton, V. "The Medical School of Velia," *La parola del passato* 25 (1970) 211–225.

O'Brien, D. "Temps et intemporalité chez Parménide," *Les études philosophiques* 3 (1980) 257–272.

———. *Études sur Parménide,* Vol. I, ed. Aubenque, P. (Paris: Vrin, 1987).

Oguse, A. "À propos de la syntaxe de *peíthō* et de *pisteúō*," *Revue des études grecques* 78 (1965).

Owen, G. E. L. "Eleatic Questions," *Classical Quarterly* 10 (1960), 84–102.

Palmer, J. H. *Plato's Reception of Parmenides* (Oxford: Oxford University Press, 1999).

Pasquinelli, A. *I Presocratici* (Turin: Einaudi, 1958).

Patin, A. "Parmenides im Kampfe gegen Heraklit," *Jahrbuch für klassische Philologie,* Supplementband 25 (1899), 489–660.

Pellikaan-Engel, M. E. *Hesiod and Parmenides: A New View on Their Cosmologies and on Parmenides' Poem* (Amsterdam: Adolf M. Hakkert, 1974).

Peyron, A. *Empedoclis et Parmenidis fragmenta ex codice Taurinensis Bibliothecae restituta et illustrata* (Leipzig: I. A. G. Weigel, 1810).

Pfeiffer, R. "Gottheit und Individuum," *Ausgewählte Schriften* (Munich: Beck, 1960).

Phillips, E. D. "Parmenides on Thought and Being," *Philosophical Review* 64 (1955) 547–559.

Pieri, A. "Parmenide e la lingua della tradizione epica greca," *Studi Italiani di filologia classica* 49 (1977).

Popper, K. *The World of Parmenides* (London/New York: Routledge, 1998).

Pugliese Carratelli, G. "*Phōlarkhós*," *La parola del passato* 18 (1963).

———. "Parmenídes *phusikós*," *La parola del passato* 20 (1965).

———. "Ancora su *phōlarkhós*," *La parola del passato* 25 (1970).

———. "Nascita di Velia," *La parola del passato* 25 (1970).

Ralfs, G. "Der Satz von Widerspruch bei Parmenides," *Lebensformen des Geistes,* ed. Glockner, H. *Kant-Studien,* Ergänzungsheft 86, 1964.

Ranulf, S. *Der eleatische Satz vom Widerspruch* (Copenhagen: Gyldendal, 1924).

Raven, J. E. *Pythagoreans and Eleatics* (Cambridge, England: Cambridge University Press, 1948).

Reale, G. in Zeller, E., and Mondolfo, R., *La filosofia dei Greci,* Part I, Vol. 3, (Florence: La Nuova Italia, 1967).

———. *Melissus: Testimonianze e frammenti* (Florence: La Nuova Italia, 1970).

———, trans. Parmenides, *Poema sulla natura* (Milan: Rusconi, 1991).

Redard, G. *Recherches sur khrê, khresthai* (París: H. Champion, 1953).

Regvald, R. "Parménide: Le trajet de la non-coïncidence," *La revue philosophique* 176 (1986), 13–29.

Reich, K. "Parmenides und die Pithagoreer," *Hermes* 82 (1954) 287–294.

Reinhardt, K. *Parmenides und die Geschichte der griechischen Philosophie* (Frankfurt: Vittorio Klostermann, 1916).
Riaux, F. M. *Essai sur Parménide d'Élee* (Paris: Librairie de Joubert, 1840).
Riezler, K. *Parmenides* (Frankfurt am Main: Klosterman, 1934).
de Rijk, L. M. "Did Parmenides Reject the Sensible World?" *Graceful Reason,* ed. Gerson, L. P. (Toronto: Pontifical Institute of Mediaeval Studies, 1983), 29–53.
Riniéri, J. J. *Le Poème de Parménide* (Paris: Presses Universitaires de France, 1955).
Robin, L. *La pensée grecque et les origines de l'esprit scientifique,* 3rd ed. (Paris: La Renaissance du Livre, 1963).
Robinson, T. M. "Parmenides on the Ascertainment of Real," *Canadian Journal of Philosophy* 4 (1975) 56.
———. "Parmenides on the Real in Its Totality," *The Monist* 62 (1979) 54–60.
Ruggiu, L. *Parmenide* (Venice: Marsilio, 1975).
Rüstow, A. "Über Parmenides," *Verhandl. d. 52 Vers. deutsch. Philol. u. Schulm. zu Marburg* (1913).
Ryle, G., ed. *Knowledge, Experience and Realism* The Aristotelian Society, Vol. Supp. 9 (1929).
Sartre, J. P. *L'être et el Néant* (Paris: Gallimard, 1943).
Schwabl, H. "Sein und Doxa bei Parmenides," *Wiener Studien* 66 (1953), reprinted in *Um die Begriffswelt der Vorsokratiker,* ed. Gadamer, H. G. (Darmstadt: Wissenschaftliche Buchgesellschaft, 1968).
———. "Hesiod und Parmenides," *Rheinisches Museum* 106 (1963) 134–142.
Schwyzer, E. *Griechische Grammatik,* Vol. II (Munich: C. H. Beck, 1950).
Seligman, P. *Being and Not-being: An introduction to Plato's* Sophist (The Hague: Martinus Nijhoff, 1978).
Sider, D. "Textual Notes on Parmenides' Poem," *Hermes* 113 (1985) 362–366.
Sigwart, C. *Logik,* 5th ed. (Tübingen: Mohr, 1924).
Snell, B. "Aischylos und das Handeln in Drama," *Philologus,* Supp. 20, I (1928).
Solmsen, F. "The Tradition About Zeno of Elea Re-examined," *Phronesis* 16 (1971) 116–141.
Solovine, M. *Démocrite* (Paris: Alcan, 1928).
Somigliana, A. "I versi 4 ss. del fr. B 6 di Parmenide e la supposta polemica antieraclitea," *Rivista di filosofia neoscolastica* 67 (1975).
Somville, P. *Parménide d'Élée: Son temps et le nôtre* (Paris: Vrin, 1976).
Stahl, J. M. *Kritisch-historischer Syntax des griechischen Verbums der klassischen Zeit* (Heidelberg: C. Winter, 1907).
Stein, H. "Die Fragmente des Parmenides *Perí Phúseo̱s,*" *Symbola philologrum Bonnensium in honorem F. Ritschelii* (Leipzig: Teubner, 1864–1867).
Stevens, A. *Postérité de l'être: Simplicius interprète de Paeménide* (Brussels: Ousia, 1990).
Tarán, L. "El significado de *noeîn* en Parménides," *Anales de filología clásica* 7 (1959) 122–139.
———. *Parmenides* (Princeton, NJ: Princeton University Press, 1965).
———. "Perpetual Duration and Temporal Eternity in Parmenides and Plato," *The Monist* 62 (1979) 43–53.
Thiede, J. *Über die Negation, den Widerspruch und den Gegensatz,* dissertation, (Berlin, 1883).
Trabattoni, F., trans. Parmenides, *I frammenti.* (Milan: Marcos y Marcos, 1985).

Trendelenburg, F. A. *Logische Untersuchungen,* Vol. I, 3rd ed. (Leipzig: S. Hirzel, 1870).

Tugwell, S. "The Way of Truth," *Classical Quarterly* 14 (1964), 36–41.

Tzavaras, G. *Tò Poíe̱ma toû Parmeníde̱* (Athens: Domos, 1980).

Überweg, F. *Grundriss der Geschichte der Philosophie,* Vol. I, 12th ed. (Basel: Schwabe, 1953).

Untersteiner, M. *Parmenide. Testimonianze e frammenti* (Florence: La Nuova Italia, 1958).

———. *Problemi di filologia filosofica,* ed. Sichirollo, L., and Venturi Ferriolo, M. (Milan: Cislapino-Goliardica, 1980).

———. *Les Sophistes* Vol. I, (Paris: Vrin, 1993).

Vallet, V., and **Villard**, F. "Les Phocéens en Méditerranée Occidentale à l'époque archaïque et la fondation de Hyélè," *La parola del passato* 21 (1966) 166–190.

Verdenius, W. J. *Parmenides: Some Comments on His Poem* (Groningen: Hakkert, 1942).

———. "Parmenides B 2.3," *Mnemosyne* 15 (1962) 237.

———. "Der Logosbegriff bei Heraklit und Parmenides," II, *Phronesis* 12 (1967) 99–117.

Vernant, J. P. "Hestia-Hermès," *Mythe et pensée chez les Grecs,* Vol. 1 (Paris: Maspéro, 1971).

———. "Raisons du mythe," *Mythe et société en Grèce ancienne* (Paris: Maspéro, 1974), 195–250.

Vitali, R. *Parmenide di Elea: Perì phúseo̱s* (Faenza: Lega, 1977).

Vlastos, G. "Parmenides' Theory of Knowledge," *Transactions and Proceedings of the Amer. Philol. Assoc.* 77 (1946) 66–77.

———. "Equality and Justice in Early Greek Cosmologies," *Classical Philology* 42 (1947).

de Vogel, C. "Platon a-t-il ou n'a-t-il pas introduit le mouvement dans son monde intelligible?" *Actes du XIe Congrès International de Philosophie* XII, Brussels (1953) 61–67.

Vuia, O. *Remontée aux sources de la pensée occidentale: Héraclite, Parménide, Anaxagore* (Paris: Centre Roumain de Recherches, 1961).

Wackernagel, J. *Vermischte Beiträge zur griechischen Sprachkunde* (Basel: 1897).

Wahl, J. *Vers la fin de l'ontologie* (Paris: Société de l'Enseignement Supérieur, 1956).

Wiersma, W. "Notes on Greek Philosophy (Parm. 1.17, 2.4, 8.61)," *Mnemosyne* 20 (1967).

Wiesner, J. "Die Negation der Entstehung des Seienden: Studien zu Parmenides B 8.5–21," *Archiv für Geschichte der Philosophie* 52 (1970) 125–146.

———. "Überlegungen zu Parmenides, fr. VIII, 34," *Études sur Parménide,* Vol. II, ed. Aubenque, P. (Paris: Vrin, 1987), 170–191.

———. *Parmenides: Der Beginn der Aletheia* (Berlin/New York: Walter de Gruyter, 1996).

Wilamowitz, U. v. "Lesefrüchte," *Hermes* 34 [1899] 203–230.

Wittgenstein, L. *Tractatus* (Frankfurt/Main: Suhrkamp, 1989).

Woodbury, L. "Parmenides on Names," *Harvard Studies in Classical Philology* 63 (1958), 145–160.

———. "Apollodorus, Xenophanes and the foundation of Massilia," *The Phoenix* 15 (1961) 134–155.

Wyatt, W. F. "The Root of Parmenides," *Harvard Studies in Classical Philology* 94 (1992), 113–120.

Zeller, E. *Die Philosophie der Griechen in ihrer geschichtlichen Entwicklung* (Leipzig: G. R. Reisland, 1892).

Zucchi, H. *Estudios de filosofía antigua y moderna* (Tucumán: Universidad Nacional de Tucumán, Instituto de Filosofia, 1956).

List of Ancient Authors Cited

List of Modern Authors Cited